IMAGES
of America

SAN GABRIEL

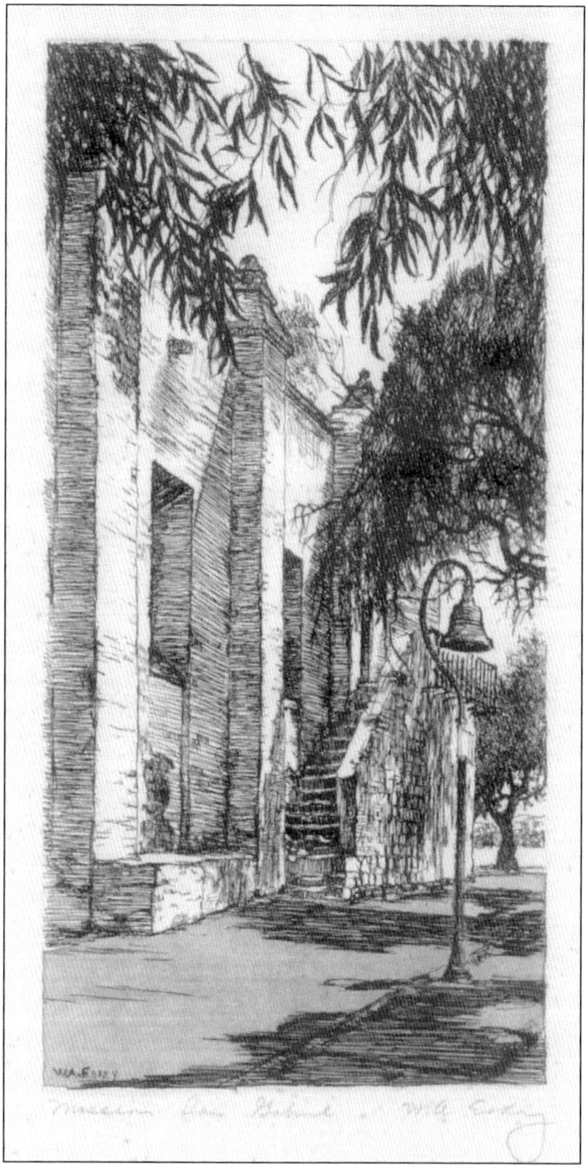

El Camino Real (King's Highway) was the original 700-mile road linking the 21 missions, 4 presidios, and 3 pueblos between San Diego and Sonoma. Preservationist Harrye Rebecca Forbes designed the El Camino Real bell guideposts placed at each mile along the route to indicate the distance between the missions and the mission locations. The first bell was erected in front of the Plaza Church in Los Angeles on August 15, 1906. William A. Eskey, a local artist, completed this etching of the San Gabriel Mission in the early 1930s. (Richard Arnold Collection.)

On the Cover: In 1895, Prof. Thaddeus S.C. Lowe established a service to carry patrons to his Mount Lowe Railway and the grand hotels atop Echo Mountain in the San Gabriel Mountains. His horse-drawn Tally-ho coaches made rounds to various hotels and local tourist attractions, such as the San Gabriel Mission (pictured). (Michael A. Patris Collection.)

IMAGES
of America

SAN GABRIEL

Richard J. Arnold

ARCADIA
PUBLISHING

ISBN 978-1-4671-3061-5

Published by Arcadia Publishing
Charleston, South Carolina

Printed in the United States of America

Library of Congress Control Number: 2013935601

For all general information, please contact Arcadia Publishing:
Telephone 843-853-2070
Fax 843-853-0044
E-mail sales@arcadiapublishing.com
For customer service and orders:
Toll-Free 1-888-313-2665

Visit us on the Internet at www.arcadiapublishing.com

For Mom

Contents

ACKNOWLEDGMENTS

I would like to acknowledge the many individuals who provided assistance, in some manner, with this book. Initial credit is owed to my dear father, Lawrence Arnold, whose love of California history was passed on to me, for the great interest and enthusiasm he showed in my book on San Gabriel, and the valuable input he provided throughout the project. Sadly, he unexpectedly passed away last year and did not get to see the completed project.

To Alan Jutzi, chief curator of rare books at Huntington Library, I give a great deal of thanks for his years of guidance and for allowing me into the wonderful collection of rare books and photographs at the Huntington Library.

To Ernie Marquez; Gary Cowles; Constance L. Rothstein; Michael Patris; Michael J. Hart; Dace Taube, regional history collection librarian at the University of Southern California; Paul R. Spitzzeri, collections manager at the Workman and Temple Family Homestead Museum; Paul Apodaca, associate professor of sociology, Chapman University; Roy Rose; Craig Rasmussen; Mary Swanton; Ken Tcheng, vice president and general manager of Sunny Slope Water Company; Erin Chase, assistant curator, and Susan Oatey, project archivist, Huntington Library; Kathleen Correia, manager of the California History Section at the California State Library; Christina Rice, senior librarian, Photo Collection at the Los Angeles Public Library; Pamela Quon, reference librarian, Los Angeles Public Library; Monica Orozco, PhD, director at the Santa Barbara Mission Archive-Library; John Macias; Jennifer Vega, photograph librarian, Colorado Historical Society; Susan Snyder, head of public services, The Bancroft Library, University of California, Berkeley; Marilyn Kim, rights and reproductions coordinator, Braun Research Library, Autry National Center; Mike Province, the George S. Patton Jr. Historical Society; Steve Wilkinson and Josh Fairman, San Gabriel Mission Playhouse; Pat Breyer, San Gabriel Valley Humane Society; and Steve Phelan, San Gabriel Post Office. To Jared Nelson, acquisitions editor, and Ryan Easterling, senior production editor, a special thanks for their hard work preparing *San Gabriel* for publication.

A special acknowledgement goes to members of my family who have been extremely supportive of this book project. To my wife, Dawn, for her enthusiastic support and for listening to my many stories of San Gabriel, to my sons—Stephen, for introducing me to Images of America and for encouraging me to write *San Gabriel*; Michael, for his technical assistance and computer skills used while preparing photographs, and to Kenneth, whom I regularly discussed ideas with during our drives to and from school each day.

Introduction

A countless number of books have been written about San Gabriel, most all of which have touched on the historic San Gabriel Mission. Few books, however, have been written about the town that grew from an ancient Indian settlement to a prosperous community or about the Gabrieleño Indians, the "First Angelinos" as author William McCawley has so appropriately described them. Little has been written about the early pioneers who traveled by wagon train to seek better opportunities or those who entered politics after first leaving their mark on the small community. San Gabriel had its share of well-known members of the military, including Civil War general George Stoneman, who became the 15th governor of California. On March 25, 1865, Union general Stoneman led 6,000 cavalrymen from Tennessee into western North Carolina and southwestern Virginia, deep into the heart of the Confederacy, destroying sections of the Virginia & Tennessee Railroad, the North Carolina Railroad, and the Piedmont Railroad and mines, ironworks, and bridges in an effort to deprive Confederate armies of supplies and avenues of retreat. Traveling more than 600 miles through enemy territory, they also assisted with the capture of Confederate president Jefferson Davis. Stoneman's raid was memorialized by songwriter Robbie Robertson of The Band, whose 1969 song "The Night They Drove Old Dixie Down" referred to one of Stoneman's 1865 raids.

It is ironic that *San Gabriel* tells the story of the community with black-and-white images when the history of the community is so colorful. At the same time, the history of San Gabriel is filled with conflict. Early writers filled their notes with facts that were more romantic or mythical than historical and often tinged them with personal bias. Historians and writers alike are continually reassessing the past, as has been done with this book, weighing the facts and providing more accurate information.

One of the more sensitive conflicts in history is the naming of the Mission Indians referred to as the Gabrieleños. Historically, the tribe was known as the Gabrieleños following the Spanish custom of naming local Mission Indians after the nearby mission—Fernadenos were named for Mission San Fernando Rey de Espana, and Juanenos were named for Mission San Juan Capistrano. Since Spanish missionaries imposed that name upon the natives, it carries a negative connotation to many in the tribe. The name "Tongva" has been used in recent times to describe the peoples who inhabited the Los Angeles basin prior to the arrival of the Spanish and has been used throughout academic writings and literature as fact, even though there is no real historical support for the name Tongva. There is, however, historical support and legitimacy for the Kizh (Kij or Kichireno), which is a name being used by many of the Gabrieleño today. In his 1996 book *The First Angelinos*, author William McCawley cites a statement made to him by Raimundo Yorba, who was a consultant to John P. Harrington, a linguist, ethnographer, and specialist on native peoples of California, that "the natives living in the Old Mission area were what they called a Kichireno, one of a bunch of people that lived at that place just this side of San Gabriel which is known as La Misión Vieja. Kichireno is not a placename, but a tribename, the name of a kind of people."

San Gabriel has been referred to as being the "birthplace of the Los Angeles region." September 4 marks the traditional anniversary of the 1781 founding of El Pueblo de la Reina de Los Angeles, and for a number of years, descendants of the pueblo's original colonists—along with members of the communities of San Gabriel and Los Angeles—walk the route from the San Gabriel Mission to the Los Angeles Plaza to commemorate and reenact the founding of Los Angeles by the original 44 *pobladores* (townspeople). It is now clear that this story is also more likely a myth than fact. The original *pobladores* actually arrived separately, not as a group, and settled the town as early as June 1781, not September 4.

The site of the original founding is also in question, just like La Misión Vieja, the original San Gabriel Mission. Historians are unclear about where settlers built their first adobes and the exact location of the pueblo, as no monument exists to mark the original site. It is likely that the site moved once or even twice before it was settled on its current location in 1818.

The exact location of La Misión Vieja (Old Mission) has never been verified, as original structures were made of tule and wood, which are subject to decay and were likely washed away during subsequent flooding, farming, and ranching. In May and June 1987, archaeologists identified a potential location, known as CA-LAN-1311H, just to the north and slightly west of the Montebello Hills. A marker placed at the southwest corner of San Gabriel and Lincoln Boulevards in the city of Montebello proclaims this to be the site. In July 1921, on the 150th anniversary of the mission's founding, Walter P. Temple commemorated the occasion and arranged for a granite marker to be placed at the site. The likely location of the original site is across the street from where the plaque was placed, and the reason the granite marker was put there was because Temple owned the land (and not the property to the north).

The 1852 murder of Joshua Bean was an example of the bias and discrimination present in the early years of San Gabriel. Bean served as the first mayor of the city of San Diego until he was unceremoniously run out of town when he tried to sell city hall. Bean came to San Gabriel and opened the Headquarters Saloon but was mortally wounded around midnight on Sunday, November 7, 1852. According to one tale, this was the result of a love triangle. The first person on the scene of the murder—the town cobbler, Cipriano Sandoval—met up with the killer, Felipe Reid, who was still holding the murder weapon and confessed, even offering to bribe Sandoval with hush money. Felipe Reid was the son of Hugo Reid, a popular, upstanding citizen and writer for the large *Los Angeles Star* newspaper, and politics of that era prevented Felipe being named (let alone convicted) of the crime. Sandoval and Benito Lopez were convicted of the murder and hung at Fort Hill in Los Angeles. Five years later, while dying of smallpox, Felipe Reid made a deathbed confession confirming that he had, in fact, murdered Bean. Roy Bean heard about the murder and came to San Gabriel, where he became the proprietor of the Headquarters Saloon once owned by his brother Joshua. Roy Bean remained in San Gabriel until he was run out of town in 1857 after killing a man who challenged him to a duel over a woman. An enraged mob hanged Bean from a nearby tree, but after the rope stretched, the woman in question was able to cut him free. He eventually moved to southwest Texas, where he built his famous saloon, the Jersey Lilly, and founded the hamlet of Langtry.

The pages that follow are a compilation of photographs that help to tell the story of San Gabriel. Much effort has been put into gathering images that have never been seen and images that have never before been published in books or periodicals. Unfortunately there is not sufficient space to tell the entire story of San Gabriel or include the tons or beautiful and interesting images collected over the years by individuals and institutions across the states. San Gabriel, in this form can only touch the surface of the history of this interesting and historical community. It is my desire that the reader will discover information that they never knew about San Gabriel or will be able to confirm their suspicions about facts they thought were correct from the details I have provided.

One

Gabrieleño Indians

The Gabrieleño are the indigenous people who inhabited the area in Los Angeles County and Orange County, California, before the arrival of Europeans. Historically, the tribe has been known as the Gabrieleños following the Spanish custom of naming local Mission Indians after the nearby mission. Since Spanish missionaries imposed that name upon them, it carries a negative connotation to many in the tribe today.

The first known contact between the Gabrieleño and Europeans (Spaniards) took place in 1542 with Juan Rodriguez Cabrillo's arrival at Santa Catalina Island. Cabrillo sailed up the California coast and landed on Catalina Island. At the time, the Gabrieleño Indians populated a territory covering almost 4,000 miles, including both the offshore islands known today as Santa Catalina and the San Clemente. The Gaspar de Portolá expedition of 1769 was the first expedition to reach Gabrieleño territory and marked the beginning of Spanish colonization. Within two years of the Portolá expedition, Fr. Junipero Serra established four missions in Alta California, including the San Gabriel Mission.

Four extremely important Gabrieleño communities were located in the vicinity, including Shevaanga, Sonaanga, Sheshiikwanonga, and Akuuronga. The four communities were situated in a fertile, well-irrigated region so became an excellent location for the permanent site of the San Gabriel Mission. It was not by chance that the San Gabriel Mission became one of the most productive of the missions as the padres chose fertile ground once belonging and inhabited by the Gabrieleño people to establish their mission.

Perhaps the greatest impact the arrival of European vessels had upon the Gabrieleño was the decimation of the native population through the spread of contagious diseases. Events of the late 1700s and early 1800s proved that contact with foreigners exposed the Gabrieleño to bacterial and viral infections for which they had no immunities.

Disease and mistreatment of Gabrieleño by the Spanish missionaries, soldiers, and Europeans dealt a serious blow to their population. Over the next 40 years, following the founding of the San Gabriel Mission, deaths far exceeded the number of births. The subsequent growth of the missions, the pueblo, and the private ranchos would eventually be responsible for the decline of the Gabrieleño communities and the destruction of their original culture. Those that at one time composed the majority of the population became the major source of labor, watching as their hunting grounds were soon transformed into ranchos.

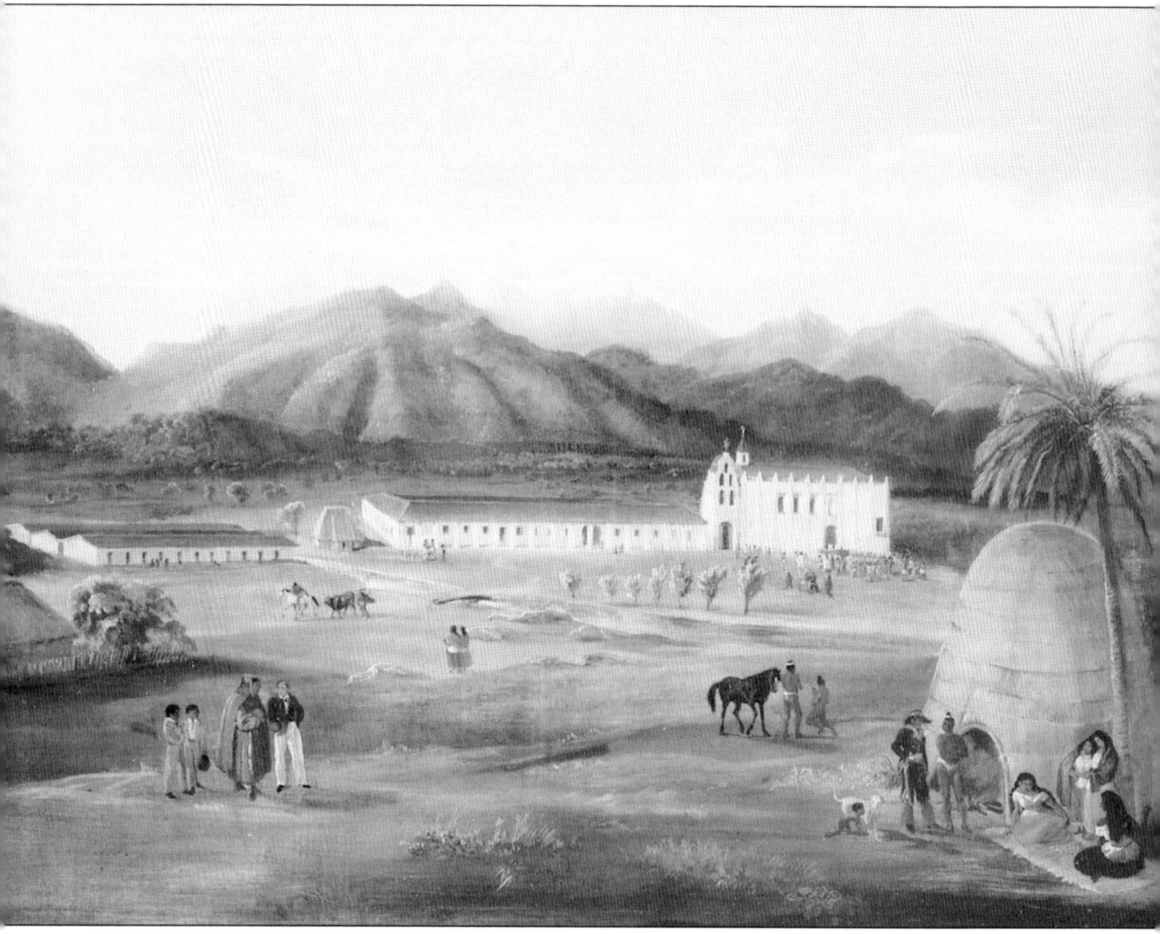

Ferdinand Deppe, a German agent for the Mexican mercantile house of Henry Virmonde y Cia and an accomplished painter, visited the San Gabriel Mission in 1828 and sketched the Corpus Christi Procession. In 1832, Deppe transferred his sketch onto canvas, the results of which is the only known painting of any Alta California mission before the secularization decrees of 1834. The lantern on top of the original arched roof allowed additional light over the altar because several of the windows were filled in after the 1812 earthquake. The traditional house of the Gabrieleño, shown in the lower right of this painting, had circular floor plans and was constructed in a dome shape. The framework was made of bent willow branches that were buried in the ground at the base to form a circle of poles. The tops of the poles were bent and tied together with yucca fiber. The frame was then covered with a thatch of tules. The largest would house 50 people. The dome-shaped designs were eventually replaced by rectangular-shaped floor plans with gabled roofs. The neophytes (mission Christian Indians) lived in adobe buildings on the mission grounds. Fr. Jose Sanchez, who was the *presidente* of the California missions, is shown in the lower left-hand portion of the painting, talking with James Scott, a Yankee supercargo from Boston. Two Indian children are shown standing behind Father Sanchez. In the right foreground next to the house, mayordomo Claudio Lopez talks to a male Gabrieleño. The Gabrieleño women shown in the lower right of the painting are dressed in blouses and petticoats, likely the result of trade with visiting Europeans. The date palm shown next to the dome-shaped house was blown down in a windstorm in 1891. (Santa Barbara Mission Archive-Library.)

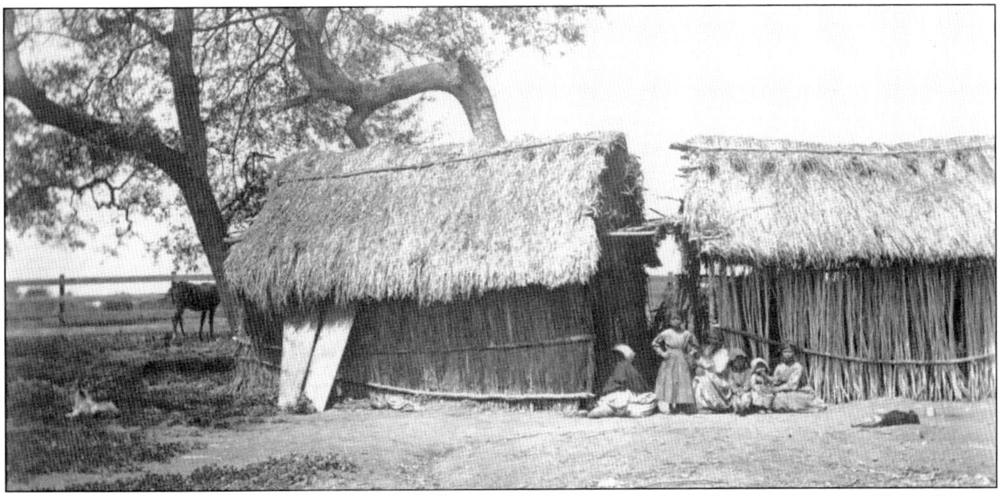

This is the Acurag-na rancheria, located near the La Presa dam on the Sunny Slope Farm. The heavily wooded settlement was referred to as Acurag-na, derived from the word *akura*, meaning "wood." The Wood clan likely settled in the area because of the presence of natural spring water that flowed constantly, forming marshy ponds that supported plant and animal life. (Huntington Library.)

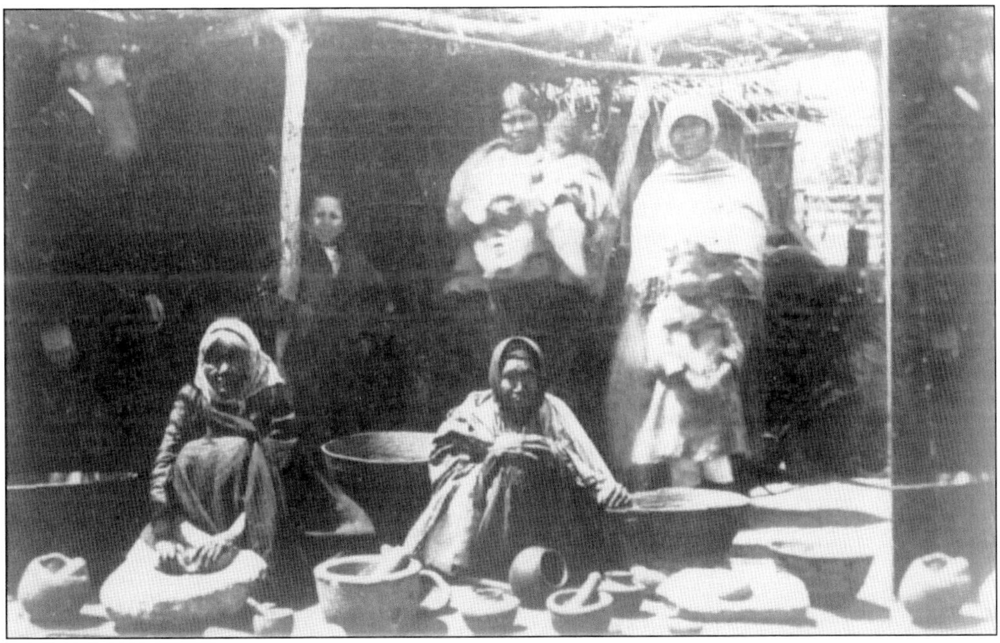

Retired Civil War major Horatio Nelson Rust is shown standing on the left side of this photograph during one of his many visits with Gabrieleño women and children. Rust was a lifelong antiquarian and amateur archaeologist who began collecting archaeological and ethnographic items as a traveling salesman. Shown in the foreground are the baskets, sandstone, granite mortar, and pestle that were known to have been used on a daily basis. Baskets were manufactured in a variety of shapes and styles, both coiled and woven. Tightly coiled watertight baskets were often used for cooking, serving, and storing of food. While the baskets made of split rushes were waterproof, they were normally used for only dry purposes. When used, they were plastered inside and outside with bitumen or pitch called *sanot*. (Huntington Library.)

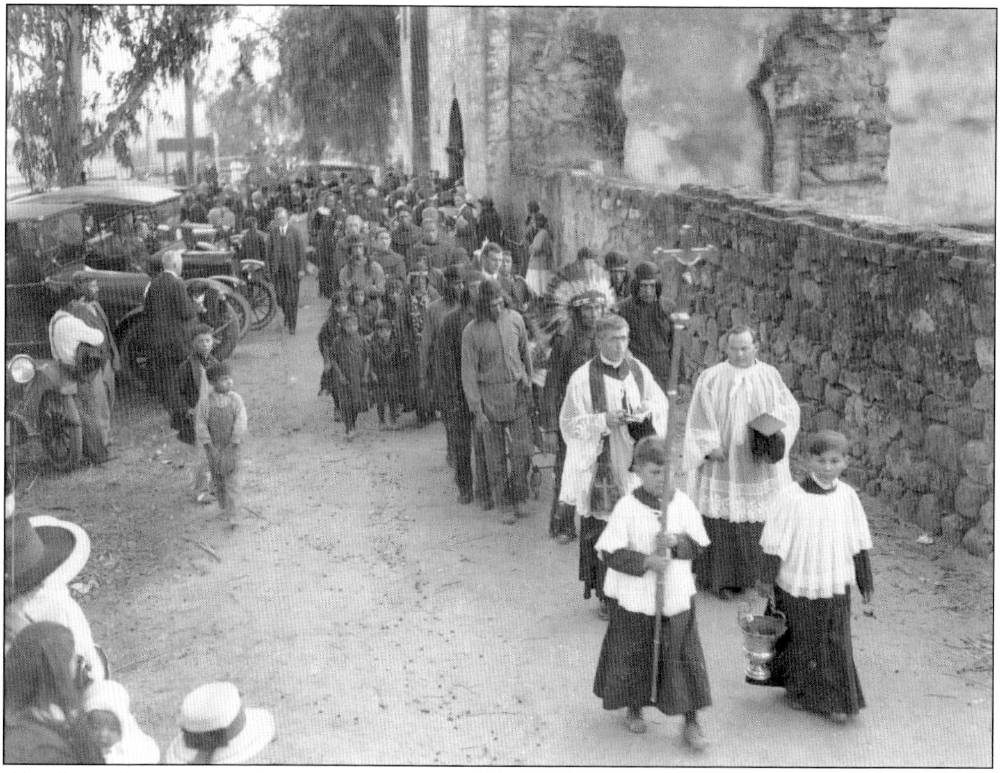

The funeral cortege of Santo Juncio proceeds slowly along the wide walkway leading from the historic mission church to the burial ground where his ancestors are buried. The church was filled to overflowing, and a crowd waited outside while a short ceremony took place for Santo Juncio, the last Gabrieleño born within the mission walls. Juncio was born at the Old Mission in 1815 and spent his youth and young manhood in the confines of the mission. (*Los Angeles Times* photographic archives, Charles E. Young Research Library Department of Special Collections, UCLA.)

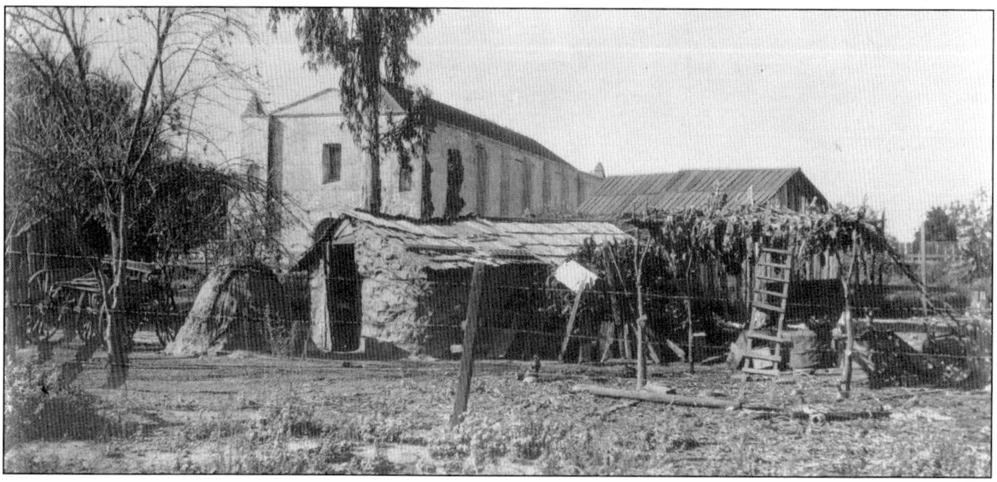

What is believed to be the last Gabrieleño settlement is pictured around 1885 looking southwest from the marshland. Remnants of the original campanile (bell tower) are visible on the north-facing side of the mission where it once was attached to the facade. (Regional History Center, Special Collections Department, University of Southern California.)

Two

San Gabriel Mission

The original site chosen for the fourth of the California missions, San Gabriel Arcángel, was well inland from the ocean along the banks of the river now called Santa Ana in present-day Orange County. Upon their arrival, Fr. Pedro Benito Cambón and Angel Somera decided to look for a better location and continued traveling northwest. The missionaries crossed the San Gabriel River and founded the mission near the present-day city of Montebello on September 8, 1771. Five years later, when they realized the need for better, more fertile ground, they moved the site to its current location. They could not have chosen a better spot, as San Gabriel became the wealthiest of the early missions.

Through the years, San Gabriel Mission fell victim to greedy politicians and land-hungry colonists. With the decrees of secularization from the Mexican government, the mission was turned over to a civil administrator in 1834. In the 10 years that followed, everything of value was removed. Gov. Pío Pico began selling the California missions to finance a local defense at the start of the Mexican War, and on June 8, 1846, he granted Mission San Gabriel, including the church and surrounding property, to William Workman and Don Hugo Reid. In the summer of 1846, however, the United States sent troops to occupy California. With the signing of the Treaty of Cahuenga on January 13, 1847, the United States took control of California. Pres. James Buchanan gave the mission property back to the Catholic Church in 1859.

For nearly 20 years, the mission remained neglected and deserted. The church was used as a parish church from 1862 until 1908, when the Claretian Missionary Fathers came to San Gabriel and began the job of rebuilding and restoring the mission. A new era of growth and vitality began with the arrival of the Claretian Missionaries. Following the charisma of their founder, Saint Anthony Claret, the Claretians restored, rebuilt, reorganized, and rejuvenated the mission.

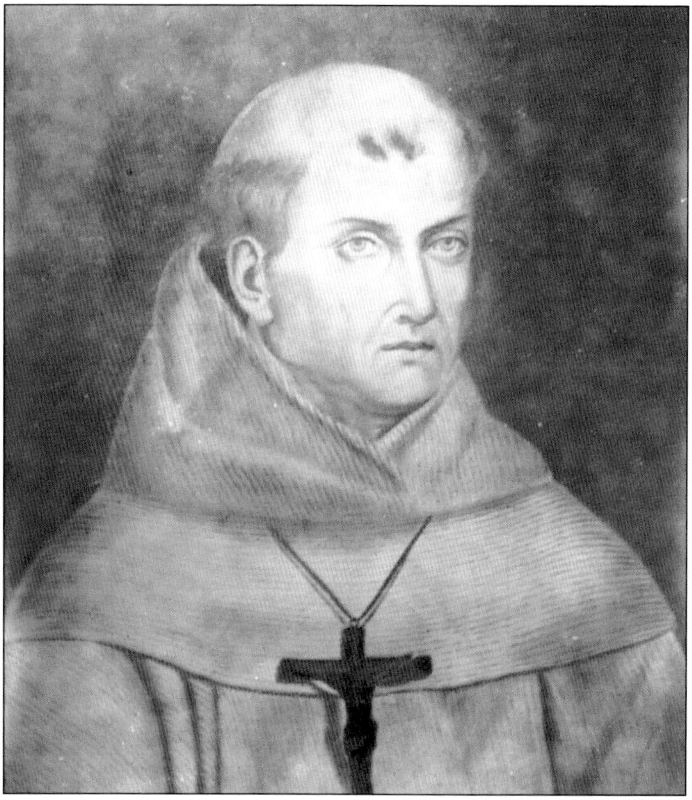

Fr. Junipero Serra was one of the most important Spanish missionaries in the New World. Joining the Franciscan Order at the age of 16, he soon gained prominence as an eloquent preacher and eventually became a professor of theology. After becoming a missionary to America, Father Serra established his first mission at the present-day site of San Diego. (Regional History Center, Special Collections Department, University of Southern California.)

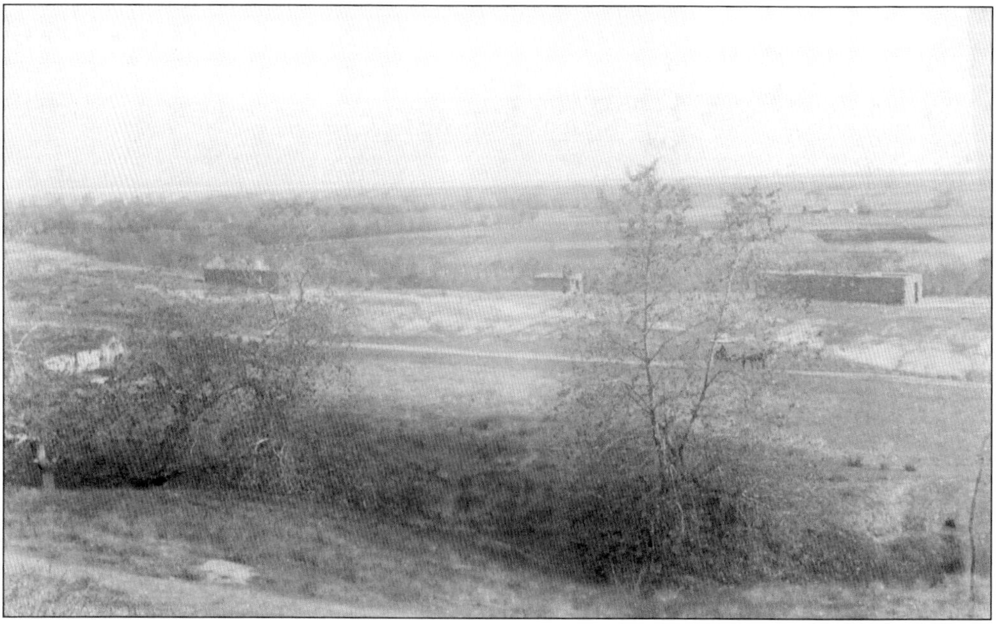

This photograph was taken looking towards the Rio Hondo River and is believed to show the site of La Misión Vieja (Old Mission). The adobe structures in this photograph were ranchos built in subsequent years but were not part of the original mission structures. (Ernest Marquez Collection.)

The adobe ruins in this photograph were often mistaken by tourists as being the foundation of the original La Misión Vieja. They were actually ruins of a ranch house built at the site in the mid-1800s. All of the La Misión Vieja buildings were constructed of logs and covered with either tule thatch or earthen roof. (Regional History Center, Special Collections Department, University of Southern California.)

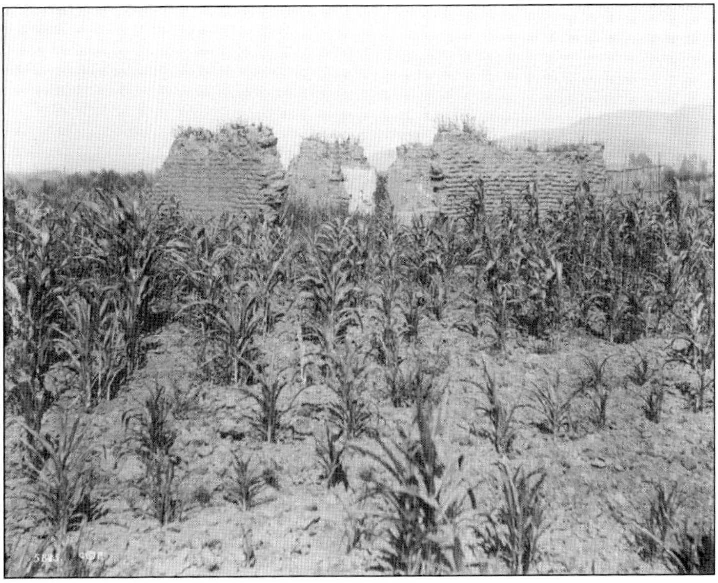

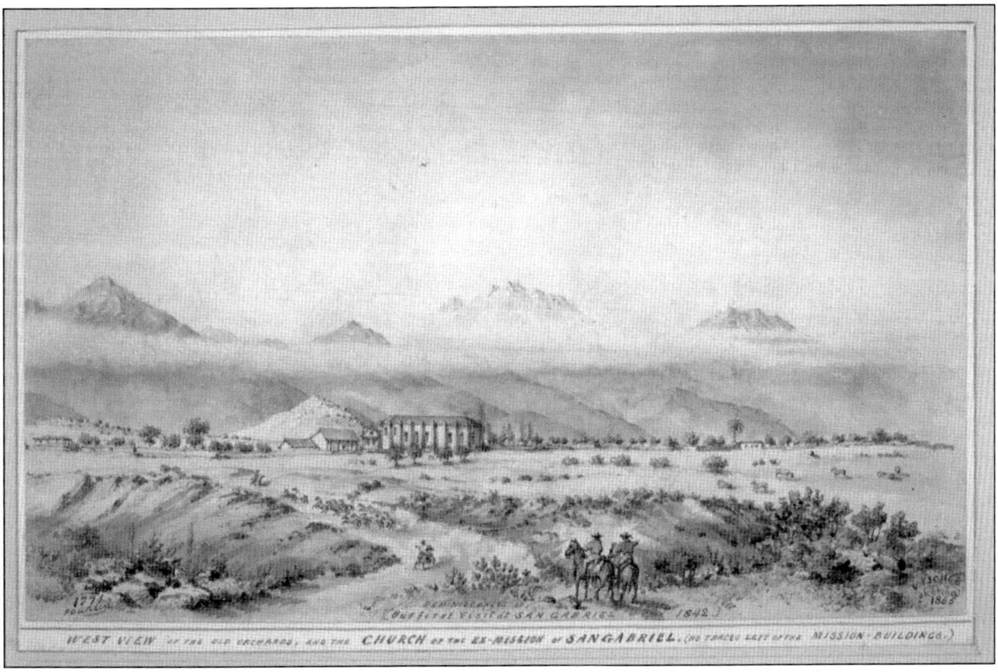

Edward Vischer (1809–1878), was a German-born painter and photographer who migrated from Germany to Mexico at the age of 19 where he became employed by the enterprising trader Heinrich Virmond. Vischer was best known for his pencil sketches of California landscapes from the 1860s through the 1870s that he completed during his vast travels throughout the state. Vischer sketched this west view of the old orchard with the San Gabriel Mission in the background in 1865; however, his initial working sketches were from his first visit to San Gabriel in 1842. It was his practice to make rapid sketches on the spot of scenes that interested him and later complete his final works from watercolor, pencil, or pen. (Bancroft Library, University of California, Berkeley.)

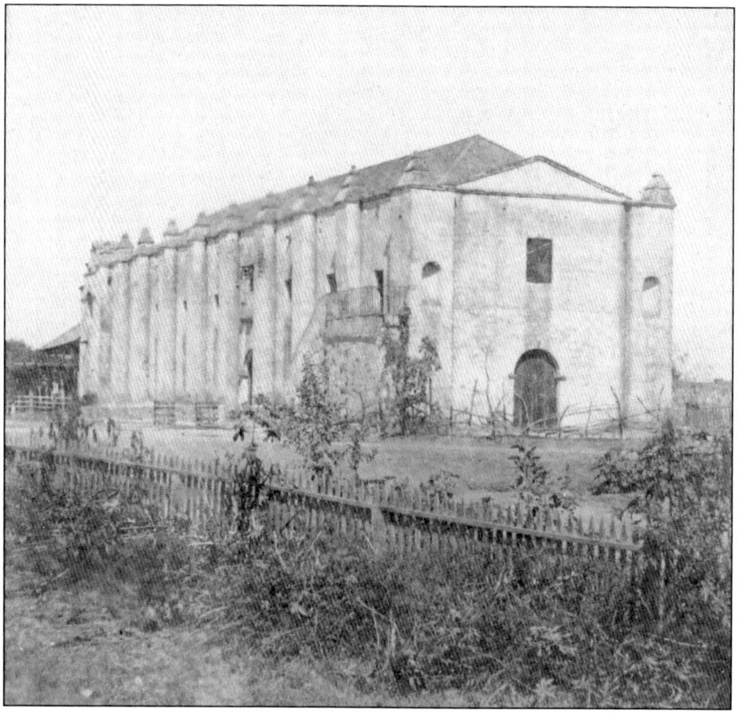

This c. 1869 image of the San Gabriel Mission, taken by William M. Godfrey, is one of the earliest known photographs of the mission. Born in New York, Godfrey set out for California in 1850 with his family, driving an oxen team across the plains with intentions to dig for gold. After failing as a prospector, he bought a daguerreotype camera from a fellow miner and started earning his living as a photographer. (Constance L. Rothstein Collection.)

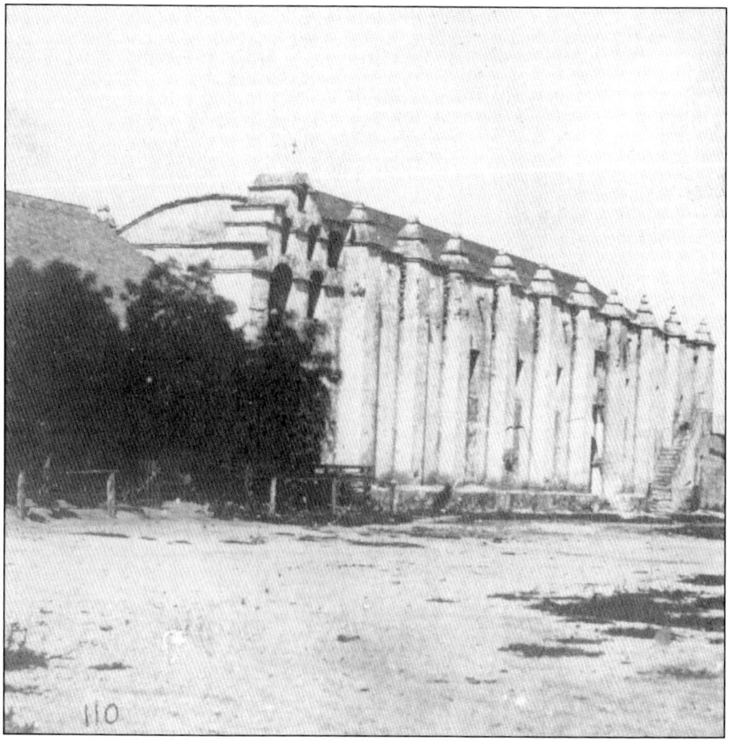

William M. Godfrey photographed the mission around 1872 after the restoration from the earthquake damage of 1864. The restoration included filling in several of the windows to add structural integrity to the building, including the first window to the right of the campanile, which is visible in this photograph. In 1886, under the direction of Fr. Joaquin Bot, the windows were enlarged and new windows were added to admit more light; the third pitched-style roof was also added. (Constance L. Rothstein Collection.)

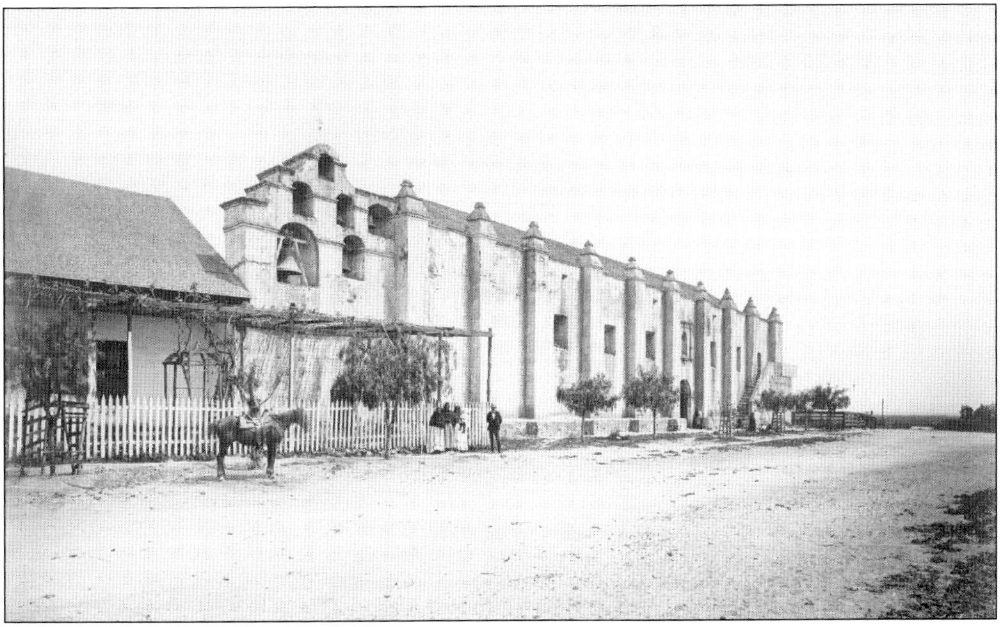

This photograph of the mission was taken by photographer Carleton E. Watkins in 1877. Watkins, perhaps the most famous of the early western photographers, was best known for his "mammoth-plate photographs," of which he produced more than 1,100. This image clearly shows the original, smaller windows that were eventually enlarged in 1886 under the direction of Fr. Joaquin Bot. Also visible in the photograph is the first window to the right of the campanile that was filled in after the earthquake damage of 1864 to add structural integrity to the walls of the building. (Huntington Library.)

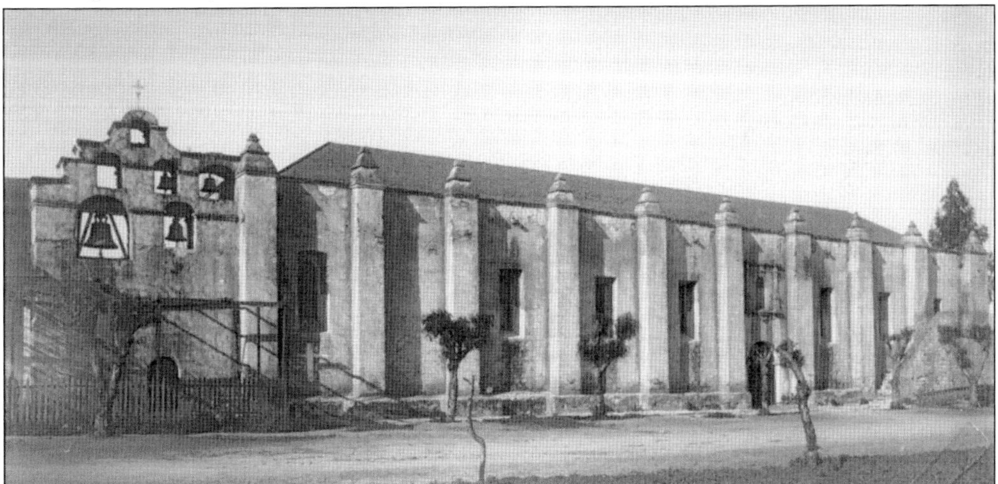

This 1890 photograph of the San Gabriel Mission shows the hand-painted cross once visible on the exterior wall directly below the first window next to the campanile. In 1996, during the restoration of the mission, the cross was covered by a textured coating. The purpose of the cross or its significance has not been determined; however, it may have been in recognition of original Indian burial grounds outside the mission walls. Skeletal remains of an adult and child were discovered in 1914 by Pacific Electric workers replacing tracks. At the time of the discovery, it was determined that this area was used for Indian burial grounds. (Richard Arnold Collection.)

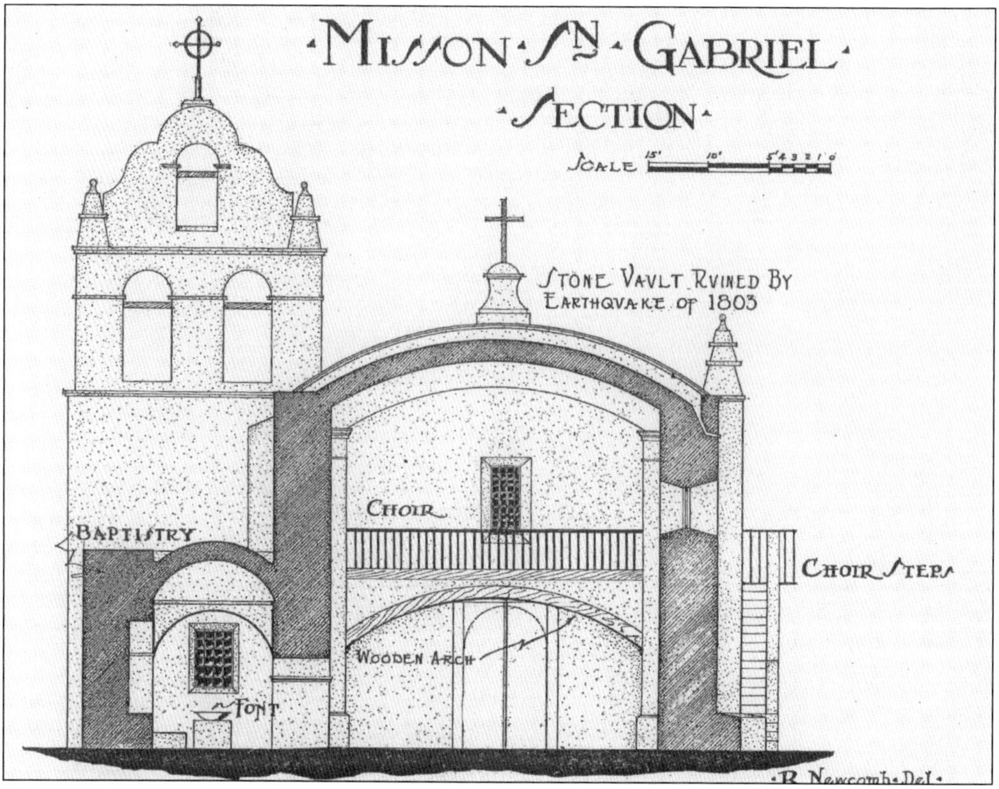

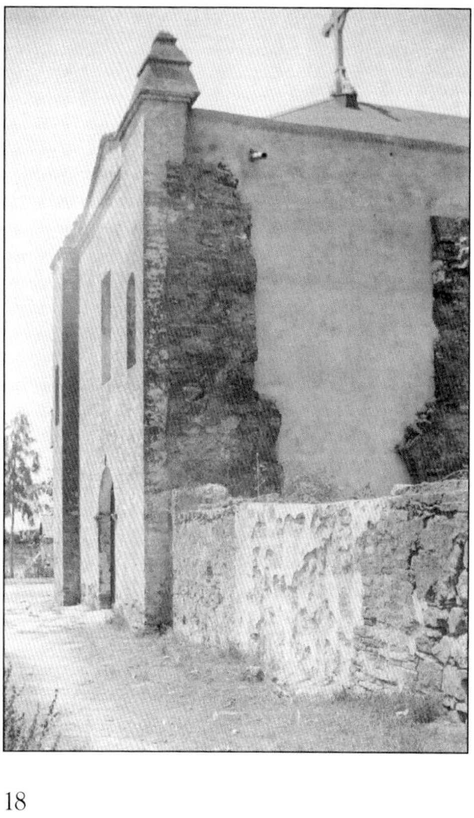

This is architectural historian and artist Rexford Newcomb's "conceptual elevation sketch" of the San Gabriel Mission campanile that originally abutted the facade. On December 8, 1812 (the Feast Day of the Immaculate Conception of the Blessed Virgin), a series of massive earthquakes shook the region, causing the three-bell structure to collapse. Although there are no existing records of the original design of the bell tower, Newcomb deduced the design and included this image in his 1916 publication *The Franciscan Mission Architecture of Alta California*. (Regional History Center, Special Collections Department, University of Southern California.)

Remnants of the original campanile are visible on the north-facing side of the mission, where the campanile was originally attached to the facade. This photograph shows that the door that once led outside to the original campanile was filled in after the campanile was destroyed. After a subsequent restoration, the door was replaced and is visible today, although it exits into air. (San Gabriel Historical Association.)

Pío de Jesus Pico, son of a mission guard, was born at the San Gabriel Mission and was the last governor of Alta California under Mexican rule. Pico twice served as governor, first replacing Gov. Manuel Victoria in 1832 when Victoria was deposed for refusing to adhere to orders to secularize the missions; Pico only served for 20 days. In 1845, Pico succeeded Gov. Manuel Micheltorena, making Los Angeles the capital of the "province." As federal troops began to occupy Los Angeles and San Diego during the Mexican-American War, Pico fled to Baja California, Mexico, but returned after the signing of the Treaty of Guadalupe Hidalgo on February 2, 1848. (Security Pacific National Bank Collection, Los Angeles Public Library.)

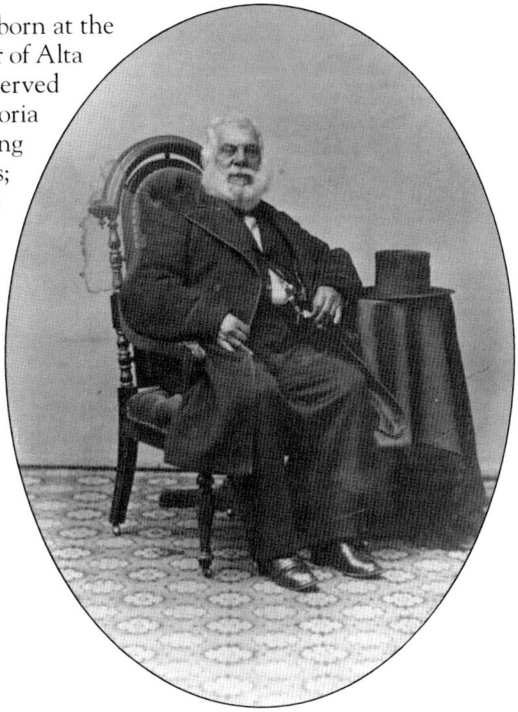

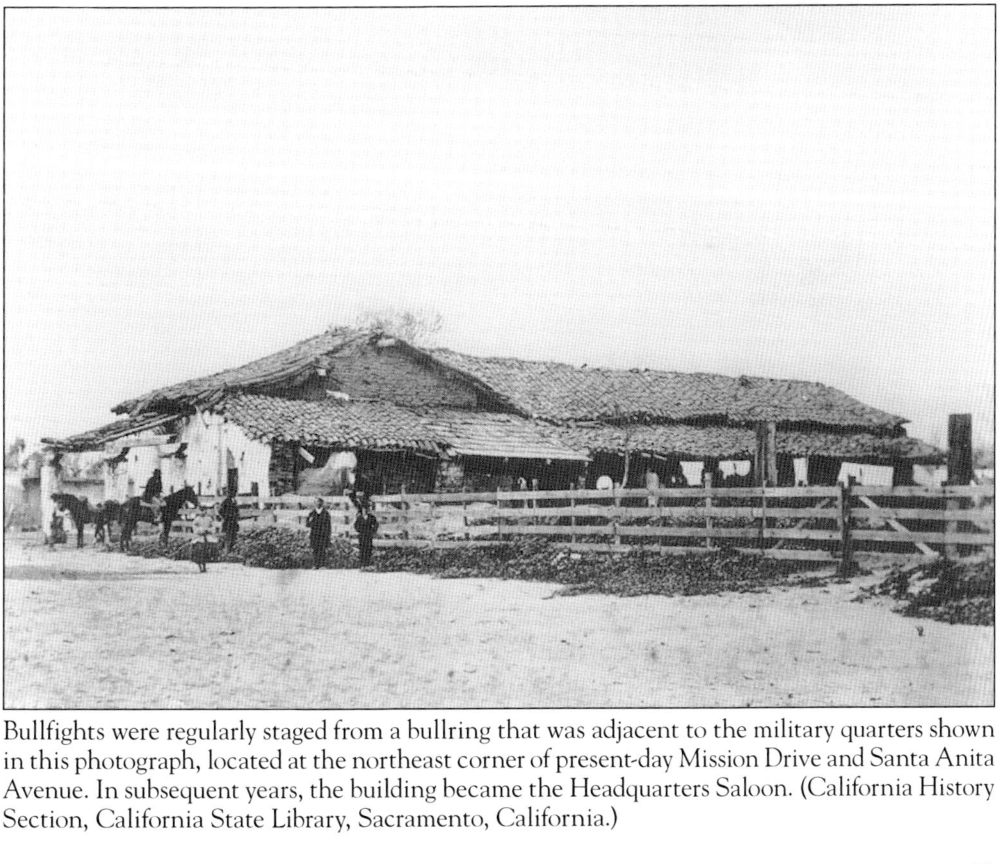

Bullfights were regularly staged from a bullring that was adjacent to the military quarters shown in this photograph, located at the northeast corner of present-day Mission Drive and Santa Anita Avenue. In subsequent years, the building became the Headquarters Saloon. (California History Section, California State Library, Sacramento, California.)

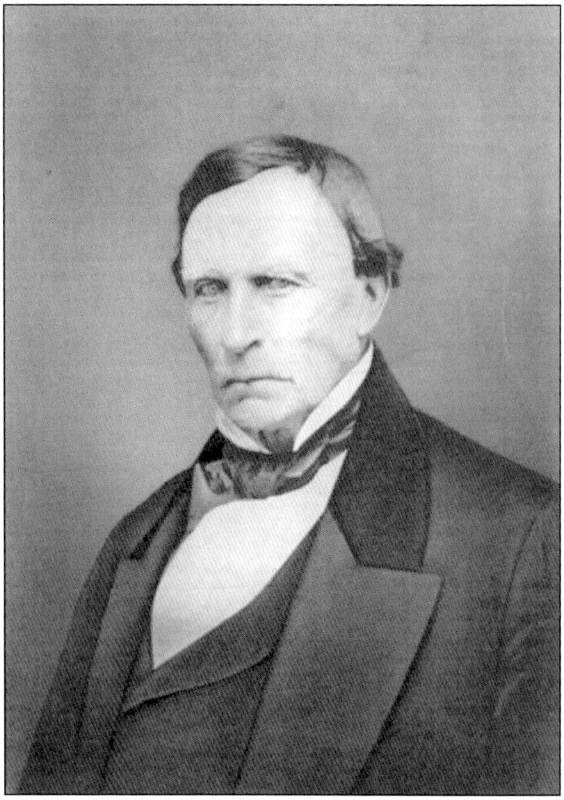

William Workman, fur trapper, merchant, farmer, rancher, and banker, came to California with John Rowland when the two led a 1,200-mile wagon train of settlers, including Benjamin D. Wilson, along the often treacherous Old Spanish Trail from New Mexico to the Los Angeles Pueblo in September 1841. The group of about 25, known as the Workman-Rowland Party, arrived at San Gabriel Mission on November 5, 1841. On June 8, 1846, Gov. Pío Pico granted the mission property to Workman and Hugo Reid for "rendering valuable services to the government." The United States Land Commission declared the 1846 sale invalid, noting that Pico had no legal authority to sell the missions. (Workman and Temple Family Homestead Museum.)

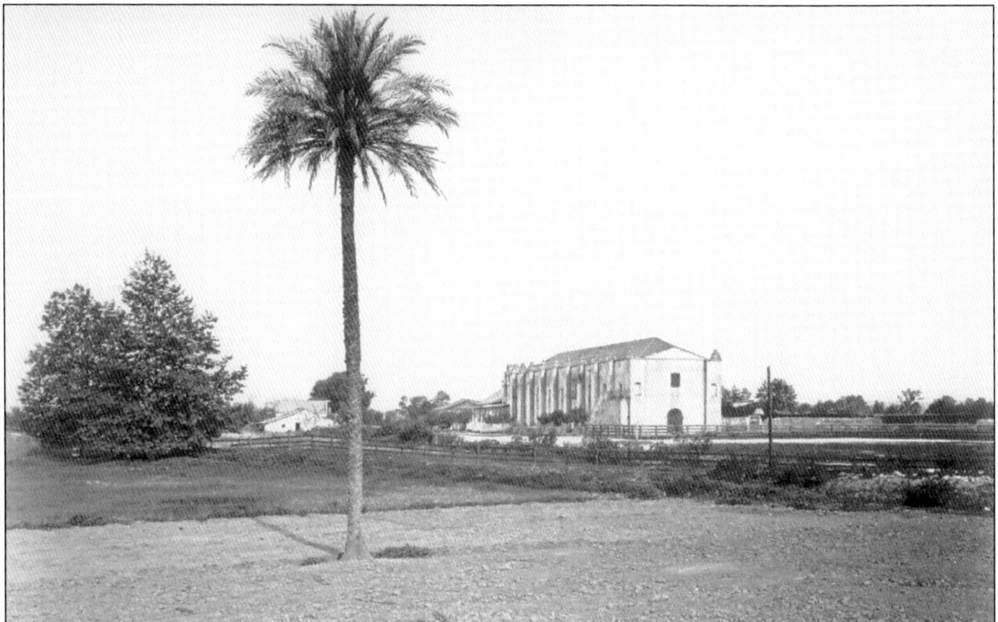

This old date palm planted by mission padres blew down in an 1891 windstorm. The fenced-in property, including the Las Tunas adobe, belonged to Volney E. Howard when Carleton E. Watkins photographed it in 1877. (Bancroft Library, University of California, Berkeley.)

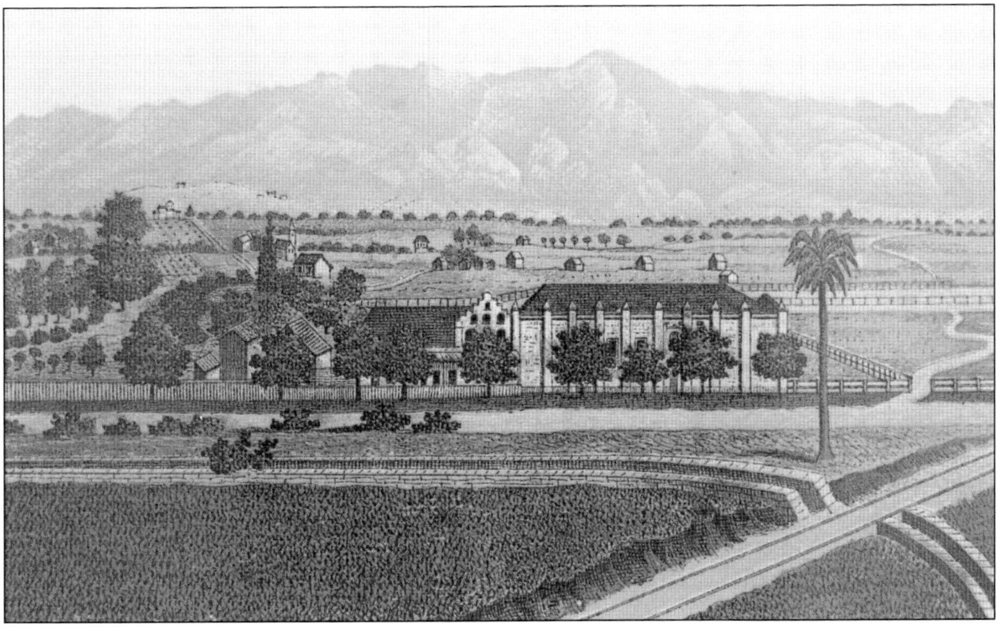

This drawing of the San Gabriel Mission shows the *zanja madre* (main ditch) crossing in front of the mission towards Chapman's Mill to the south. The Southern Pacific Railroad began operating trains between Los Angeles and Colton on July 16, 1875, and as is shown, the steel rails clearly bisected the *zanja*. In the foreground is the old date palm that was planted by the padres and blew down in a windstorm in 1891; it was located in close proximity to the Las Tunas adobe that, at the time of this drawing, was part of the Volney E. Howard ranch. (Richard Arnold Collection.)

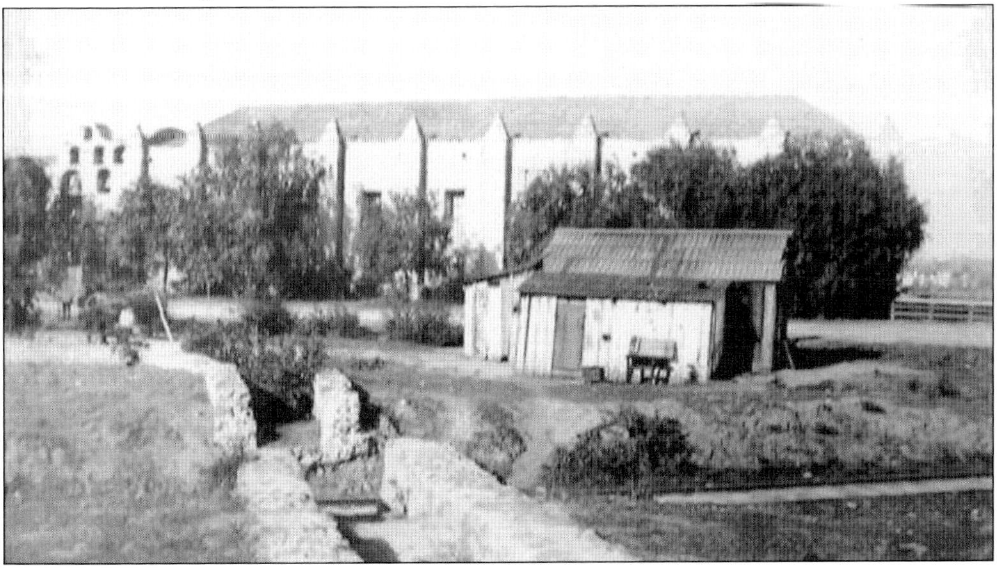

This photograph of the San Gabriel Mission, taken on April 8, 1884, shows the *zanja madre* (main ditch) crossing in front of the mission towards Chapman's Mill to the south. Although not as clear in detail as the above drawing, the steel of the Southern Pacific Railroad can be seen cutting through the *zanja*. The *zanja madre* functioned as a millrace where it entered Chapman's Mill as well as a water ditch for irrigation of the 340 acres south of the mission. (San Gabriel Historical Association.)

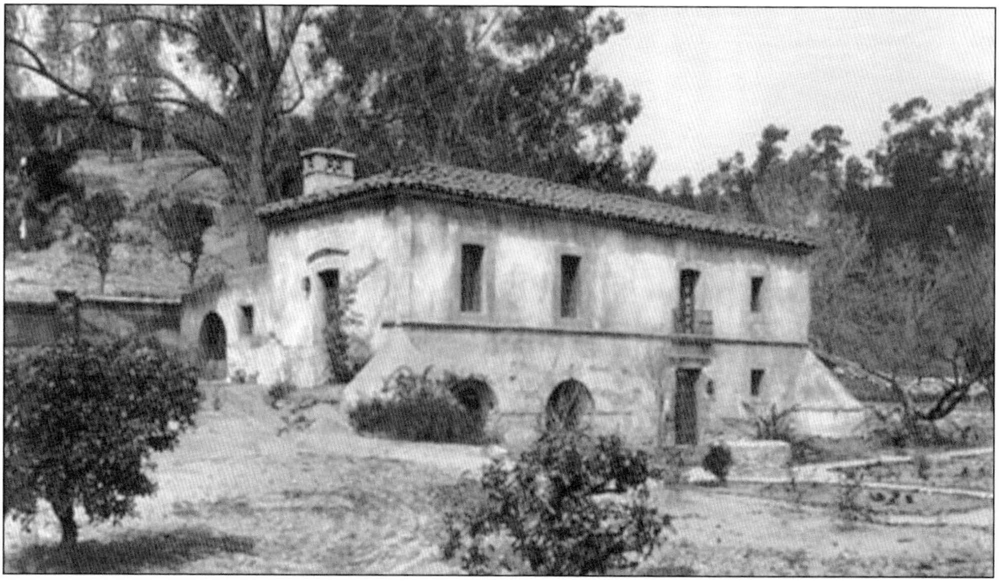

El Molino Viejo, known as "The Old Mill," is located at the bottom of a slope caused by the uplift of the Raymond Fault at the mouth of Mill Canyon (present-day San Marino). The gristmill, designed by Fr. José María de Zalvidea and built around 1816 by Mission (Gabrieleño) Indians utilized a Spanish-style mill design with a horizontal mill wheel. After turning the mill wheel, water ran out of El Molino and into Mission Lake. The flawed design of the mill allowed water to splash up the shaft leaving flour damp. In 1823, Joseph Chapman designed a New England–style mill closer to the mission, so the Old Mill was abandoned around 1824. (Regional History Center, Special Collections Department, University of Southern California.)

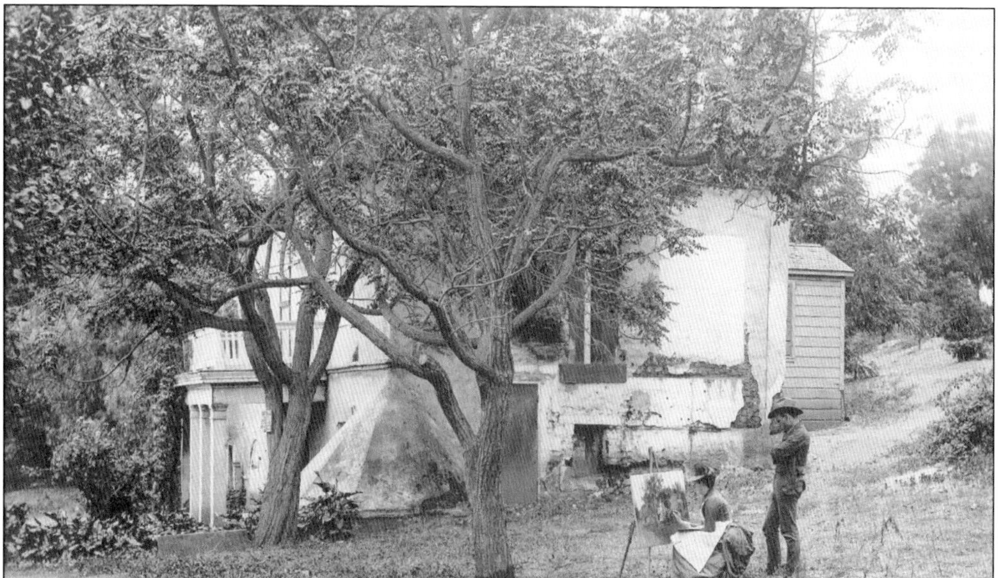

Landscape painter and art teacher Elizabeth Jaynes Putman and her fiancé, John Gutzon Borglum, posed for this photograph in 1887 alongside the El Molino Viejo. Borglum later gained fame as a sculptor, most notably of the series of presidential portraits on Mount Rushmore. (Regional History Center, Special Collections Department, University of Southern California.)

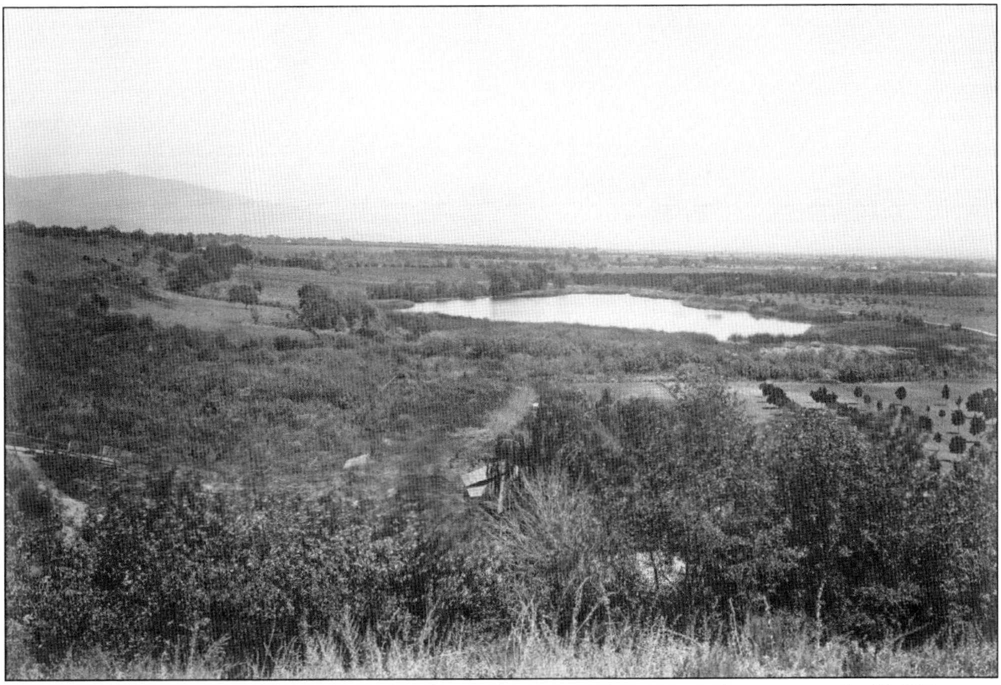

Benjamin D. Wilson's ranch, referred to by Wilson as Lake Vineyard, comprised of 1,200 acres of vineyards and extensive orange groves, much of which was planted by mission padres. Wilson owned a third of Mission Lake, also referred to as Wilson Lake and Kewen Lake after Edward J. Kewen, eventual owner of El Molino Viejo. The lake served as the water supply for the nearby Gabrieleño settlement and the major water supply for Chapman's Mill, located south of the mission. In later years, before being filled and turned into Lacy Park, it was a swimming hole for a young George S. Patton Jr. (Huntington Library.)

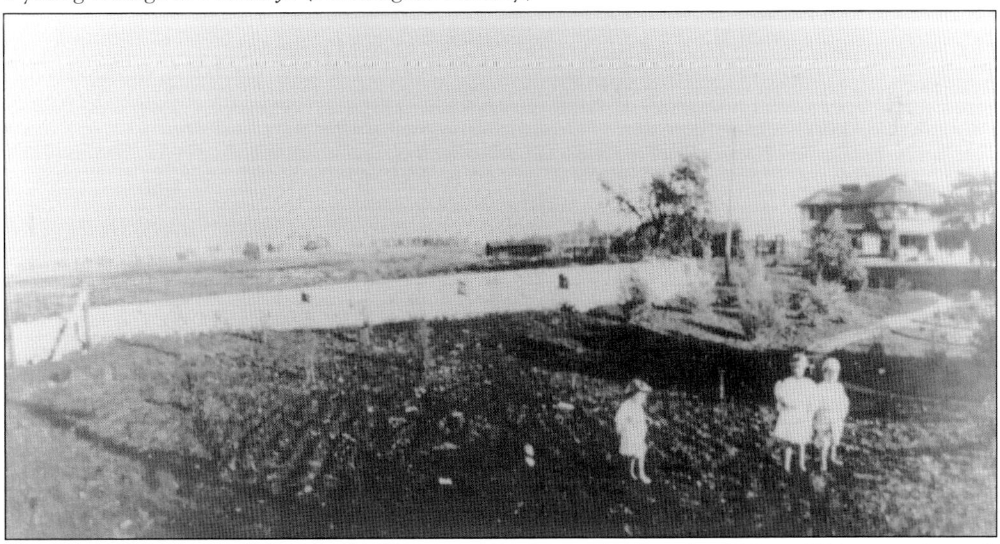

Seen here around 1907, La Presa ("the dam" in Spanish) was built in the 1780s or 1790s using Spanish and neophyte labor to capture water from natural springs and provide water to the mission gristmill located below the dam. The gristmill at La Presa, built in the late 1700s or early 1800s, no longer exists but portions of the dam are still visible at the site. (Sunny Slope Water Company.)

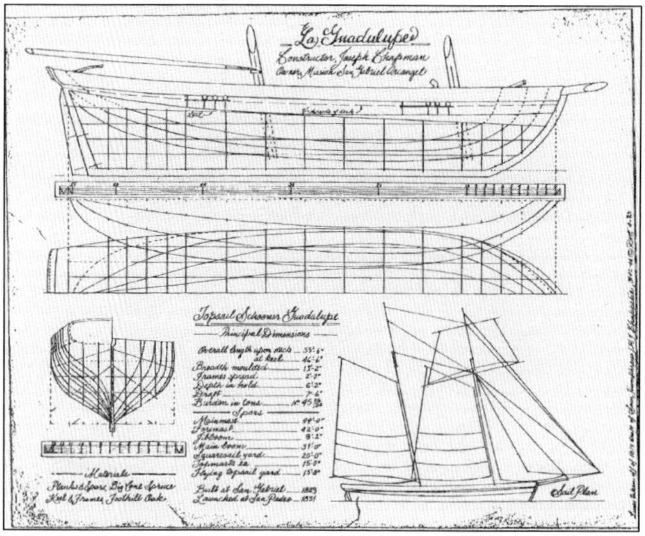

The *Guadalupe* was a 99-ton topsail schooner built at the San Gabriel Mission in 1830 by former pirate Joseph Chapman, Michael White, Thomas Pain, and Mission Indians. The schooner was then dismantled and hauled by carts before being reassembled and launched in San Pedro. The *Guadalupe* was the first ship built in California from native materials. The rusty remains of the 19th-century anchor are now on display in the gardens of the San Gabriel Mission. (Richard Cunningham Collection.)

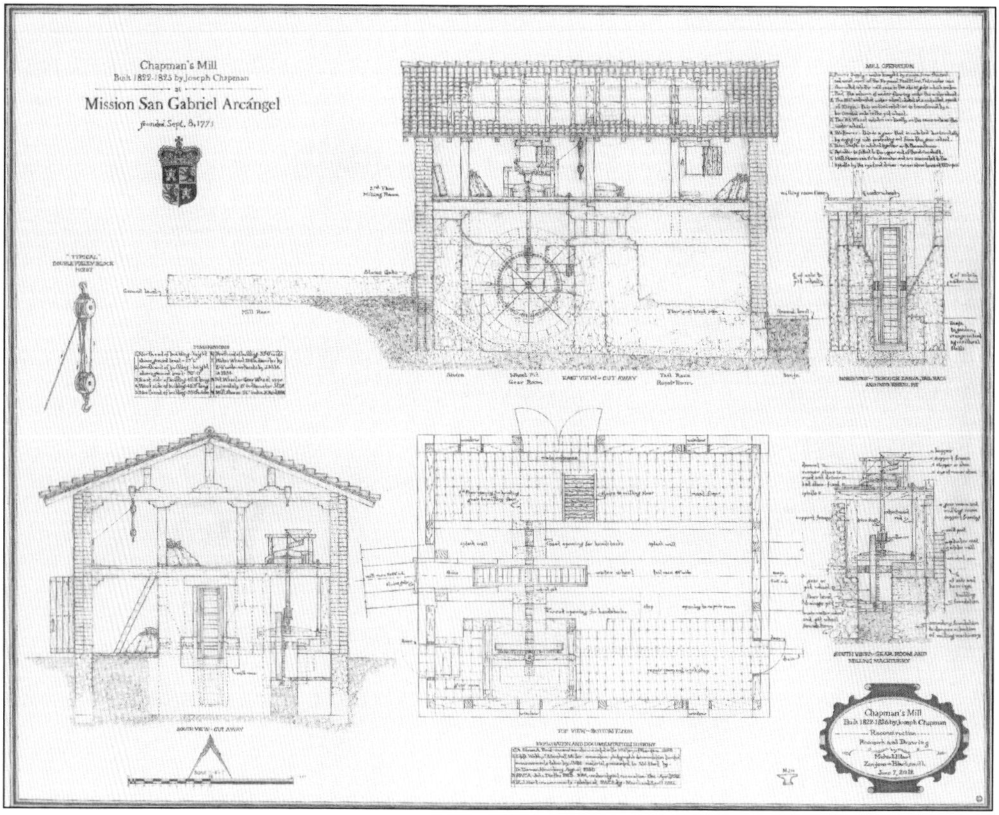

Chapman Mill, as drawn by Michael J. Hart, was built between 1823 and 1824 using a New England–style mill technology with a vertically aligned mill wheel rather than the less efficient Spanish horizontal wheel used at El Molino Viejo. The vertical wheel made better use of the lower water flow present at the mission. Joseph Chapman came to San Gabriel in 1821 at the request of Fr. Jose Maria de Zalvidea to build a more efficient mill closer to the mission. (Michael Hart Collection.)

In this 1934 photograph, Gabrielino Temple poses against the wall of the flume from the Chapman Mill ruins. Portions of the gristmill, which was built between 1823 and 1824, were exposed during the 1934 excavation conducted by Edith Webb, but none of the actual working mechanisms were found. Along with being a painter, Webb was the author of *Indian Life at the Old Missions*, a culmination of many decades of research on the missions. (San Gabriel Historical Association.)

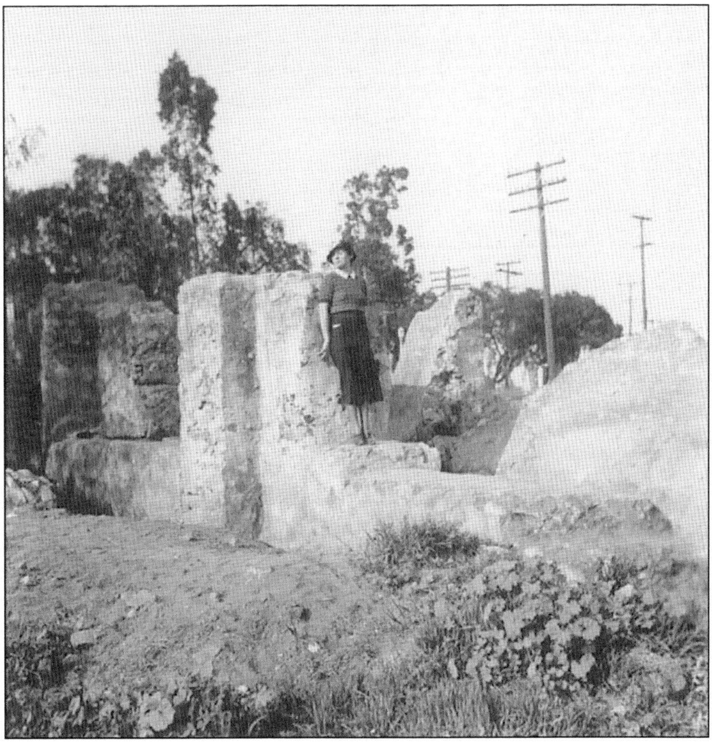

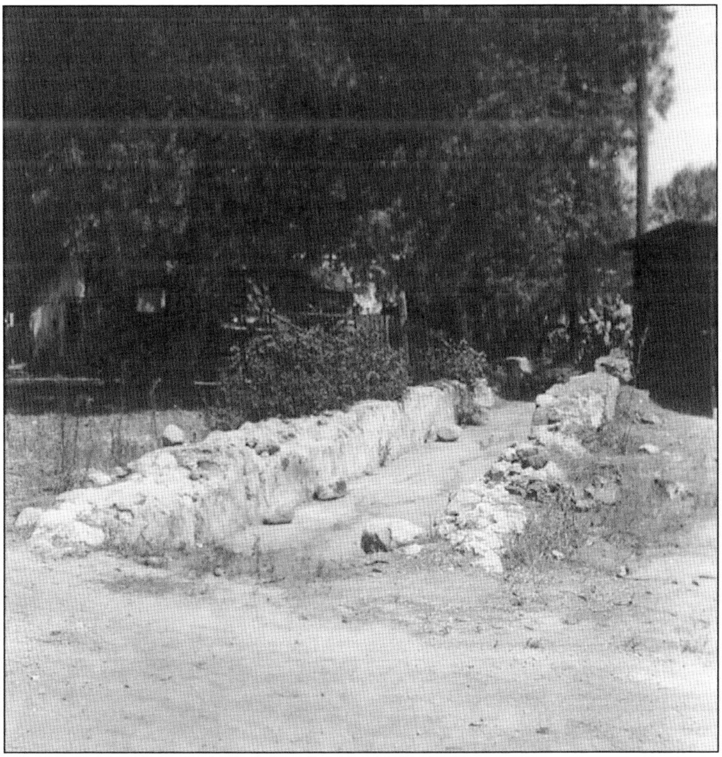

A small portion of the millrace for the Chapman Mill was exposed during the 1934 excavation conducted by Edith Webb. (San Gabriel Historical Association.)

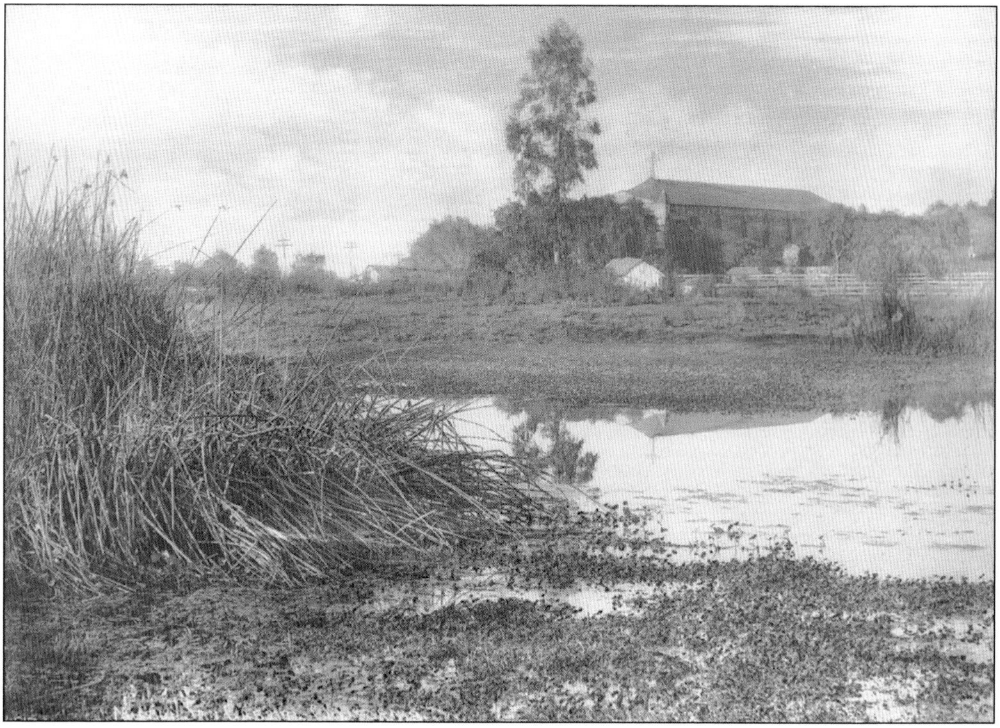

This 1889 view of the San Gabriel Mission, looking southwest, shows the natural lake and marshland. (Regional History Center, Special Collections Department, University of Southern California.)

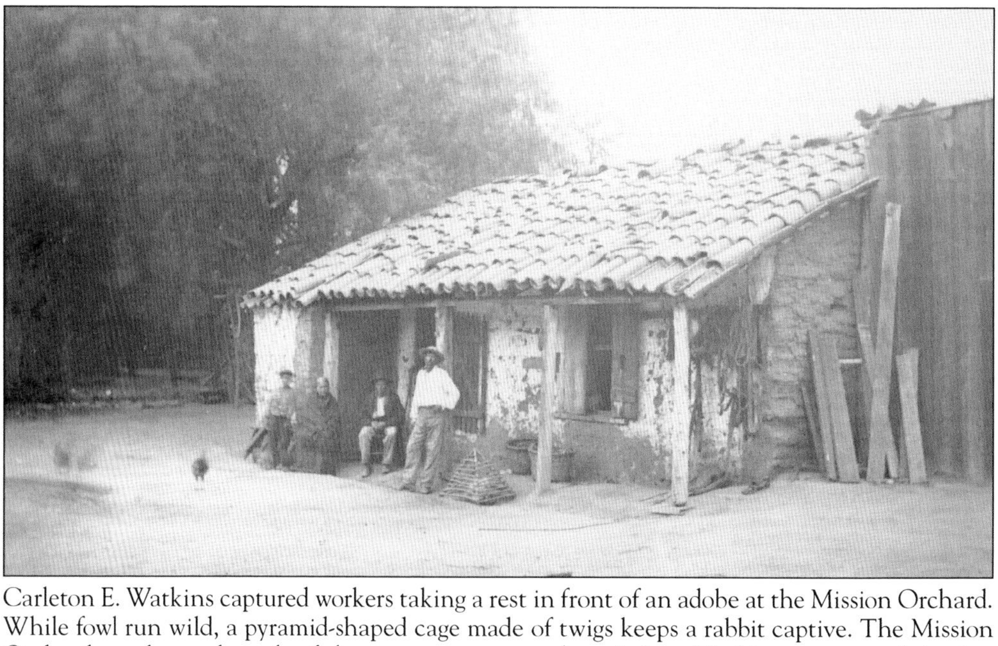

Carleton E. Watkins captured workers taking a rest in front of an adobe at the Mission Orchard. While fowl run wild, a pyramid-shaped cage made of twigs keeps a rabbit captive. The Mission Orchard was located south of the east entrance to the mission. Watkins was one of the few photographers of the time known to have taken pictures of Southern California's Indian population. (Huntington Library.)

Doña Eulalia Perez de Guillen, born at the military port of Loreto, Baja California, around 1766 traveled to Alta California as a soldier's wife and in her later years served as the *llavera* (keeper of the keys) at the mission, providing nursing and welfare activities among the Indians and soldiers. She performed her duties so well that on Easter day 1826, Fr. José María de Zalvidea supposedly presented her with a grant of 14,000 acres known as Rancho San Pasqual, present-day Pasadena, South Pasadena, Altadena, and San Marino. Today, this story seems to be more mythical than reality as no evidence of a deed in her name exists. Eulalia is buried in the mission church cemetery. (Bancroft Library, University of California, Berkeley.)

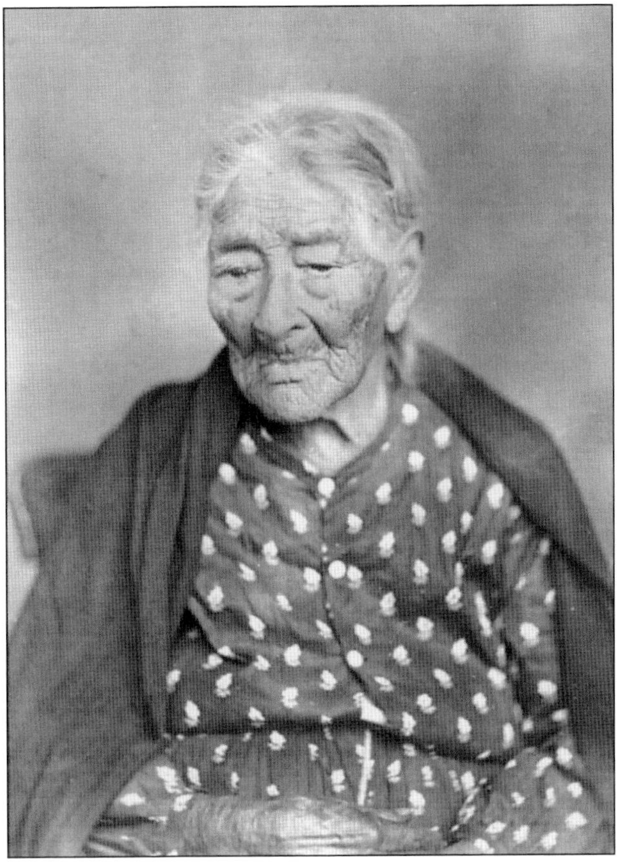

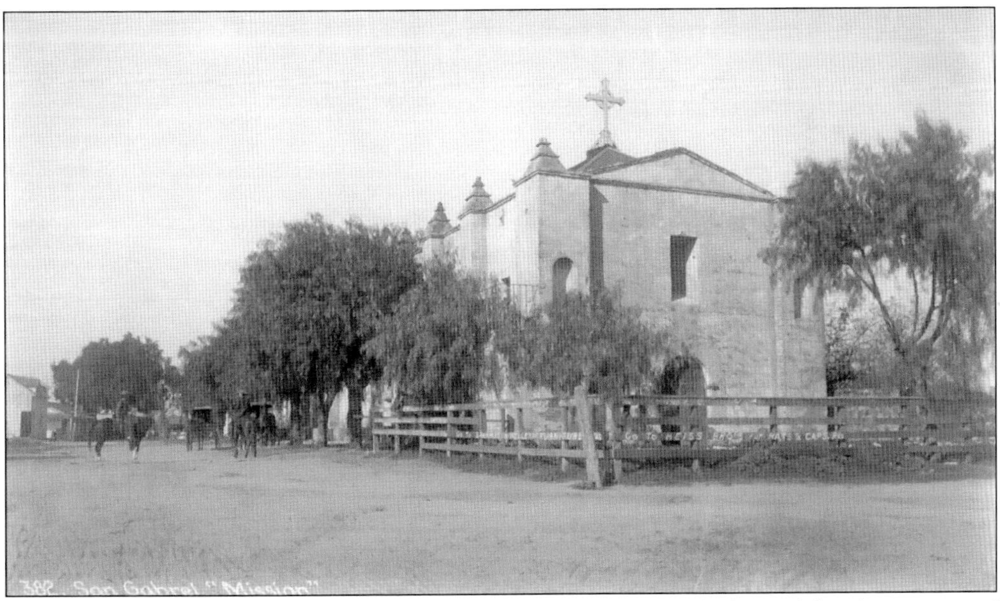

The wood fence enclosing the east end of the mission was regularly used for the posting of advertisements, including the ones shown in this image: "Booths sure death squirrel poison," and "Go to Heiss Bro's for hats and caps." (Bancroft Library, University of California, Berkeley.)

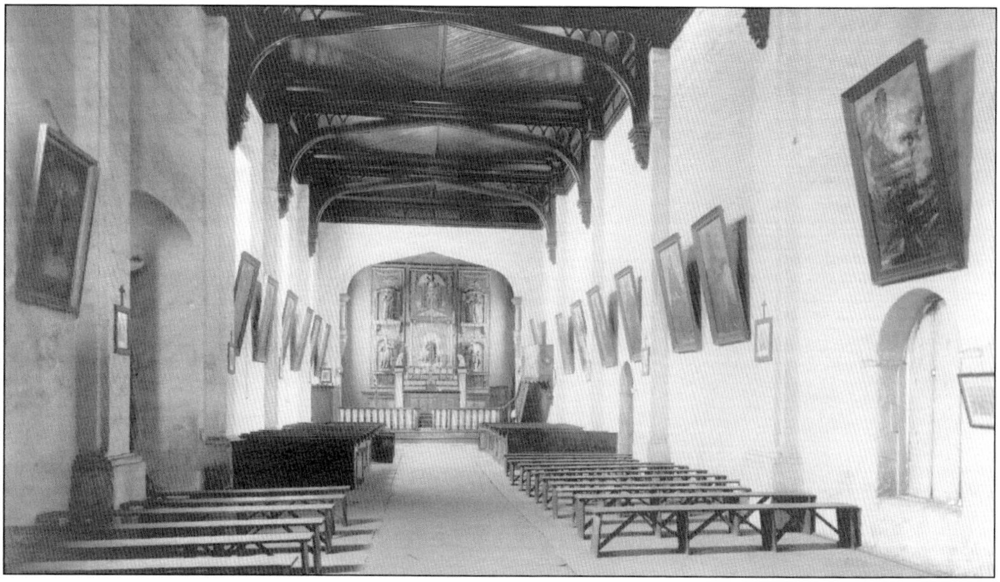

On Sunday, February 7, 1904, parishioners from all over the county gathered at the San Gabriel Mission to celebrate the first service illuminated by incandescent globes. Electricity had arrived at the historic mission, fed from the wires of the Pacific Electric Company's trolley line. Each time a trolley neared the mission, the lamps dimmed, with the candles on the altar providing the only illumination. While this was a novelty to most, others felt that a dozen candles would have been most adequate. (Regional History Center, Special Collections Department, University of Southern California.)

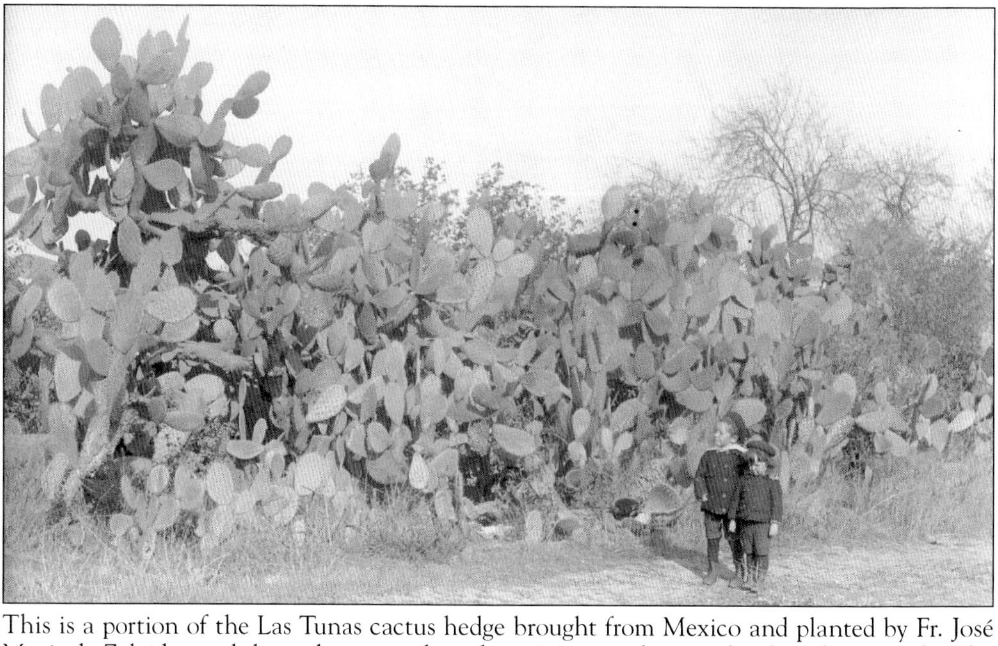

This is a portion of the Las Tunas cactus hedge brought from Mexico and planted by Fr. José María de Zalvidea and the padres to enclose the mission gardens, orchard, and vineyards. The enclosure, which was approximately a mile square, protected the grounds from roaming bands of horses and cattle that thrived on the wild oats that covered the terrain. The fruit was also used as food by the Gabrieleño Indians. (San Gabriel Historical Association.)

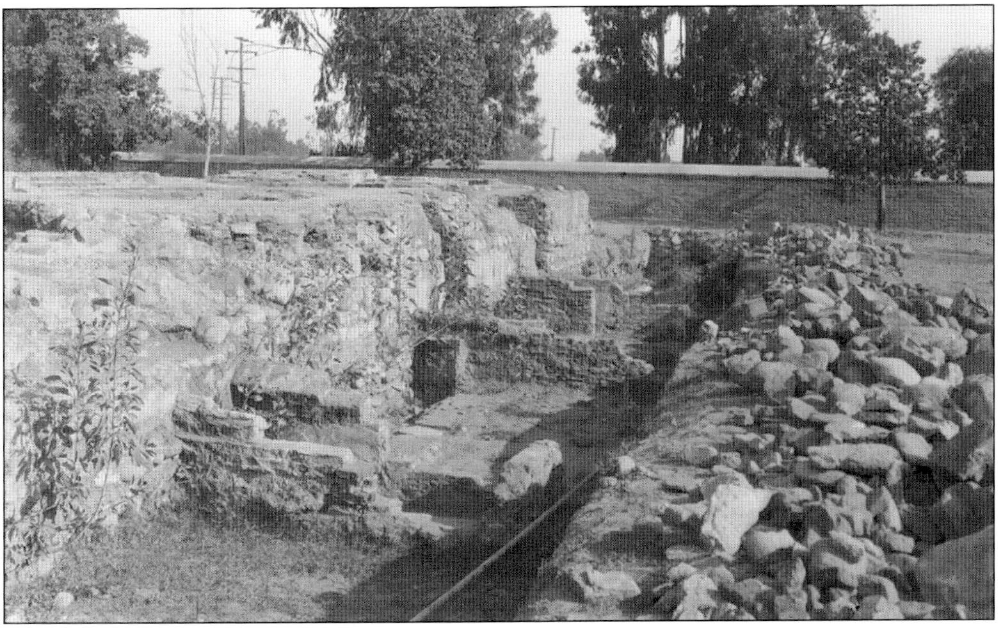

These ruins of the ancient bake ovens used by the Gabrieleño Indians were located behind the church around 1908. (Regional History Center, Special Collections Department, University of Southern California.)

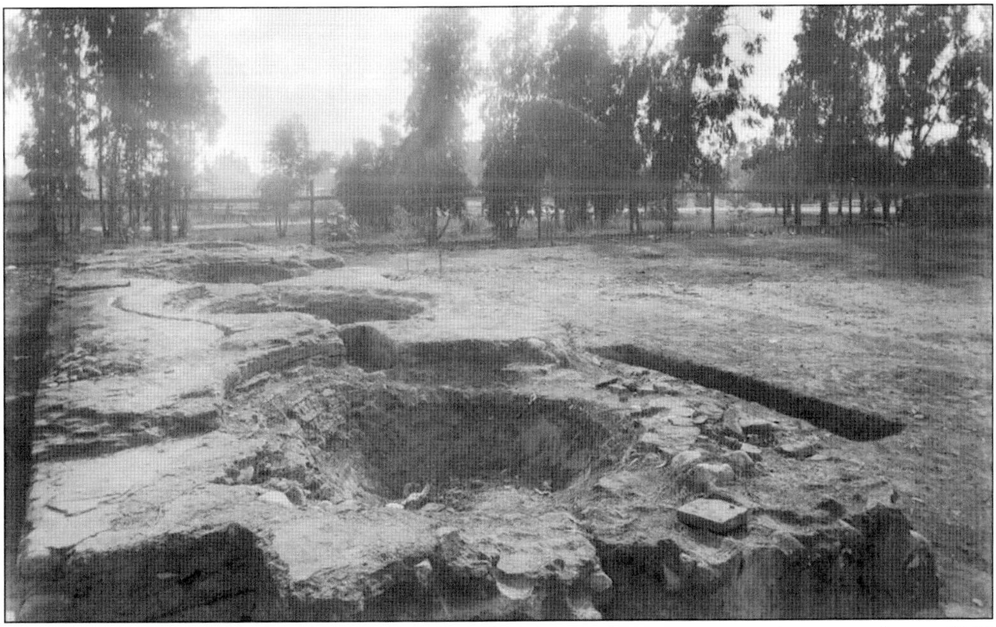

Ancient soap vats used by the Gabrieleño Indians near the mission are shown in this c. 1908 photograph. The soap factory, which supplied soap to most of the California missions, consisted of four large furnaces or boilers, each of which held from 2,000 to 2,500 gallons of water. The furnaces were made of brick, stone, and lime and were built in the shape of a sugar loaf. Strips of iron sheet metal 8 or 10 inches wide lined the mouth of each cistern and each of the pots. A large iron pot was set on each of the furnaces so the fire below could keep it boiling. (Regional History Center, Special Collections Department, University of Southern California.)

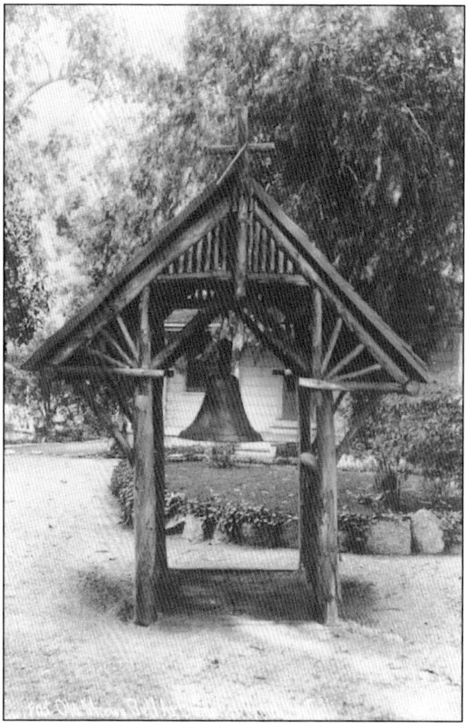

The mission bell hung proudly under this covering on the Lucky Baldwin Ranch for a number of years and was a popular tourist attraction that appeared in a number of photographs. No one knows for sure how Elias J. "Lucky" Baldwin came into possession of the "stolen" bell, but rumor has it that the bell blew into the passing buckboard—which belonged to Baldwin—during a heavy windstorm in 1870. It was eventually returned to the San Gabriel Mission by Anita Baldwin sometime after her father's death. (Richard Arnold Collection.)

This 1924 aerial photograph provides a good perspective of buildings within the San Gabriel Mission complex. The brick building on the northeast corner of Santa Anita Avenue and Mission Drive, where the military quarters once stood, was later replaced by the Billiard Saloon. The church rectory and convent was originally the fenced-in bullring attached to the east of the military quarters. (Security Pacific National Bank Collection, Los Angeles Public Library.)

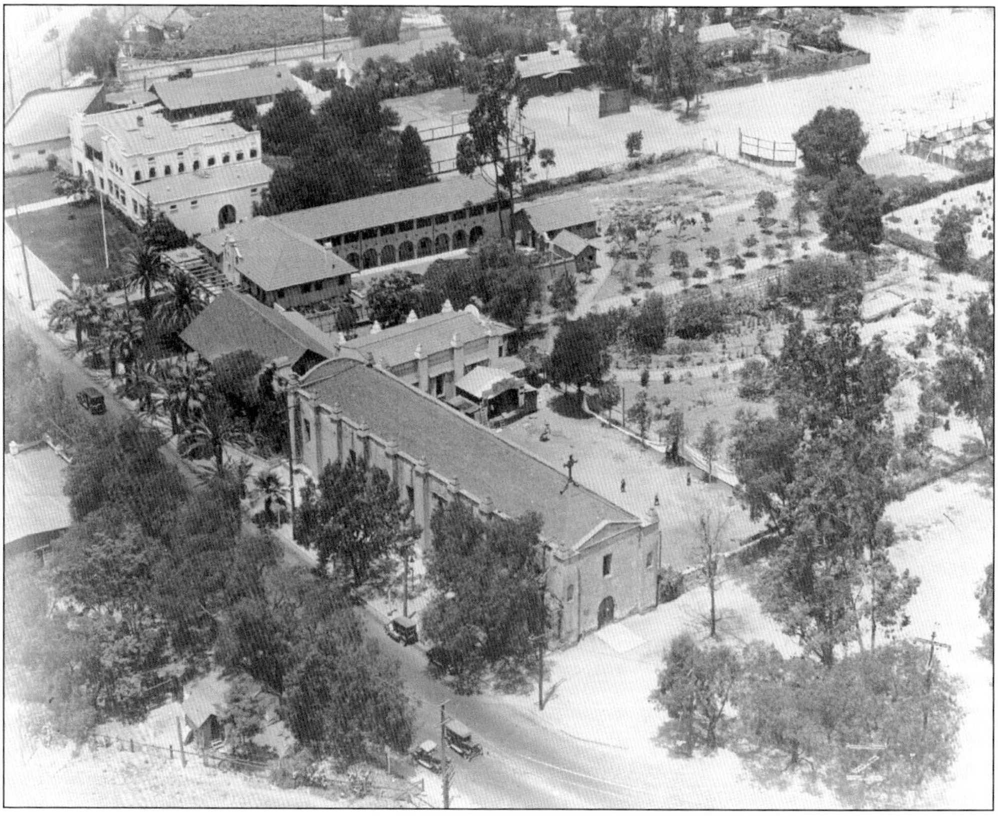

Three

San Gabriel Township

In her children's book *The Hunter Cats*—published in 1884, the same year she published *Ramona*—Helen Hunt Jackson describes San Gabriel as follows: "You can find this name San Gabriel on your atlas, if you look carefully. It is in small print, and on the atlas it is not more than the width of a pin from the water's edge; but it really is thirty miles, a good day's ride, and a beautiful day's ride too, from the sea. San Gabriel is a little village, only a dozen or two houses in it. And an old, half-ruined church, a Catholic church, that was built there a hundred years ago, when the country was first settled by the Spaniards. They named all the places they settled, after saints; and the first thing they did in every place was to build a church, and get the Indians to come and be baptized, and learn to pray."

The first American citizen to come overland to San Gabriel was Jedediah Strong Smith, who led a group of trappers down from the Great Salt Lake and across the Mojave Desert, arriving at San Gabriel Mission in November 1826. The first organized wagon train to San Gabriel brought William Workman, John Rowland, and Benjamin D. Wilson on November 5, 1841. By 1852, San Gabriel became one of the first townships in Los Angeles County, and according to the 1860 census, the population was a mere 586.

In his 1883 book *A Southern California Paradise*, R.W.C. Farnsworth described "modern" San Gabriel as follows: "To the tourist, familiar with the conventional village of the East, San Gabriel presents a peculiar aspect. The low-roofed *adobe* houses, and the dark, graved faced people, who sit in their doorways or move listlessly about their various callings, seem to form no part of our energetic republic, but rather shadow the splendor of a departed age."

San Gabriel was an inviting town, attracting many visitors and pioneers, but it was also a town typical of the "Wild West," with regular shootings and occasional murders. Outlaws often met their fates on Fort Hill in Los Angeles, where their last necktie was a rope.

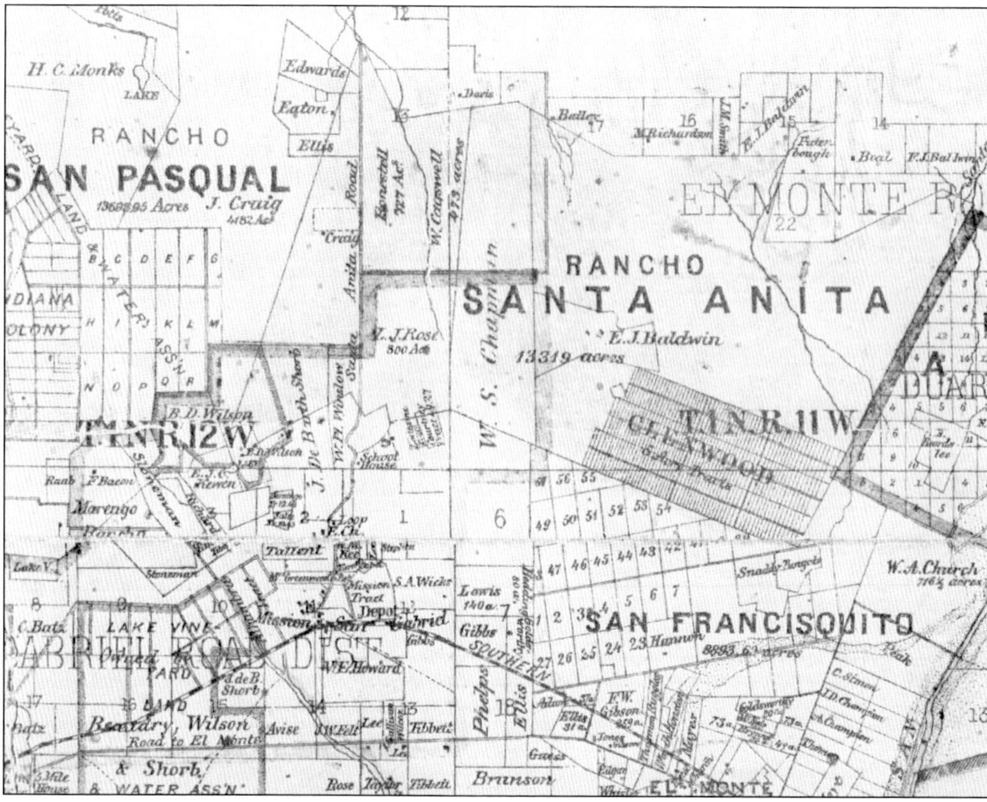

This photograph shows a section of a map of Los Angeles County compiled by J.H. Wildy in 1877. Properties of interest include those of Benjamin D. Wilson, Leonard J. Rose, Elias J. "Lucky" Baldwin (Rancho Santa Anita), Volney E. Howard, Edward J. Kewen, and George C. Gibbs. (Huntington Library.)

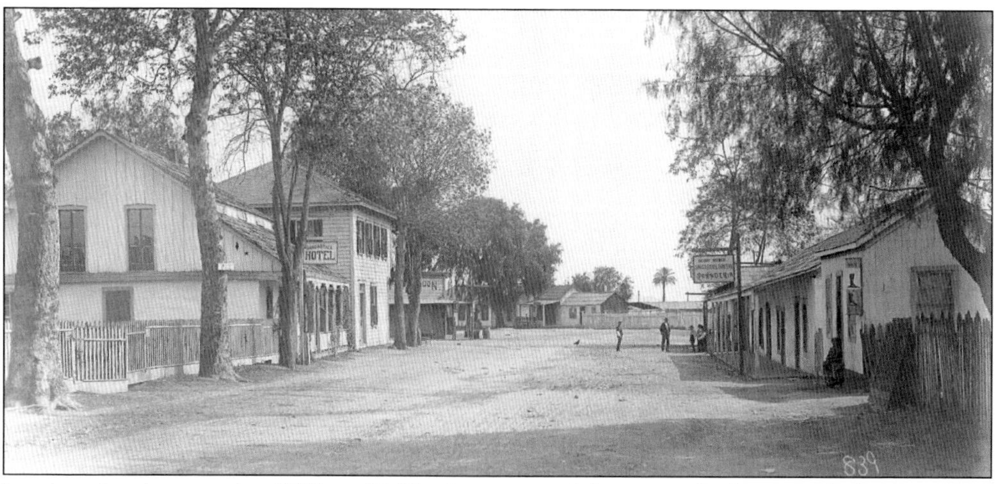

Los Angeles photographer William H. Fletcher captured this image looking south down Mission Drive in 1890. Fletcher learned photography while working in the pharmaceutical and jewelry industries and moved to Los Angeles in 1885 with plans to establish himself as a druggist. He quickly discovered that there was an overabundance of pharmacies, so he decided to change careers. (California History Section, California State Library, Sacramento, California.)

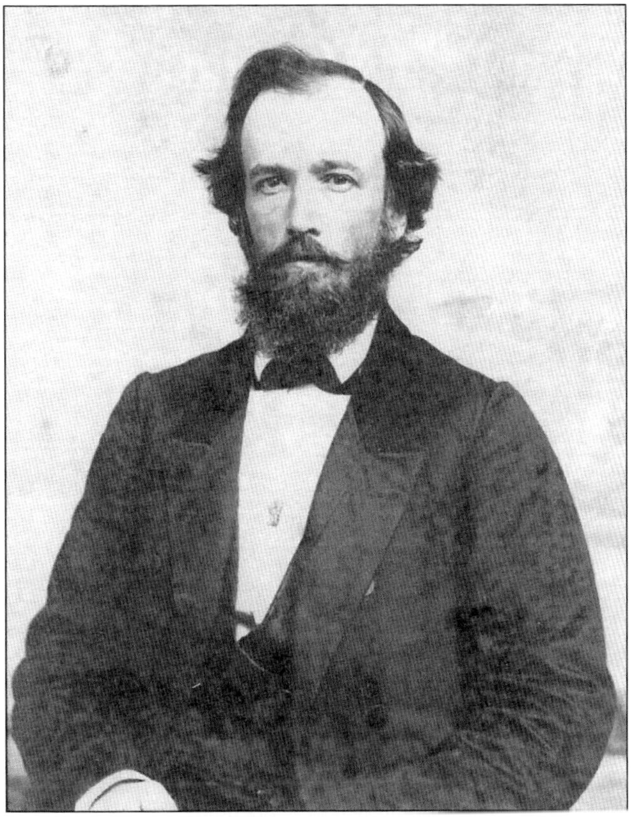

David Franklin Hall arrived in San Gabriel in 1854 and, with his friend Dr. George Rice, purchased the adobe house and lot on the east side of Mission Drive from Hipolito Cervantes. Hall opened a grocery store, and, on August 23, 1861, was appointed the second postmaster of San Gabriel, a position he held until December 29, 1874. Around 1871, Hall converted the small, three-bedroom adobe into a hotel, which he ran for 10 years as the San Gabriel Hotel—the only hotel in San Gabriel. The exact date this adobe was built is unknown but predates the 1850s. (Richard Arnold Collection.)

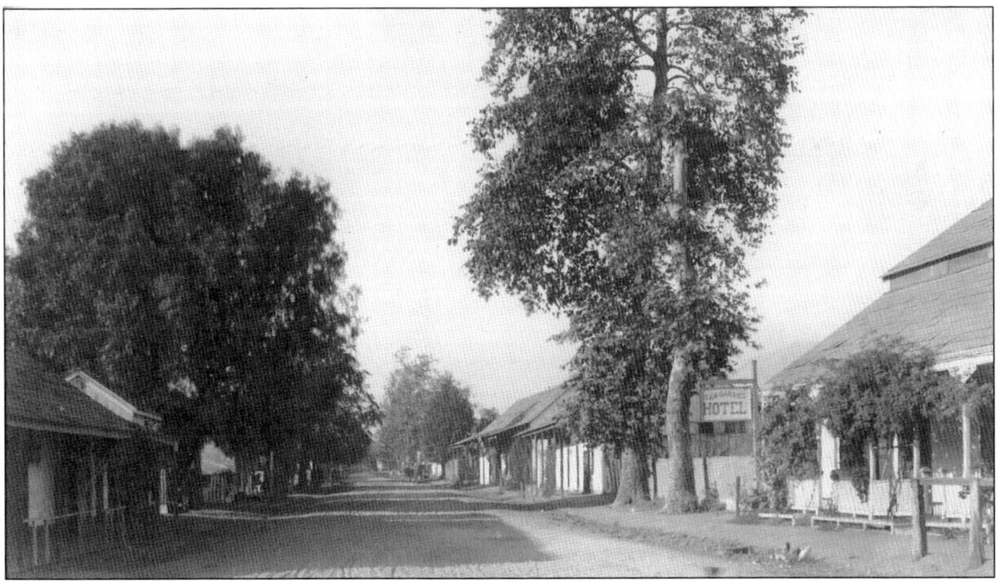

In the spring of 1861, David Hall was given a wild grapevine from L.J. Rose, which he transplanted behind his San Gabriel Hotel with the assistance of Rose. Rose had purchased land, which he improved, that included the grapevine, and he called this land Sunny Slope. The grapevine obstructed his plans, so he gave it to Hall. Proof of the planting is documented on an affidavit signed by Hall. (San Gabriel Historical Association.)

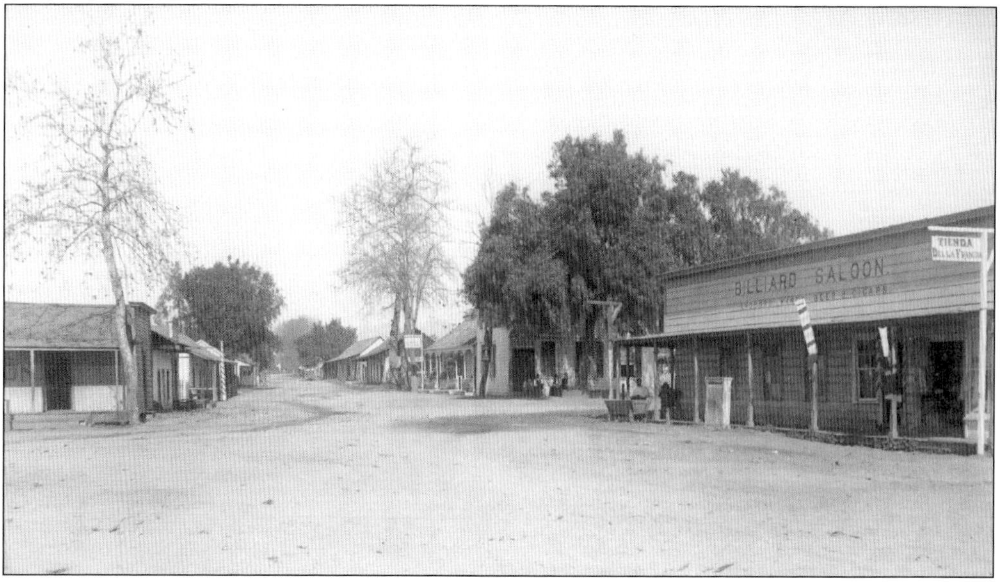

J.A. Duarte was the proprietor of the Billiard Saloon on the northeast corner of Santa Anita Avenue and Mission Drive. The wood-frame building was razed in the late 1890s and replaced with another saloon constructed with brick. Although the Butterfield stagecoach did not use the San Gabriel Hotel or the local saloon as "official" stops, it was common for establishments such as the Billiard Saloon to utilize a semaphore device similar to those used by railroads to flag down a coach for customers. This was referred to as a flag stop. (San Gabriel Historical Association.)

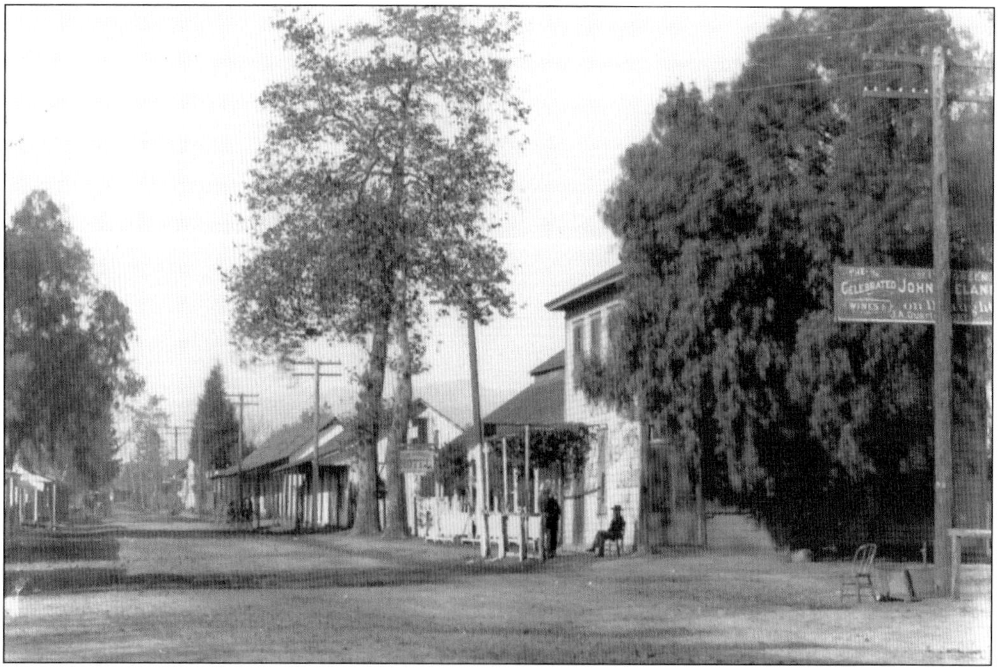

This c. 1893 photograph shows Mission Drive looking north from Santa Anita Avenue. The sign posted on the power pole belonged to the Billard Saloon and advertised for Wieland Beer. John Wieland, a gold miner, owned and operated one of the most successful and largest breweries on the West Coast from 1856 until his death in 1885. (San Gabriel Historical Association.)

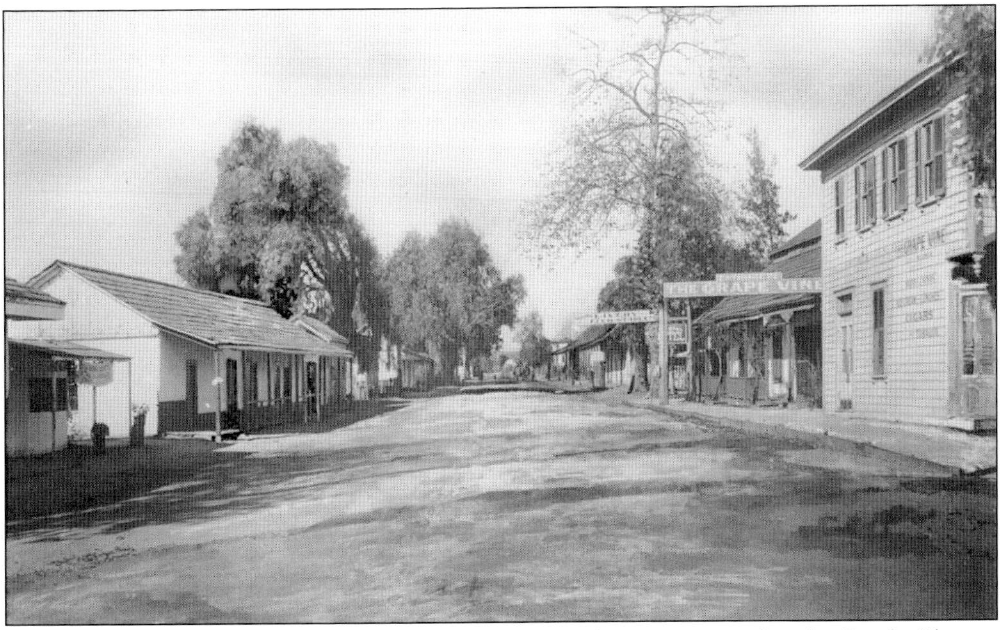

This photograph of Mission Drive was taken in the early 1900s soon after the Pacific Electric arrived in San Gabriel on June 2, 1902. For unknown reasons, the original photograph has been painstakingly retouched by an artist to remove the power poles, trolley poles, and streetcar tracks that were originally present in the photograph. The same image was printed and used for postcards with the power poles, trolley poles, and streetcar tracks visible and was artistically colored instead of the original black and white. (Regional History Center, Special Collections Department, University of Southern California.)

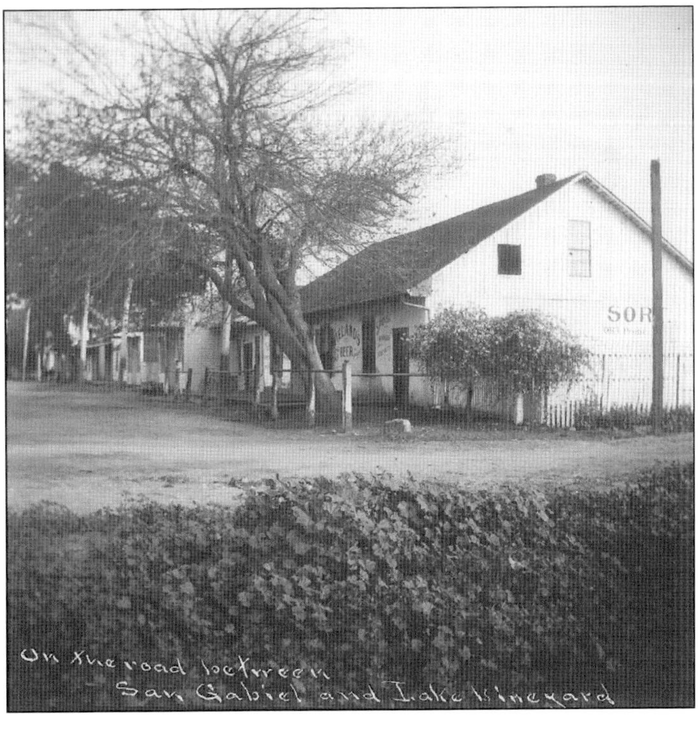

This is one of the many saloons that were commonplace along Mission Drive and Santa Anita Avenue. This particular saloon was located mid-block on Santa Anita Avenue between Mission Drive and present-day Broadway. Wieland's Beer, advertised on the front of the saloon, was manufactured at the Wieland Brewery in San Francisco. George W. Hazard took this photograph around 1885. (Ernest Marquez Collection.)

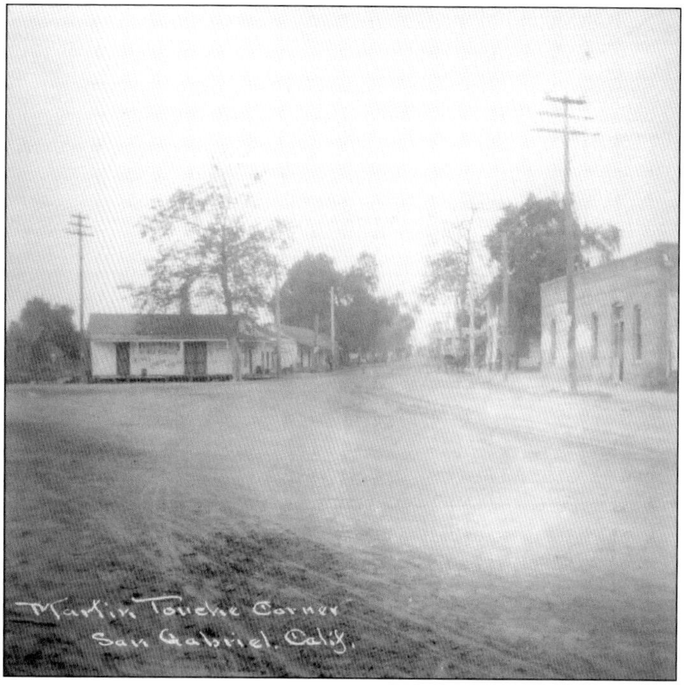

This late-1880s photograph of the corner of Santa Anita Avenue and Mission Drive was taken by George W. Hazard. Hazard was a pioneer historian and photographer who visited practically every historical landmark in Los Angeles County, obtaining photographs and data for a book he was writing on the history of the Los Angeles region. Hazard marked the negatives of each of his photographs with the location for future reference. This image was marked "Martin Touche Corner" after the name of the proprietor of the saloon pictured at left. (Ernest Marquez Collection.)

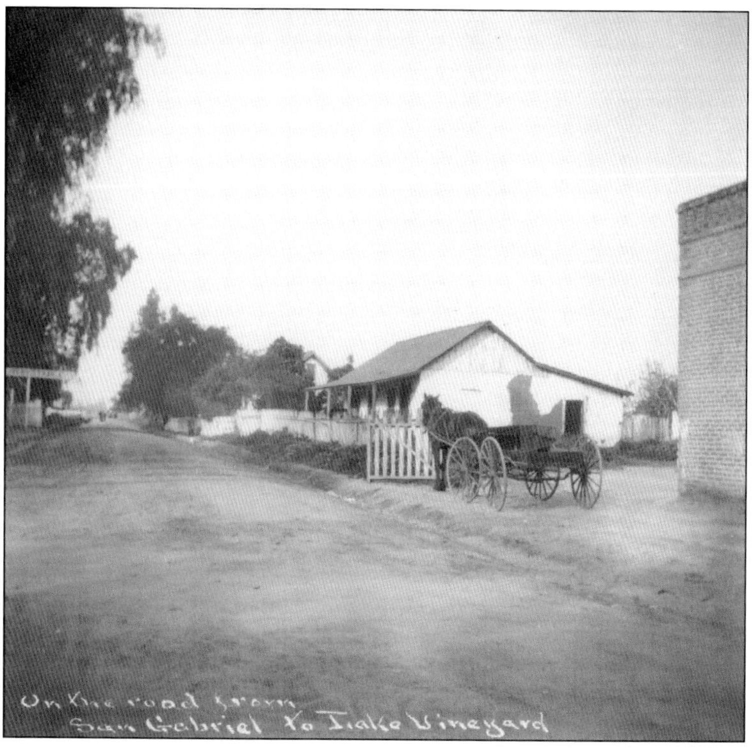

Historian George W. Hazard photographed Santa Anita Avenue looking north from Mission Drive around 1890. The brick building at the far right was constructed as a saloon to replace the wood-framed Billard Saloon occupying the corner where the military quarters for the San Gabriel Mission once stood. The two adobes on the right and north of the brick building were part of the original mission quadrangle. (Ernest Marquez Collection.)

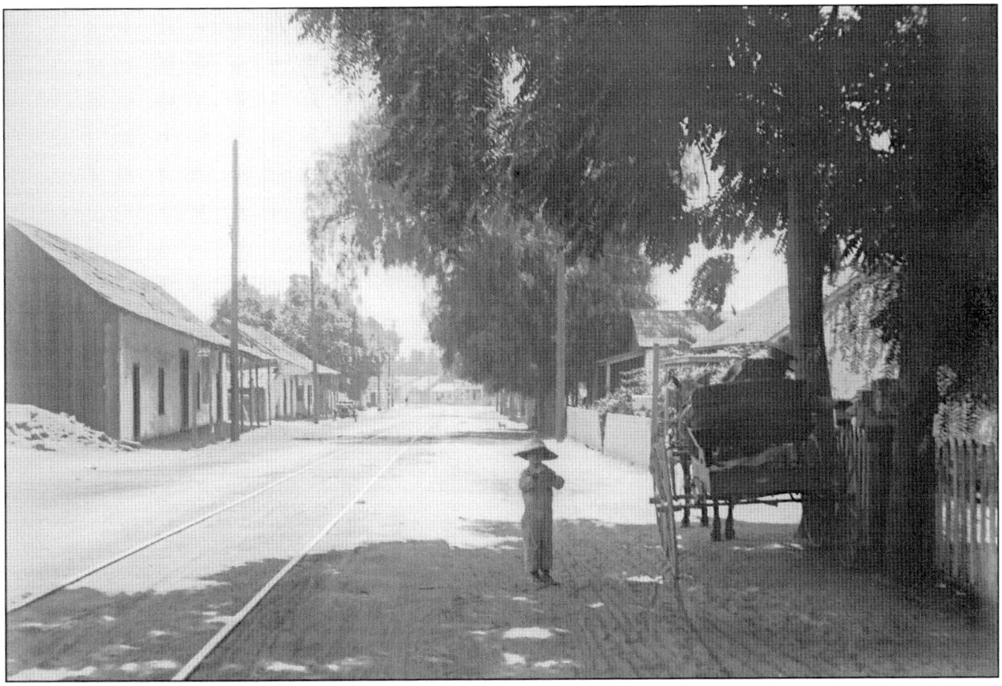

C.H. Wallace arrived in San Gabriel in 1903 and went to work for O.W. Longden, San Gabriel postmaster, as a postal clerk and store clerk. Twice a week he delivered mail on his rural route within San Gabriel Township, northeast to Arcadia and what is now Rosemead and Temple City. This photograph shows Wallace in his carriage as he works his route delivering mail along Mission Drive. Wallace later became assistant postmaster to Longden around 1905. (Colorado Historical Society.)

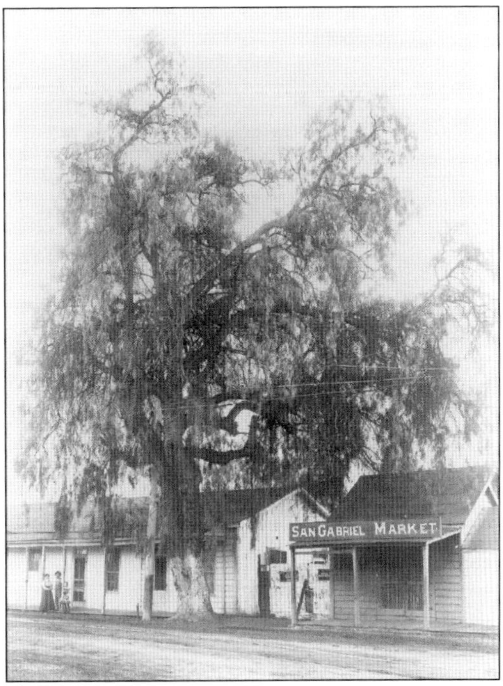

Located mid-block on Mission Drive, the San Gabriel Market was one of the few wood-frame structures on the adobe-lined street; none of the wooden buildings remain today. Although this 1905 photograph was taken two years prior to the arrival of Henry Huntington's Pacific Electric streetcars, it appears that the throngs of visitors to the historic San Gabriel Mission, located a mere block away, had yet to visit this quaint part of town. (Richard Arnold Collection.)

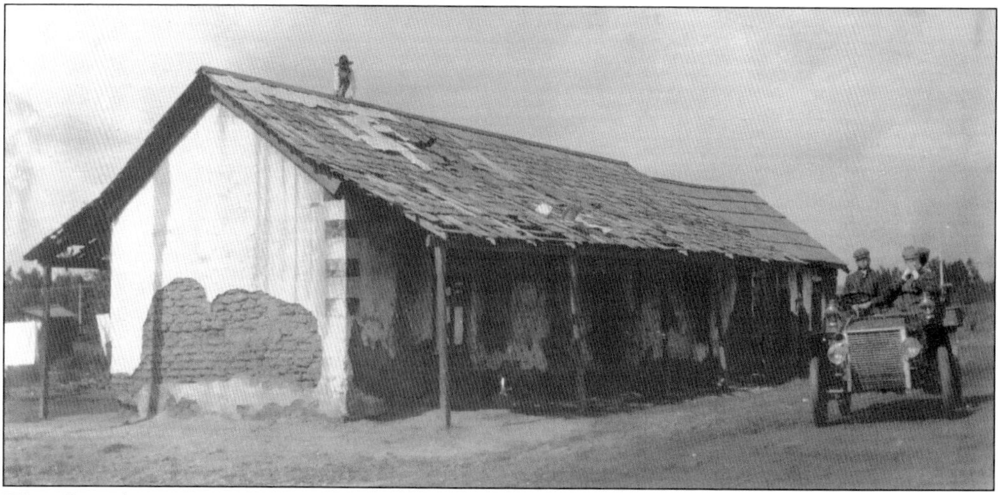

This "horseless carriage" was an unusual sight on Mission Drive around 1910 as it headed south towards the San Gabriel Mission. (Regional History Center, Special Collections Department, University of Southern California.)

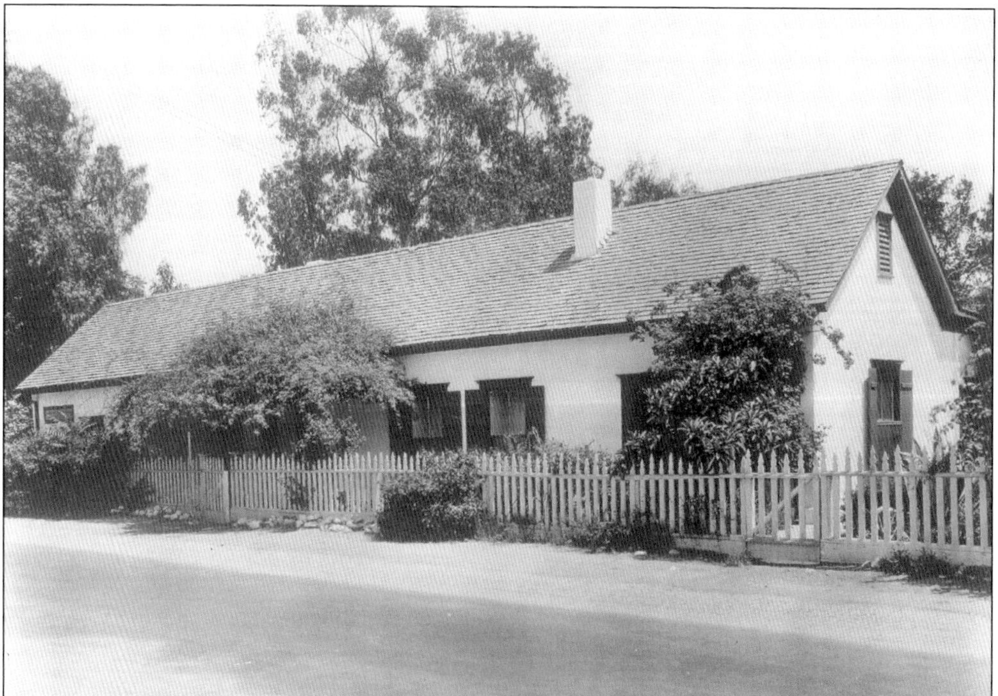

The Lopez de Lowther adobe, located at 330 Santa Anita Avenue, was built between 1800 and 1806 and was apparently one of the original structures in the west end of the mission quadrangle. The long, narrow shape suggests that the adobe may have once served as housing for soldiers or Gabrieleño Indians. The house was acquired from the Catholic Church in 1849 by Don Juan Neopomuceno Lopez, a local silversmith, and eventually passed on to one of his children, Maria Lopez. Maria married Hugh Sears Lowther in 1920, thus the name Lopez de Lowther. Maria moved to Laguna Hills in 1965 and sold the adobe back to the Los Angeles Diocese of the Catholic Church. (Richard Arnold Collection.)

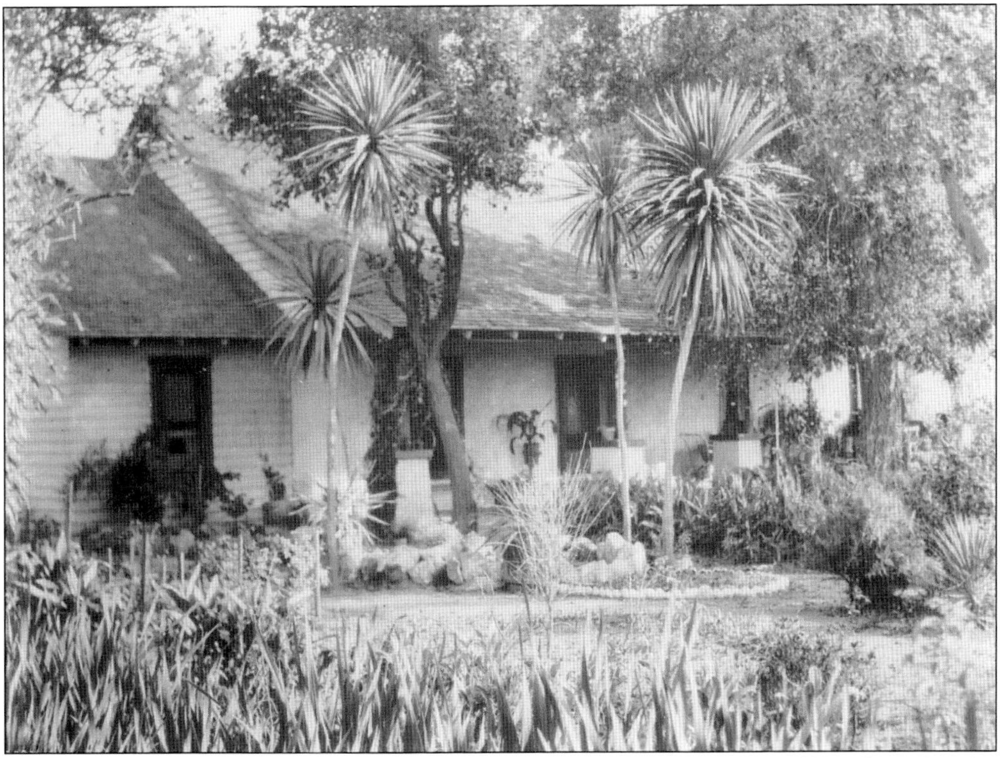

The Ortega-Vigare adobe, located at 616 South Ramona Street, was originally L-shaped and is now only half its original size. The adobe, believed to have been built by Estevan Munos in the early 1850s, became the property of Don Jean Vigare in the early 1860s. The Hancock survey map of 1853, in which the house is conspicuously absent, invites suspicion about earlier claims that the adobe was built between 1792 and 1805. (San Gabriel Historical Association.)

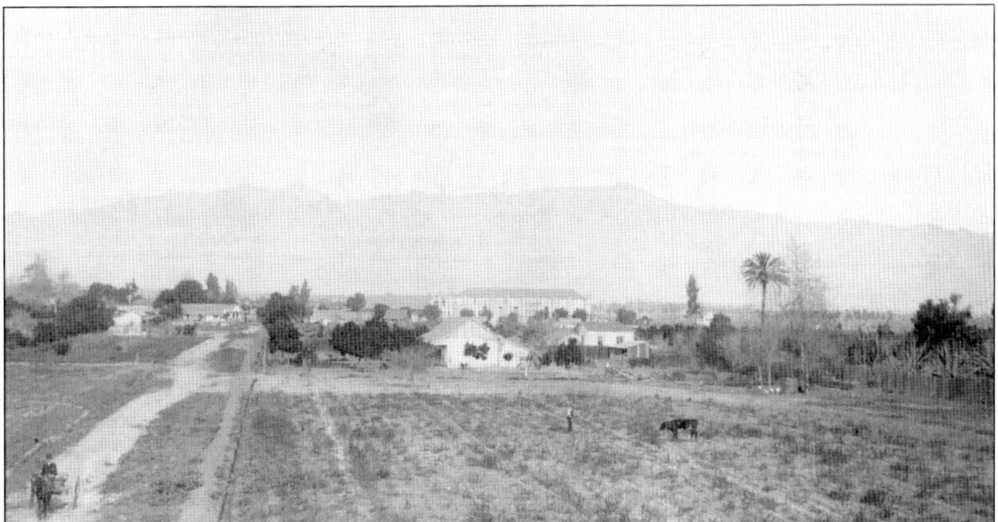

This view of Ramona Street looks north with the Ortega-Vigare adobe visible in the foreground. The downward angle of the photograph suggests that the photographer perhaps climbed a tree to get a better visual of the streetscape around 1880. (San Gabriel Historical Association.)

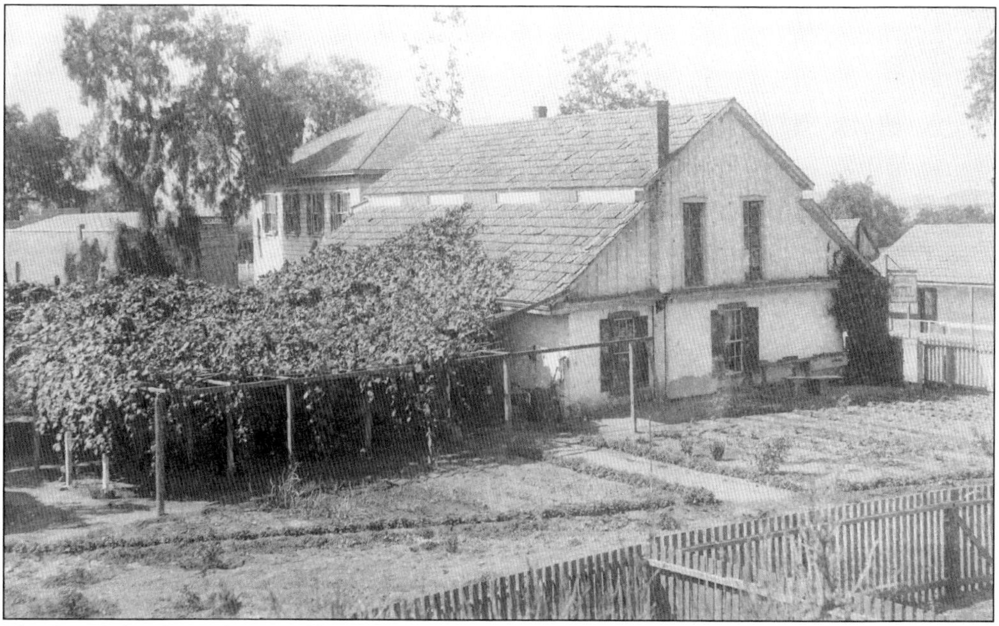

The San Gabriel Hotel, opened by David F. Hall around 1854, became the Bailey Hotel in 1882 when George Bailey purchased the adobe from Hall. Known by many names, including the Grapevine Inn when it was owned by Kate C. Bailey McCormick, the adobe became the Café de Espanola in the 1930s and eventually named Ramona's Home after *Ramona*, written by Helen Hunt Jackson. The adobe was one of many inns across the state of California that was named after *Ramona*, as proprietors cashed in on the fame of the book to attract customers. Helen Hunt Jackson was, in fact, a visitor to San Gabriel during her research on the Gabrieleño Indians; however, there is no documentation that she ever actually stayed at the hotel. (Ernest Marquez Collection.)

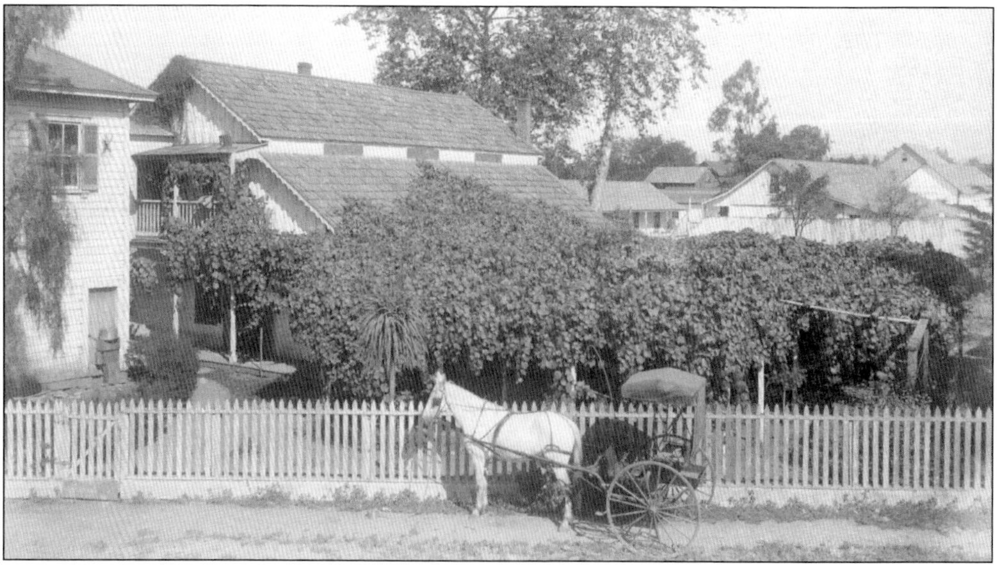

A horse with a carriage waits patiently alongside the San Gabriel Hotel. This photograph shows a rare glimpse of the back of the San Gabriel Hotel and the two-story grocery store that once stood on the northwest corner of Mission Drive and Santa Anita Street. The grocery store was demolished in the early 1900s and replaced by the Spanish-style archway. (Ernest Marquez Collection.)

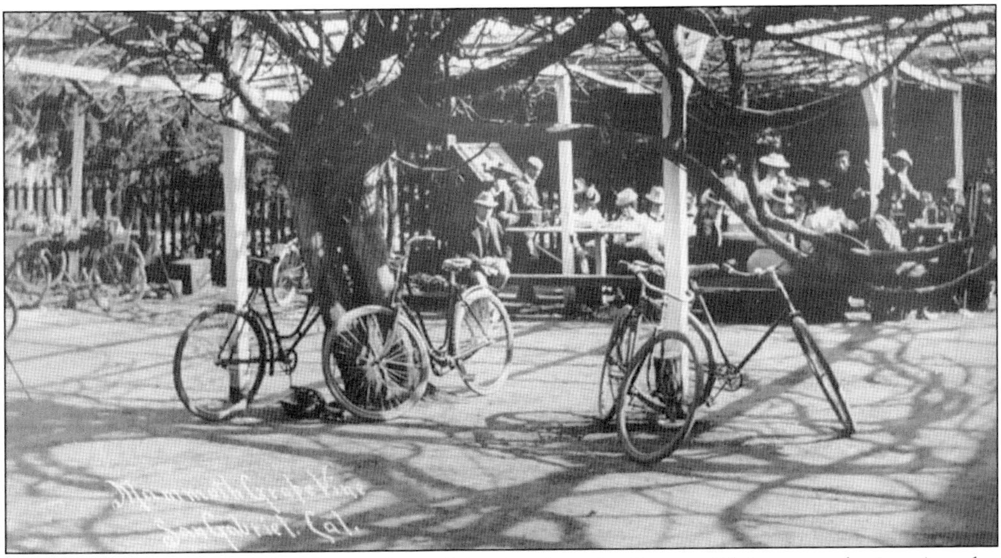

On Saturday, February 19, 1900, members of the Los Angeles Camera Club met at the Los Angeles Chamber of Commerce at 9:00 a.m. for their third outing, a trip to San Gabriel and intermediate points of interest. Anywhere from 15 to 20 members made the run on their bicycles, a dozen were passengers on a Tally-ho carriage or private carriages, and the remainder went by train; a total of 50 members participated. After stops at Eastlake Park and the F.Q. Story ranch home in Alhambra, the group arrived in San Gabriel at 1:00 p.m., where they then visited the historic mission. (Security Pacific National Bank Collection, Los Angeles Public Library.)

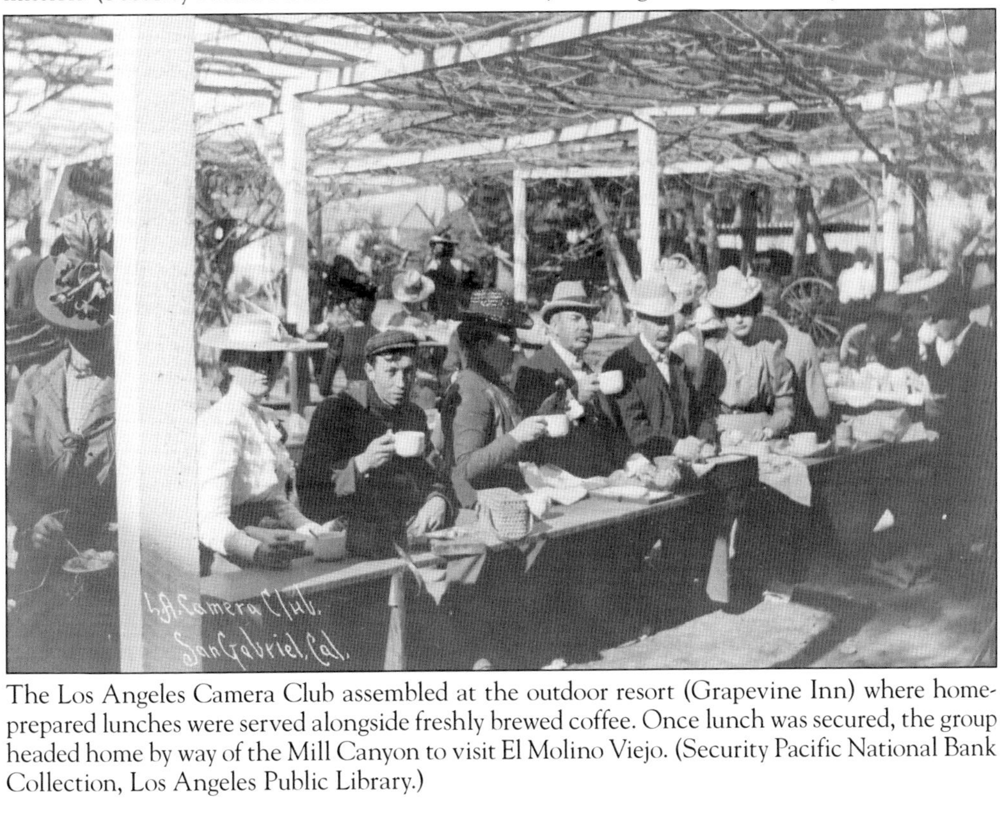

The Los Angeles Camera Club assembled at the outdoor resort (Grapevine Inn) where home-prepared lunches were served alongside freshly brewed coffee. Once lunch was secured, the group headed home by way of the Mill Canyon to visit El Molino Viejo. (Security Pacific National Bank Collection, Los Angeles Public Library.)

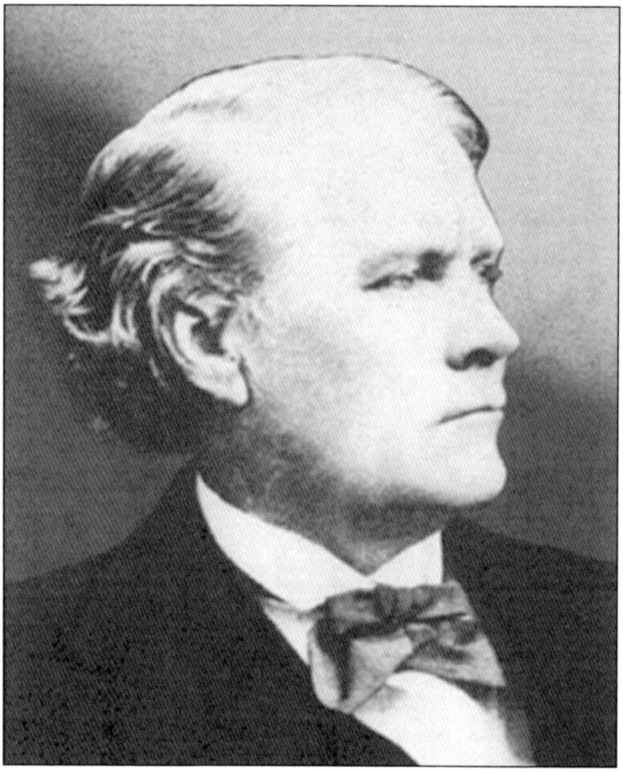

Volney E. Howard, one of many residents of the Las Tunas adobe, served in the US Congress, representing Texas from 1849 to 1853. In 1856, he was appointed major general by California governor J. Neily Johnson to head the state militia. After entering law practice, Howard participated in California's second Constitutional Convention in 1878, which reorganized the state's judicial branch. In 1879, Howard and Ignacio Sepulveda were elected as the first two judges in the newly formed Los Angeles Superior Court. (Richard Arnold Collection.)

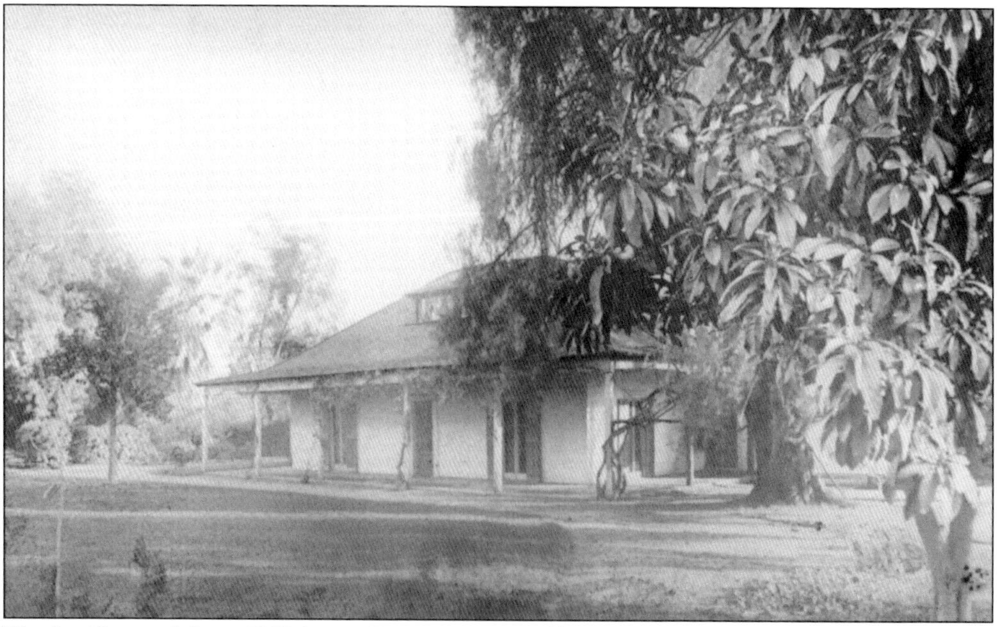

The Las Tunas adobe at 328 Mission Drive—so named because of the tuna cactus that surrounded it—is believed to have been built between 1776 and 1790 as a temporary residence for the padres overseeing the construction of the mission. The house began as a three-room structure and gradually expanded through the years. The first orange tree seedlings planted in California were in the garden of the Las Tunas Ranch around 1815. (Huntington Library.)

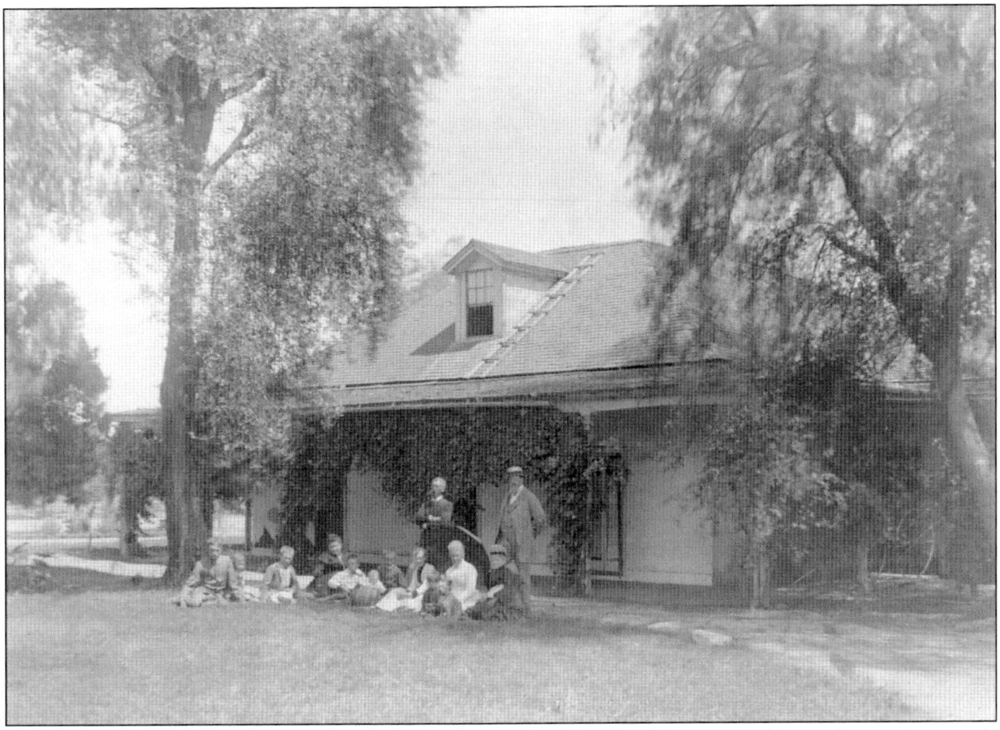

In 1846, the Las Tunas adobe became the property of William Workman and Hugo Reid, along with 16,000 acres of land deeded to them by Gov. Pío Pico. The adobe was sold to Jessie Hildreth in 1852 and Volney Howard later the same year. Howard was elected twice and served as Los Angeles district attorney from 1864 to 1867 and from 1873 to 1876 during his residence in San Gabriel. Gervaise Purcell bought the Las Tunas adobe from Howard in 1880. The Purcell family is shown on the front lawn of the ranch with William Booth, general in command of the Salvation Army, during his visit to Los Angeles on February 27, 1898. (San Gabriel Historical Association.)

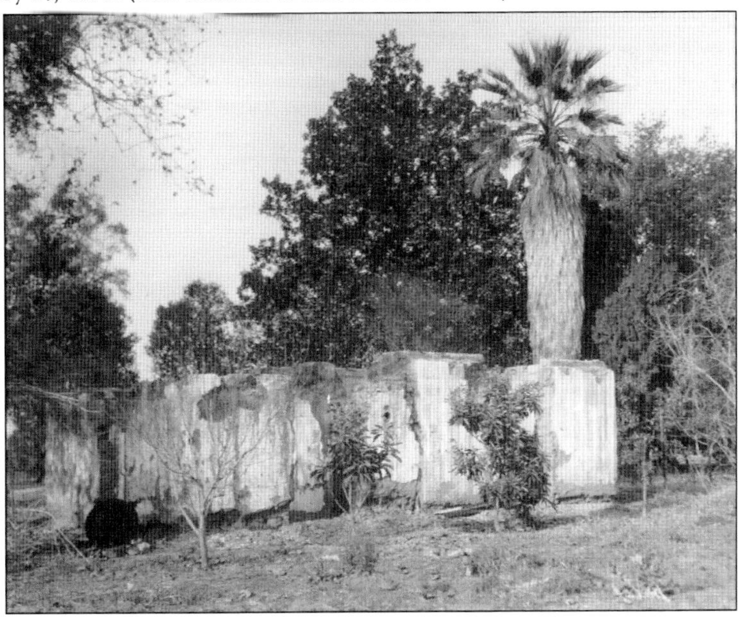

These are the ruins of the Francisco Sales adobe. Sales was one of the Gabrieleño Indians granted a small parcel of land by the governor of California in the 1840s. The Sales property was located north of present-day Roses Road and east of Mission Drive. (Huntington Library.)

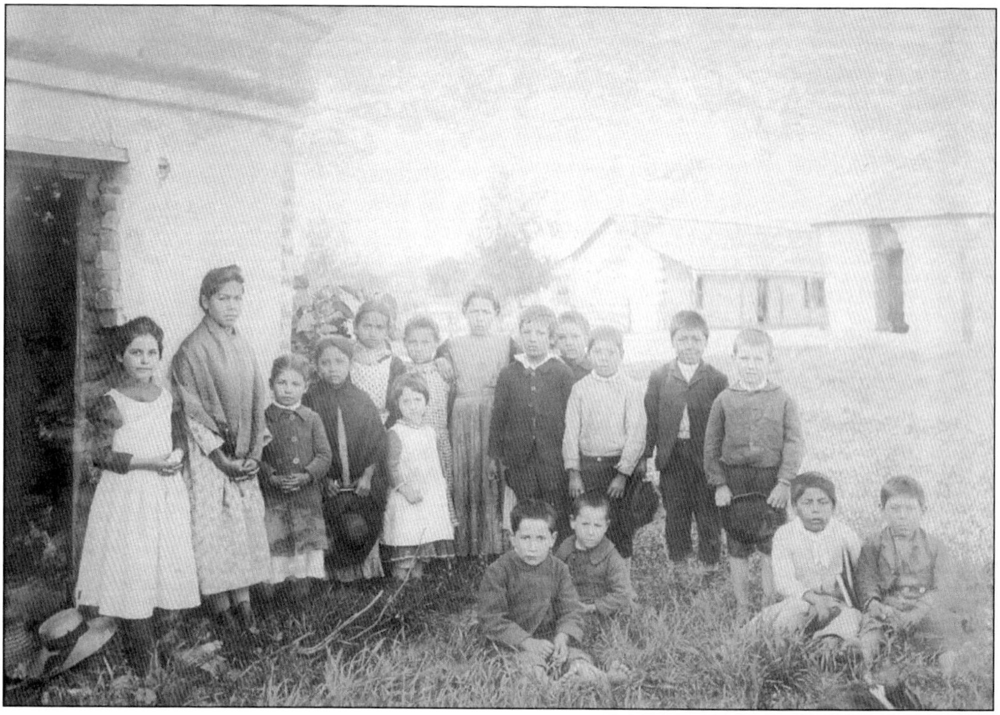

These schoolchildren are pictured around 1875 in front of the Moneyan Institute adobe, which served as a schoolhouse in San Gabriel a short period of time. The adobe belonged to William Money, a theologian, eccentric Angeleno, and the city's first documented cult leader, who had great visions of developing a great university amid the "uncultured" pioneer atmosphere of the West, but his ideas failed to impress the community, so the university never materialized. (Bancroft Library, University of California, Berkeley.)

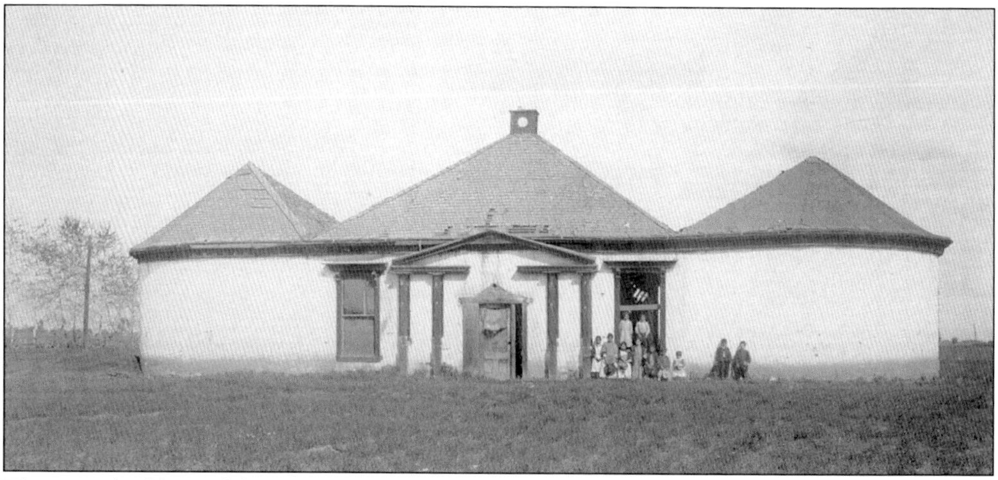

The main building of the Moneyan Institute was constructed by William Money in 1857, soon after he arrived in San Gabriel from Scotland. In 1854, while living in Los Angeles, Money published the *Reform of the New Testament Church*, which blasted the divine phenomena in Catholicism. The bilingual volume was the first book published in Los Angeles. In 1855, Money also founded the Reform of the New Testament Church, a sect with 12 converts. (San Gabriel Historical Association.)

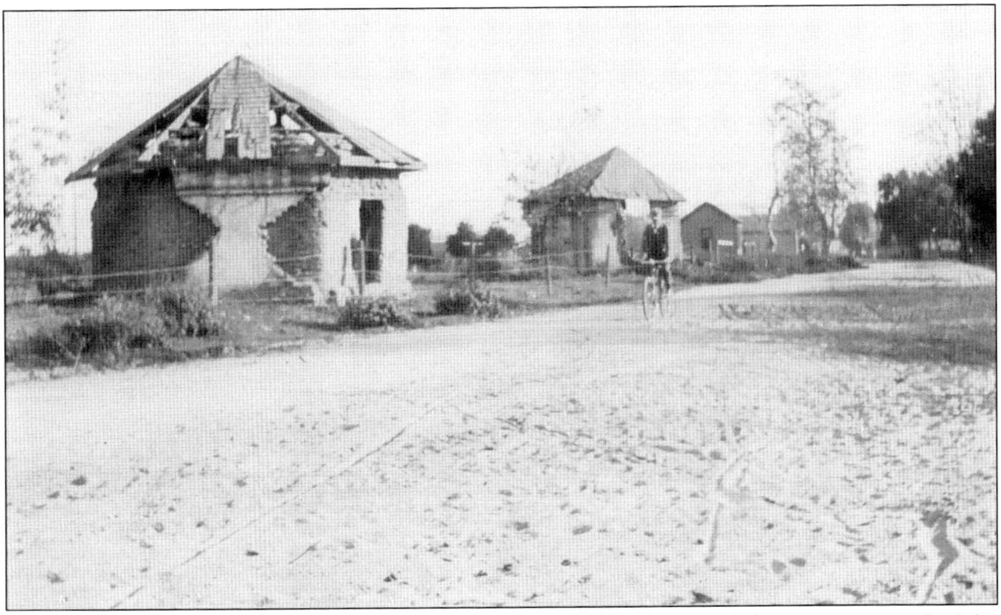

This image looks south on Mission Drive from Las Tunas Drive toward the two octagonal adobe block buildings that were the gatehouses of the Moneyan Institute. Money designed his structures so that they would survive earthquakes. Both gatehouses had eight triangular roof panels that formed pyramid-like roofs. The gatehouses and the main building were on the east side of Mission Drive between Las Tunas Drive and Padilla Street. (Braun Research Library Collection, Autry National Center.)

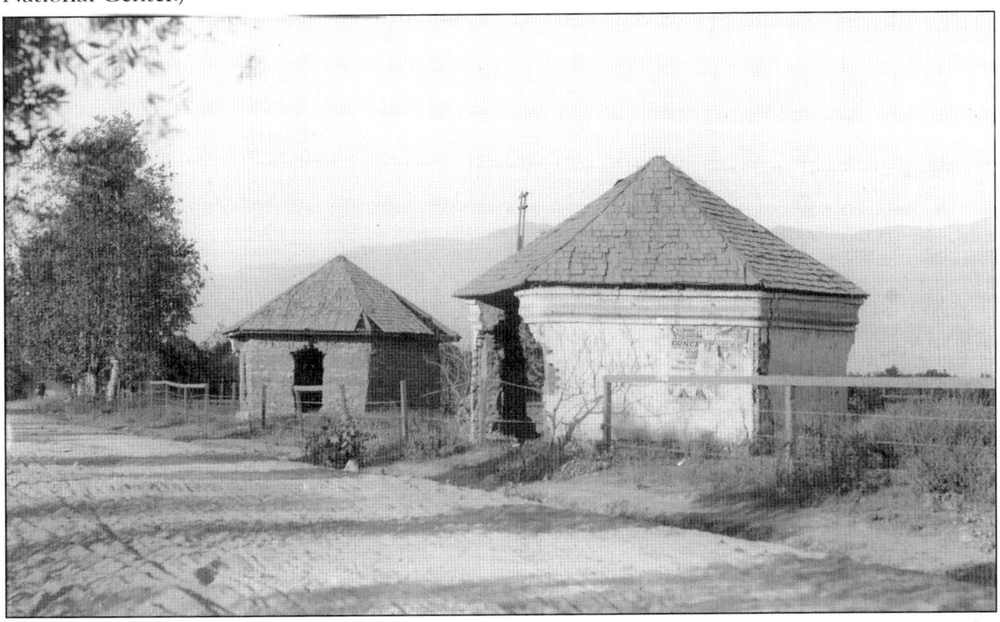

The two gatehouses are shown here looking north on Mission Drive from Padilla Street. The larger main building had an oval floor plan, somewhat in the shape of a ship's hull, placed on a north-south line to "ride out" the earthquakes. The main structure had a large center room with a smaller room on each end with three interconnected roofs. The roof was pyramid shaped, with an eight-sided pyramid on each end. (San Gabriel Historical Association.)

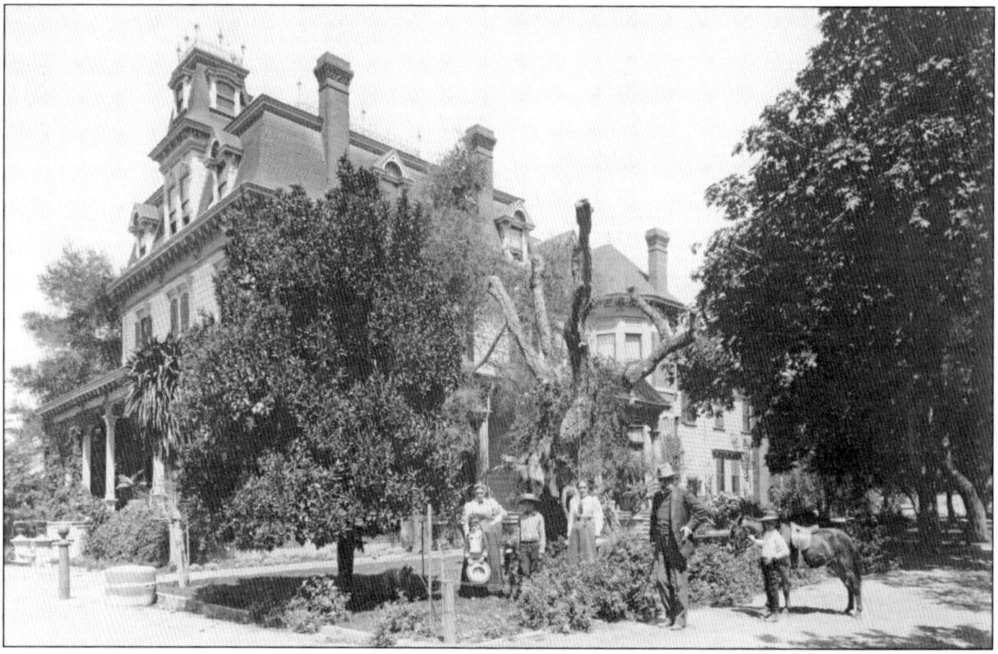

The Shorb family poses in front of their home at the San Marino Ranch, named after the family's plantation in Maryland. James de Barth Shorb, a Maryland native, married Maria DeJeaus "Sue" Wilson, daughter of Benjamin D. Wilson, in 1867. Benjamin Wilson gave his daughter 500 acres adjoining his Lake Vineyard on which the Shorbs built their house and started their ranch. The house, built sometime between 1865 and 1870, began as a simple farmhouse. After the Civil War, Shorb hired Los Angeles architecture firm Keysor & Morgan to expand the house, adding a third story; the house contained 13 bedrooms, 3 bathrooms, and a billiard room. Upon Shorb's death in 1895, Henry Huntington bought the 500-acre ranch, tore down the house, and built his own mansion, which is now home to the Huntington Library. (Huntington Library.)

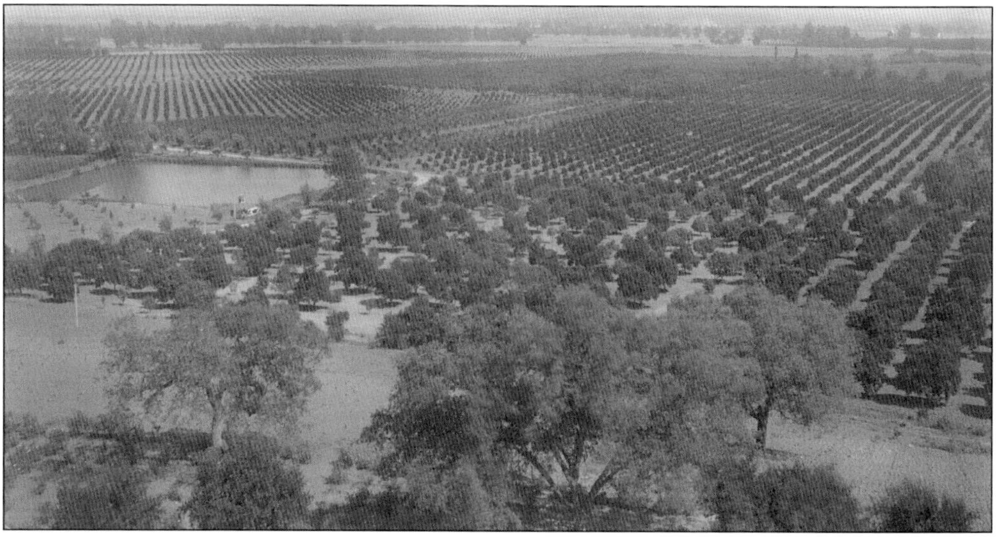

This c. 1870 photograph, looking across the 500 acre San Marino Ranch, owned and operated by James Shorb, included vineyards orchards and flowers for perfumes. (California History Section, California State Library, Sacramento, California.)

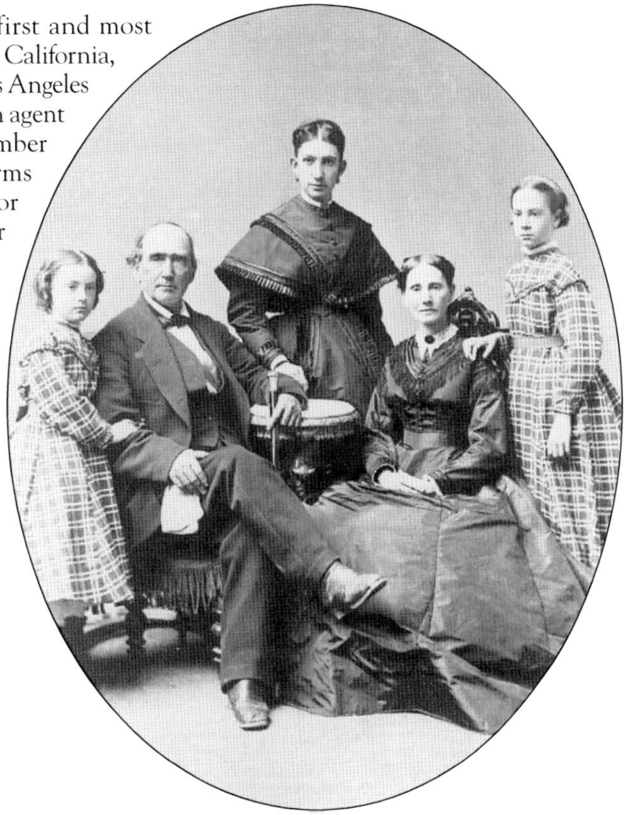

Benjamin D. Wilson, one of the first and most influential ranch owners in Southern California, was elected as the second mayor of Los Angeles in 1851 and was appointed US Indian agent for the southern district on September 1, 1852. Wilson served for three terms as Los Angeles County supervisor and three terms a state senator for California. Benjamin Wilson and his second wife, Margaret, (seated) are flanked by their two daughters, Ruth (left) and Anne (right). Wilson's daughter Maria de Jesus, stands in the center. Ruth was the mother of Gen. George S. Patton Jr. (San Gabriel Historical Association.)

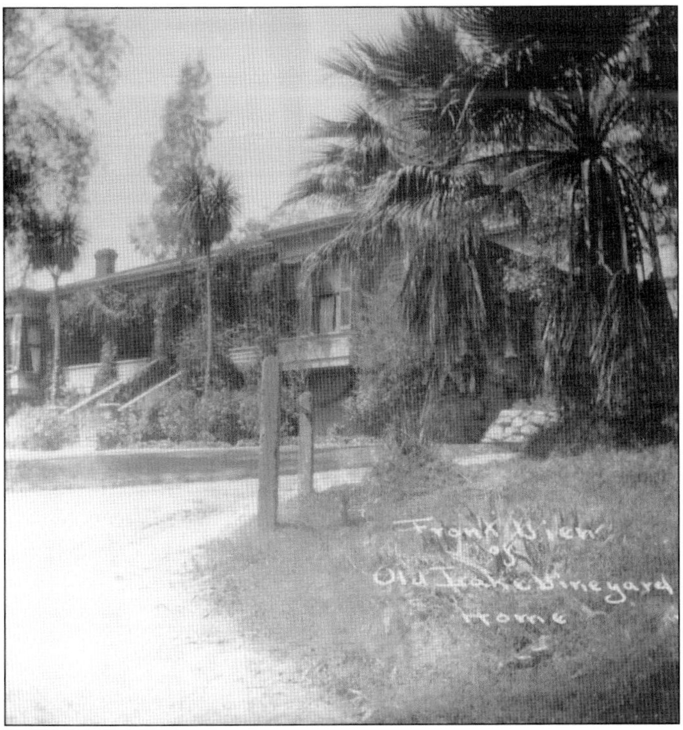

In 1856, Benjamin D. Wilson bought the 128.5-acre Huerta de Cuarti (Cuarti's Orchard) property from the Indian wife of Hugo Reid, Maria Victoria Bartholomea Reid, and built this home. The house was located on a hill above and overlooking Mission Lake, later known as Wilson Lake. Wilson named his homestead Lake Vineyard, being the land included both a lake and commercial vineyards. Lake Vineyard became one of the largest vineyards in California and one of the major citrus orchards in the Southland, with 1,650 citrus, orange, lemon, and lime trees. (Ernest Marquez Collection.)

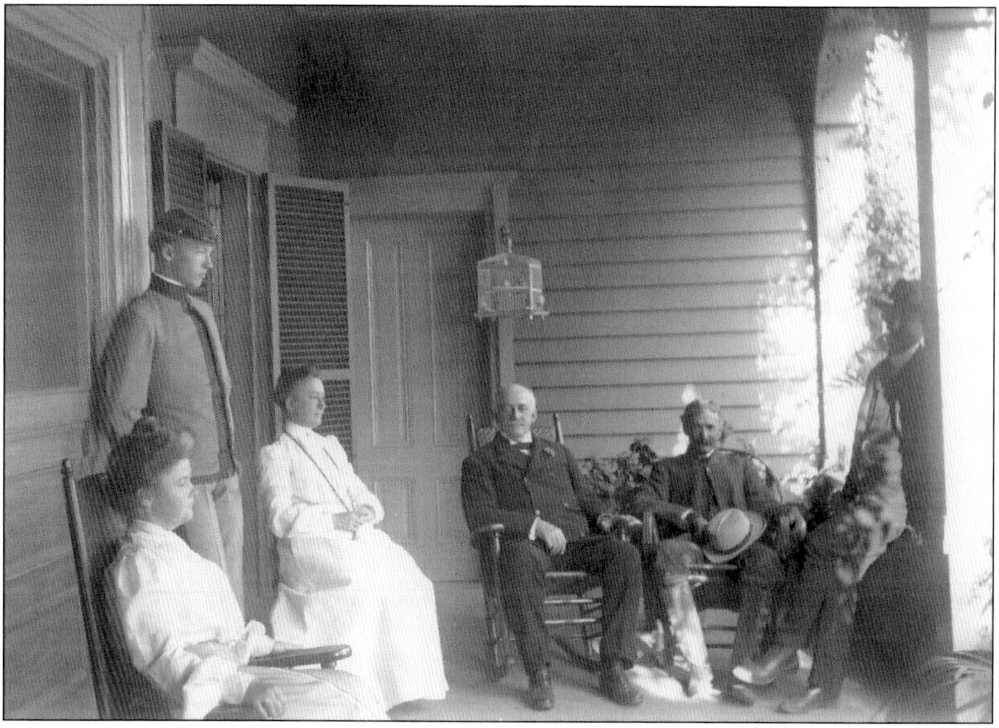

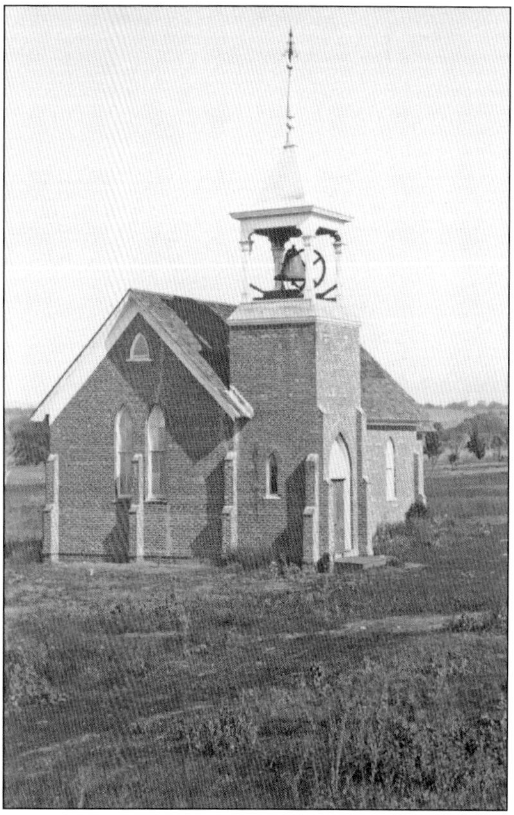

While attending the Virginia Military Institute, George Patton Jr. was able to make occasional visits to Lake Vineyard to see his parents. One such visit was documented in this November 1903 photograph on the porch at Lake Vineyard. Shown are, from left to right, Susan Patton Wills (sister of George S. Patton Sr.), George S. Patton Jr., Ruth Patton, Henry Huntington, George S. Patton Sr., and Hancock Banning. (Huntington Library.)

The Church of Our Savior is the oldest Protestant church in the San Gabriel Valley. Built at 535 West Roses Road between 1867 and 1869, the church was founded as the result of a $5,368 gift from Providence, Rhode Island, philanthropist Frances Vinton. Vinton selected three sites at random—one in New England, one in Iowa, and the third in El Monte—to build churches as memorials to her deceased children. All three were to be known as the Church of Our Savior. Benjamin D. Wilson was able to influence Vinton to change the third site to San Gabriel instead of El Monte. (Huntington Library.)

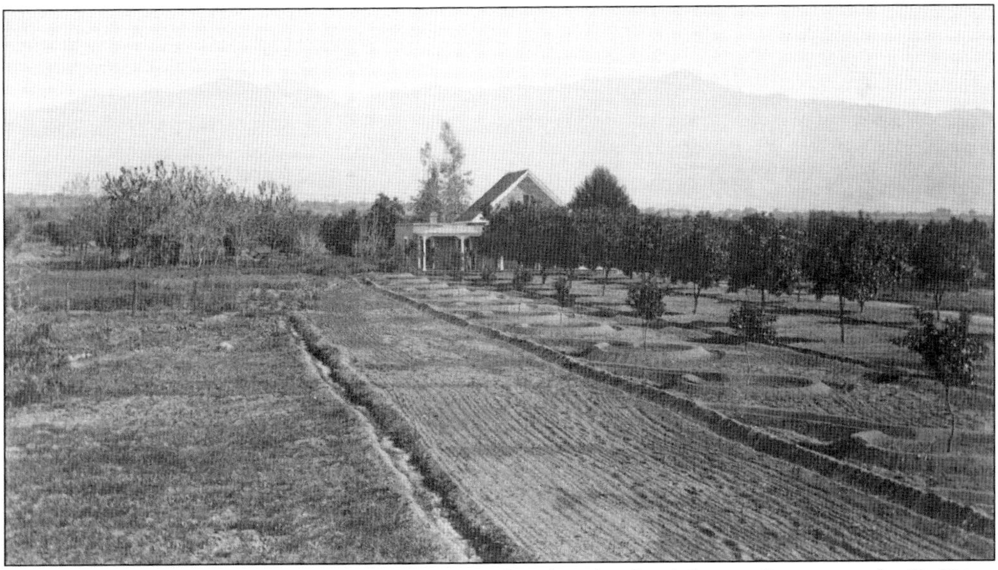

Col. John R. Dobbins and his, wife Ellen Louise, lived in this brick house (known as the Dobbins House) the longest and were responsible for wooden additions that changed the style to that of a large Victorian farmhouse. A local contractor demolished the historic Dobbins House on Labor Day 1984 after preservationists' attempts to save the house failed. (Huntington Library.)

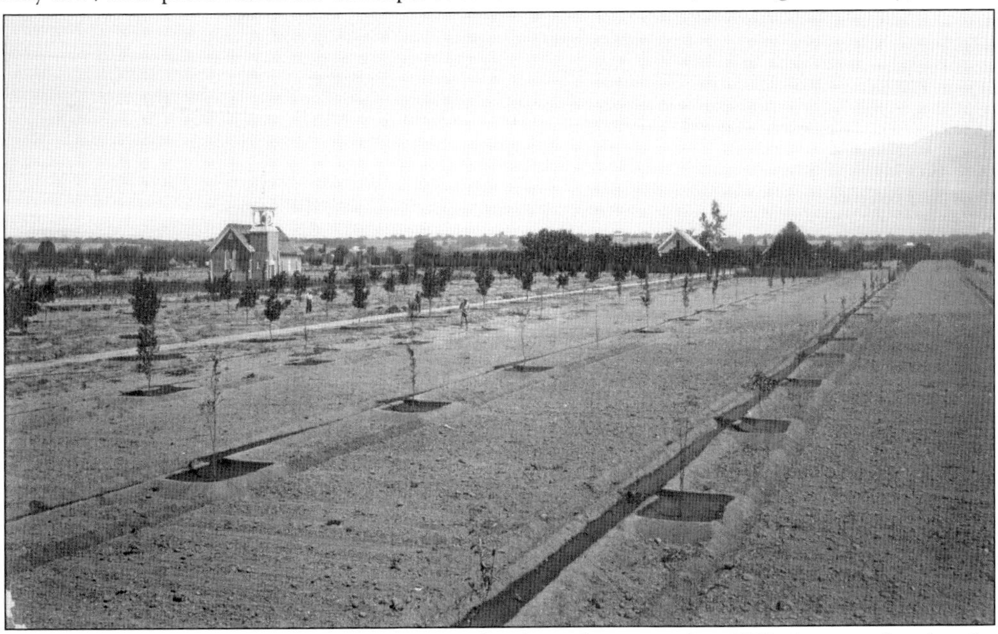

The Church of Our Savior and Dobbins Orchard are shown in this 1877 photograph taken by Carleton E. Watkins. John R. Dobbins served with distinction as a colonel during the Civil War and, upon retirement, became one of the most progressive orange growers in the country. In 1876, Dobbins and his wife, Ellen Louise, purchased from Rev. Dr. Henry Messenger a 22-acre parcel adjoining the Church of Our Savior and established orange orchards. Dobbins was a well-known orchardist and horticulturist responsible for propagating the Australian parasite (*vedolia cardinalis*) used to control white scale on citrus. (California History Section, California State Library, Sacramento, California.)

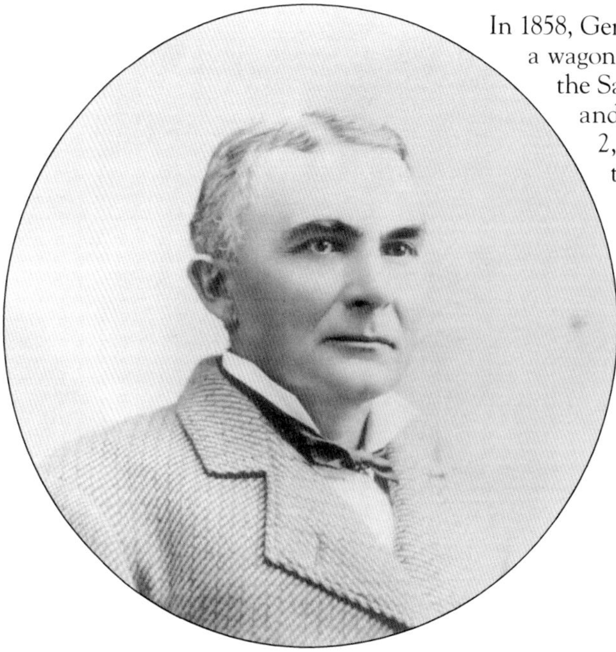

In 1858, German immigrant Leonard J. Rose led a wagon train from Iowa to California over the Santa Fe Trail with his wife, Amanda, and their 11 children. Rose acquired 2,200 acres of the western section of the Rancho Santa Anita in 1861 and established a vineyard and racehorse stud farm ranch named Sunny Slope Farm. In 1879, Rose built the Sunny Slope Winery in Lamanda Park, using more than 35 varieties of grapes, and irrigated his farm using artesian wells. (Roy C. Rose and The Irvine Museum.)

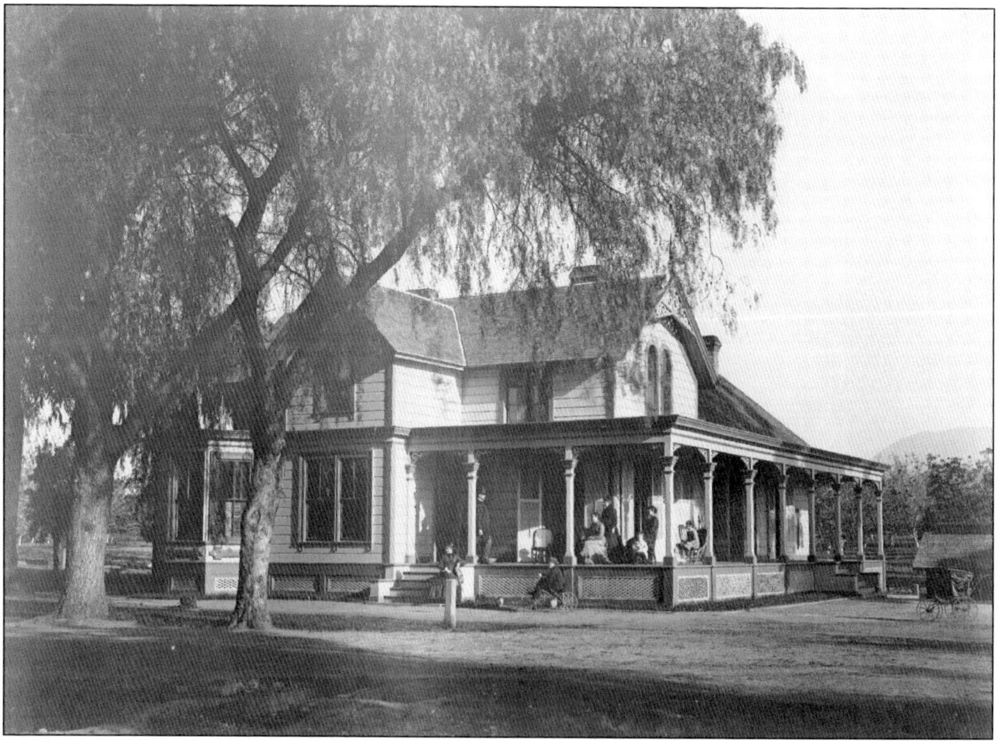

By the fall of 1862, Leonard Rose's family completed construction on their Victorian-style ranch house situated on the five-acre site just southwest of the La Presa dam. Sunny Slope served as a stopping place for friends and visitors touring the orange groves and vineyards until it was sold to an English syndicate in 1887. The house was moved to 7026 La Presa Drive around 1902. (Huntington Library.)

Guy Rose painted *San Gabriel Mission*—the only painting he ever completed of any of the missions. (Roy C. Rose and The Irvine Museum.)

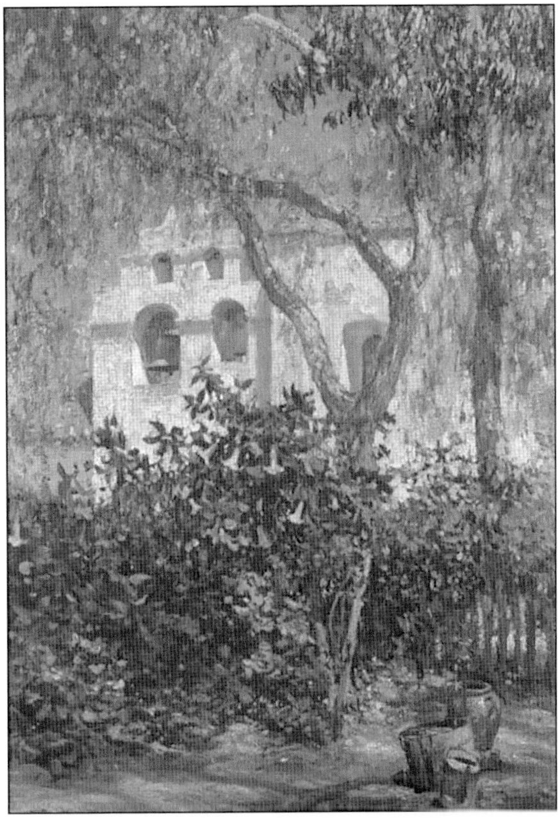

Guy Rose, born in San Gabriel on March 3, 1867, became one of California's premier impressionist painters of the late 19th and early 20th centuries. Guy was the seventh child born to Leonard J. Rose and Amanda Jones Rose on their large Southern California ranch known as Sunny Slope. After graduating from Los Angeles High School, Rose attended the School of Design in San Francisco. In 1888, he studied in Paris with famed artists Benjamin Constant, Jules Lefebvre, and Lucien Doucet. In 1899, he and his wife, Ethel, bought a cottage at Giverny, where he lived from 1904 to 1912 and became friends with Claude Monet, who was also his mentor; Guy Rose's paintings of this era reflect Monet's influences. (Roy C. Rose and The Irvine Museum.)

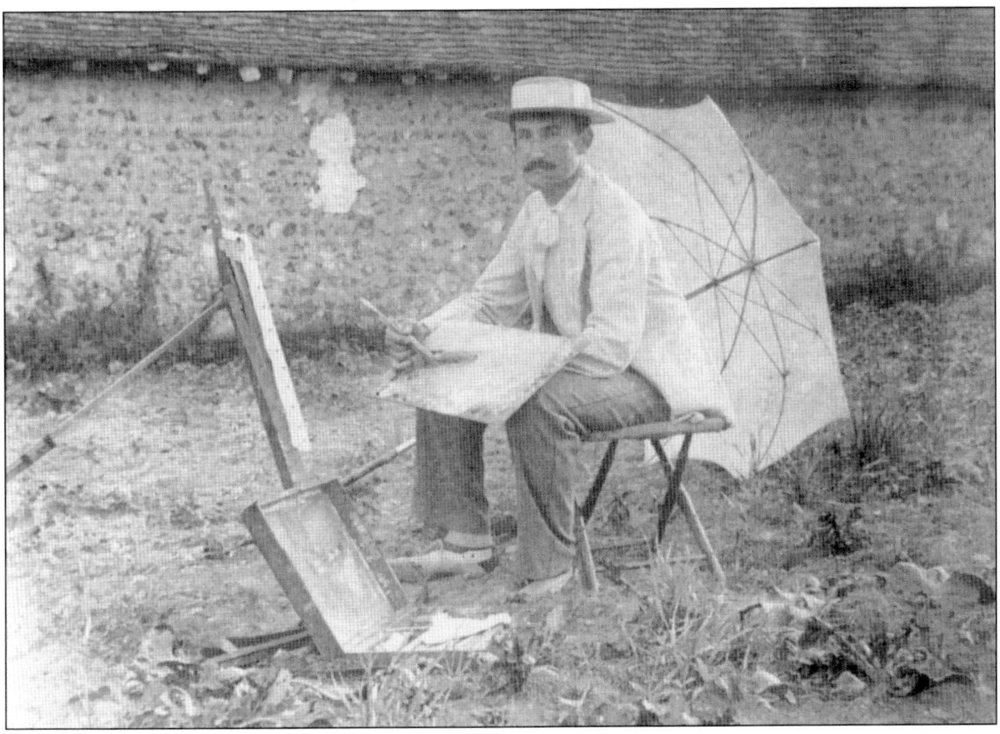

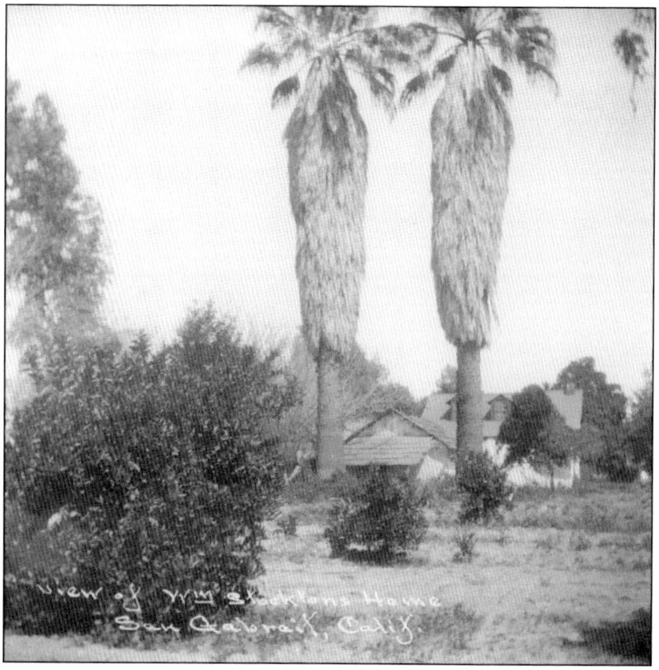

The William M. Stockton adobe (Twin Palms) was located just north of present-day Huntington Drive between Wembley and Cambridge in present-day San Marino. Stockton was one of the first people to cross Death Valley in 1849 on his way to Northern California in search of gold. Successful in his search, Stockton moved to Los Angeles and was elected as a supervisor for Los Angeles County in 1857. After retirement, Stockton moved to San Gabriel in 1851, started a nursery and vineyard, and continued his mining operations. (Ernest Marquez Collection.)

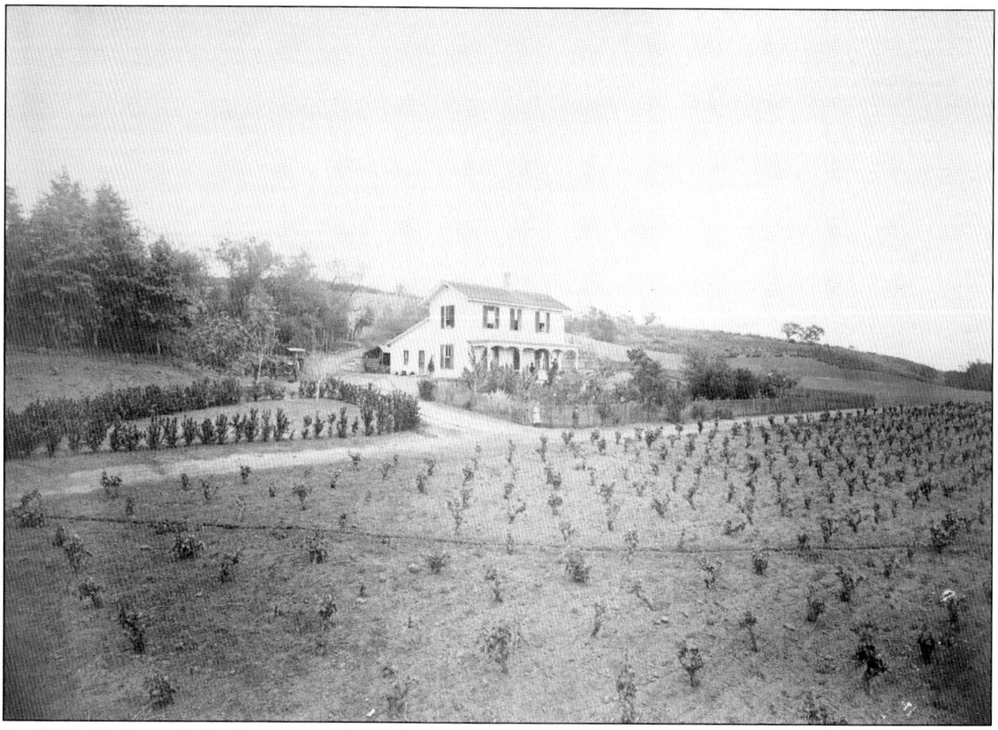

In 1872, Nathaniel C. Carter purchased and settled on a part of the Flores Ranch in San Gabriel, situated just south of the present-day Langham-Huntington Hotel in Pasadena. In 1874, he operated railroad excursions between New England and Los Angeles called "Whitcomb Excursions," bringing Easterners with lung ailments to healthier California. In 1861, Carter purchased 1,103 acres of the Santa Anita Rancho from Lucky Baldwin and founded Sierra Madre. (Richard Arnold Collection.)

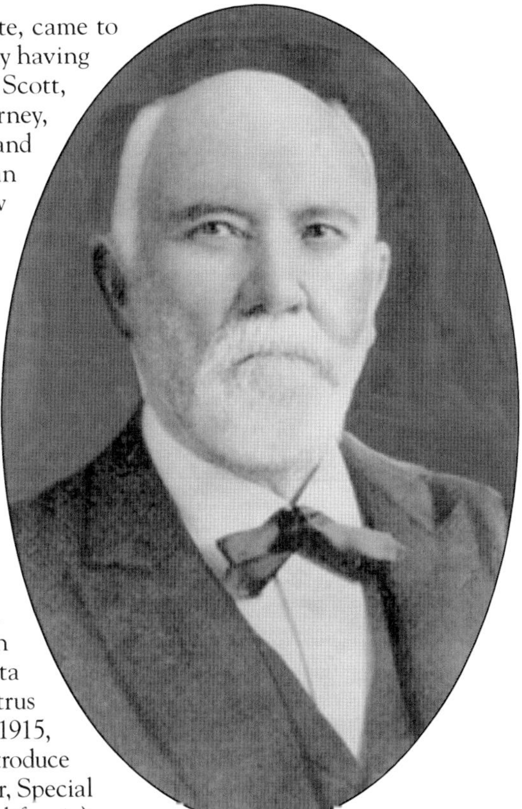

Alfred Beck Chapman, a West Point graduate, came to California in 1861 after retiring from the Army having achieved the rank of major. He married Mary Scott, the daughter of a prominent Los Angeles attorney, Jonathan R. Scott, whom he studied law with, and was admitted to the bar in California. Chapman became a prominent real estate attorney and law partner with boyhood friend Andrew Glassell. Their law firm handled real estate transactions and often took land as payment of their fees. Chapman bought Rancho San Rafael at a foreclosure sale in 1860 and was one of the developers of Glendale. In 1863, Chapman became city attorney of Los Angeles and in 1868 was elected district attorney of Los Angeles County, for which he served two terms. In 1868, Chapman and Glassell were granted a portion of Rancho Santiago de Santa Ana as payment of fees and founded the City of Orange. Chapman continued to practice law until retiring with his second wife, Mary Stephens, to manage his 700-acre San Gabriel ranch, a portion of the Rancho Santa Anita grant in 1879, and become involved in citrus production. Prior to his death on January 16, 1915, Chapman was the first person successfully to introduce the Valencia orange. (Regional History Center, Special Collections Dept., University of Southern California)

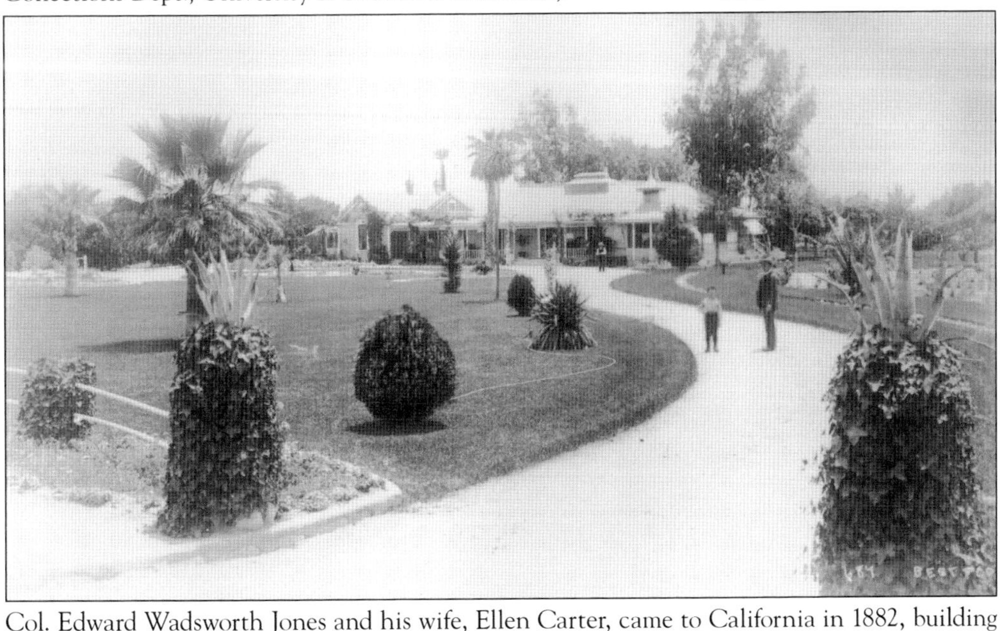

Col. Edward Wadsworth Jones and his wife, Ellen Carter, came to California in 1882, building this home on Roses Road, directly across from the Church of Our Savior. Jones served with distinction during the Civil War as a colonel in the 2nd Connecticut Artillery. (Security Pacific National Bank Collection, Los Angeles Public Library.)

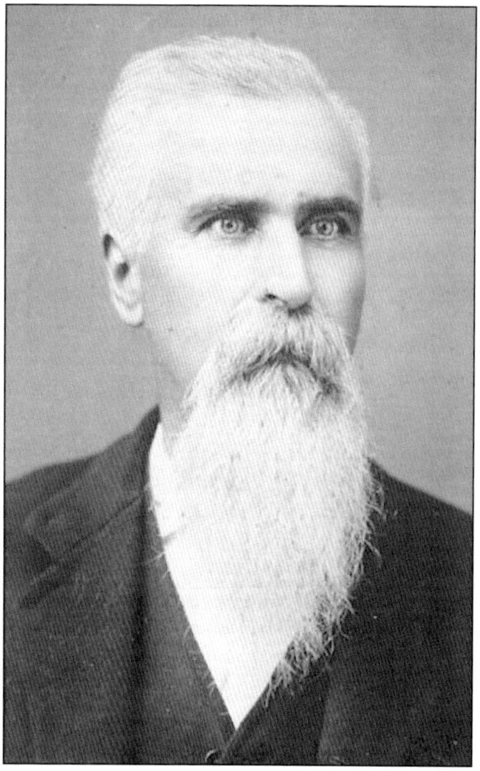

Cyrus Burdick settled in San Gabriel, opening a general store in an adobe directly across from the mission, which he ran from 1856 to 1864. In 1870, after a failed attempt at raising cattle in San Dimas, Cyrus and his wife, Amanda, settled in what is present-day Pomona and started the first citrus orchard in Pomona on 40 acres of land. Cyrus and his friend George C. Gibbs became the founders of the City of Pomona. (Richard Arnold Collection.)

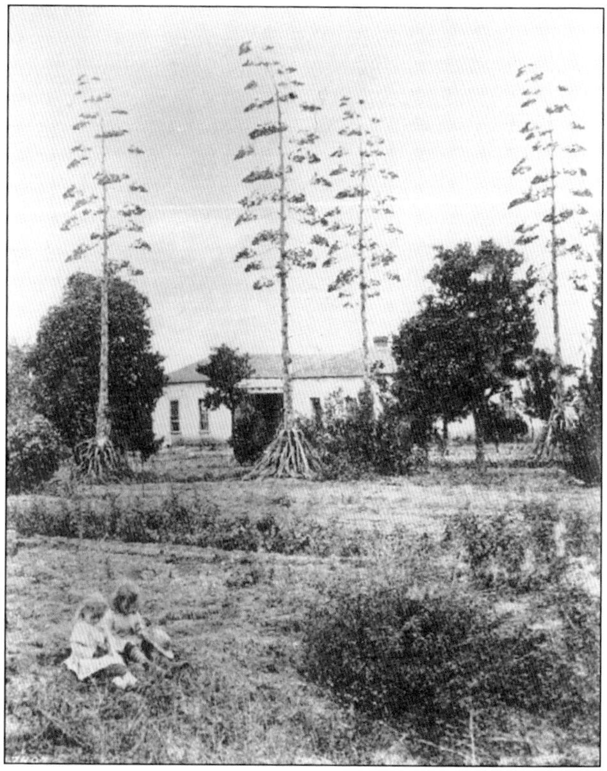

Judge George Clinton Gibbs and his wife, Elmina, lived in this residence with their seven children from 1872 to 1883. The adobe was located on acreage they owned just east of present-day San Gabriel Boulevard and south of Broadway. Judge Gibbs served in the New York Assembly before moving to California in the late 1800s and becoming a judge for the California Superior Court. He and former San Gabriel businessman Cyrus Burdick were founders of the City of Pomona. (Huntington Library.)

Orray W. Longden came from Connecticut and settled in San Gabriel, opening a mercantile business on Shorb Avenue; Longden was appointed postmaster on December 28, 1886. He operated the San Gabriel Post Office in his store during his tenure as postmaster. After serving as justice of the peace, school trustee, and deputy assessor, Longden was elected as a supervisor for Los Angeles County on January 3, 1899. Longden was a founding member of the San Gabriel Valley Country Club and served as their first president. The street now known as Longden Avenue was renamed in his honor in 1928. (Richard Arnold Collection.)

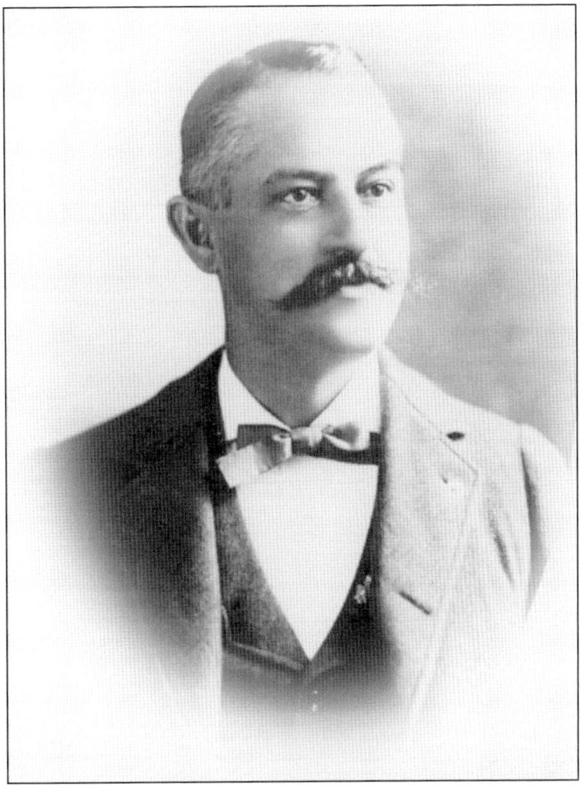

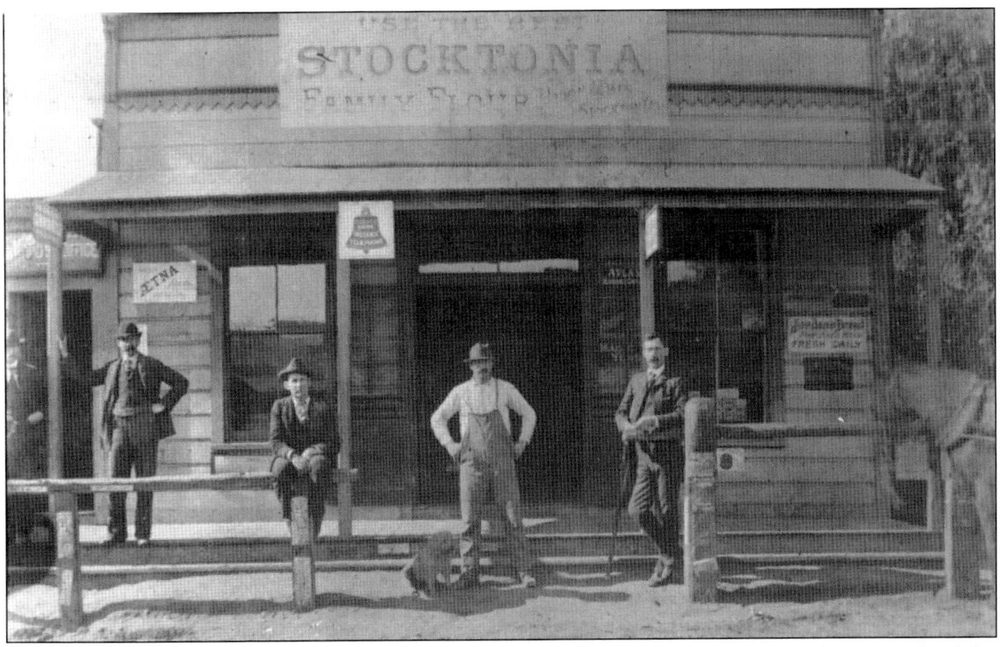

The John A. Myers general store located on Shorb Avenue (San Marino Avenue) just north of the Southern Pacific Railroad depot is often inaccurately referred to as the "Stocktonia" store because of the large Stocktonia flour sign hanging above the door. Myers was appointed postmaster on December 5, 1898, and ran the post office out of this store. (Huntington Library.)

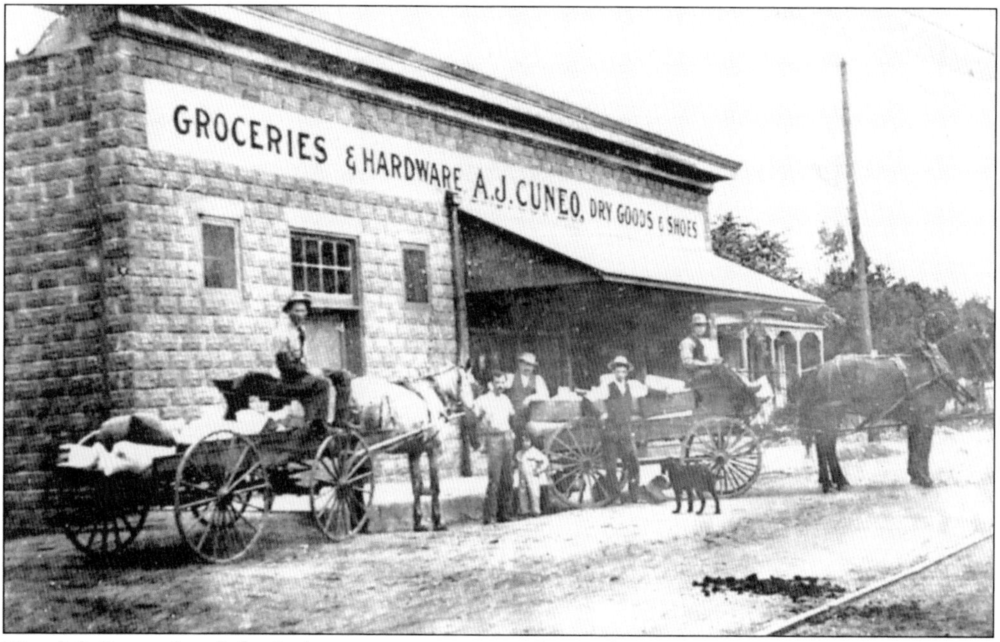

The A.J. Cuneo family built their grocery store at 250 South Mission Drive in August 1907. The building was constructed of concrete block with simulated brick finish and modern plate-glass windows. Cuneo initially worked at his mother's grocery store across the street at 265 South Mission Drive, which was eventually used as the first city hall in 1913. Cuneo married a San Gabriel girl, Mary Slack, whose father was also a merchant in San Gabriel, and he eventually became partners in the grocery business and opened this store. (San Gabriel Historical Association.)

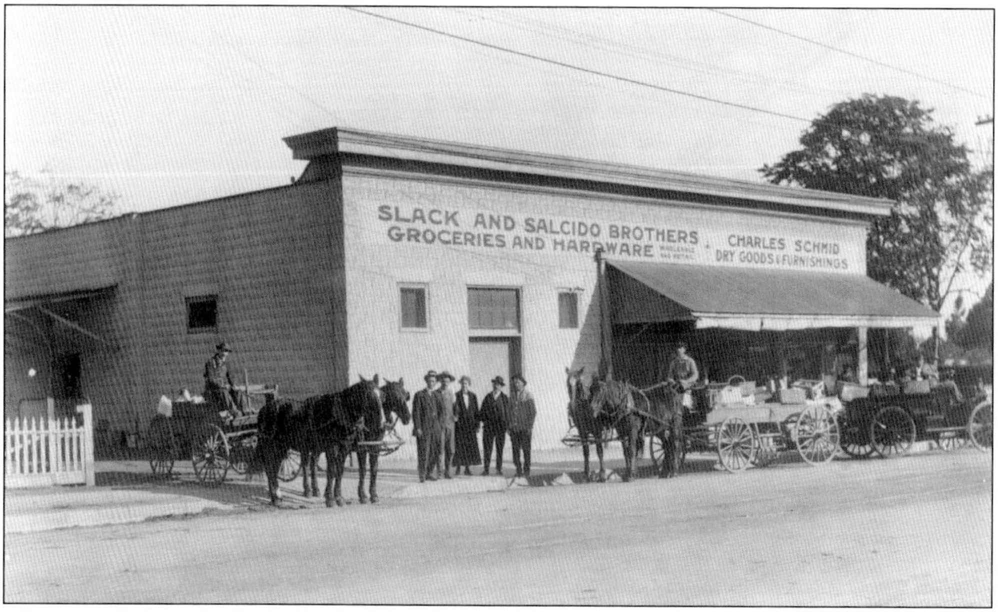

The City of San Gabriel purchased the former A.J. Cuneo Groceries & Hardware store and, later, the Slack & Salcido Brothers store from Claude Slack on April 10, 1946, for $11,000. In October 1946, the city offered the building for use as the new San Gabriel Justice Court. Prior to this, the court was held at city hall, built in 1923. (San Gabriel Historical Association.)

George Stoneman was a major general in the Union army, having graduated from West Point in 1846 where his roommate was the future "Stonewall" Jackson. Stoneman's first visit to California from his native New York was as a second lieutenant with the Morman Battalion during the Mexican-American War. Stoneman retired from the Army on August 10, 1871, after a distinguished but oftentimes troubled career because of his tendency for questioning authority and his knack for making enemies. Stoneman took up residence in San Gabriel shortly after his retirement and with his wife, Mary, would raise their four children. On January 8, 1883, Stoneman was elected as the 15th governor of the State of California, serving a single four-year term. (National Archives.)

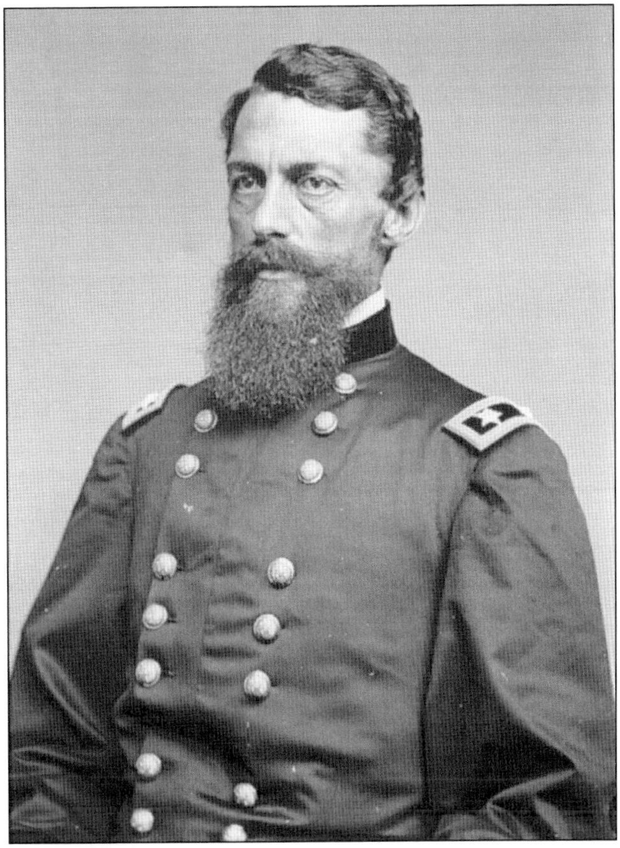

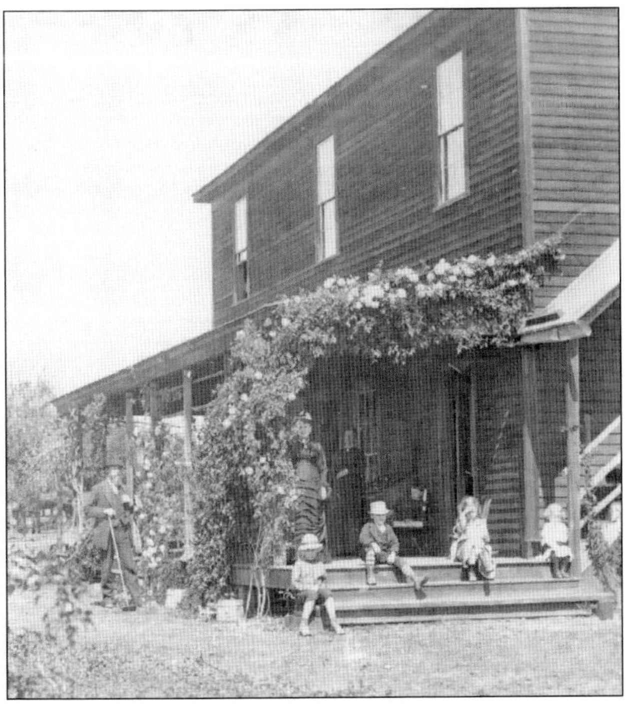

The Stoneman house, located on the 400-acre ranch known as Los Robles, was adjacent to Wilson's Oak Knoll tract (the present-day location is 1912 Montrobles Place, San Marino). The property was purchased from Benjamin D. Wilson in 1872 for $7,000. The ranch would become a prosperous vineyard and orange grove for the general and governor of California. On July 17, 1885, fire thought to be caused by his political enemies destroyed the entire ranch home, including all of their personal effects. General Stoneman is shown on the driveway of their home as Mary and their children pose one the porch. One of the general's sisters is shown standing next to his wife, Mary. (Huntington Library.)

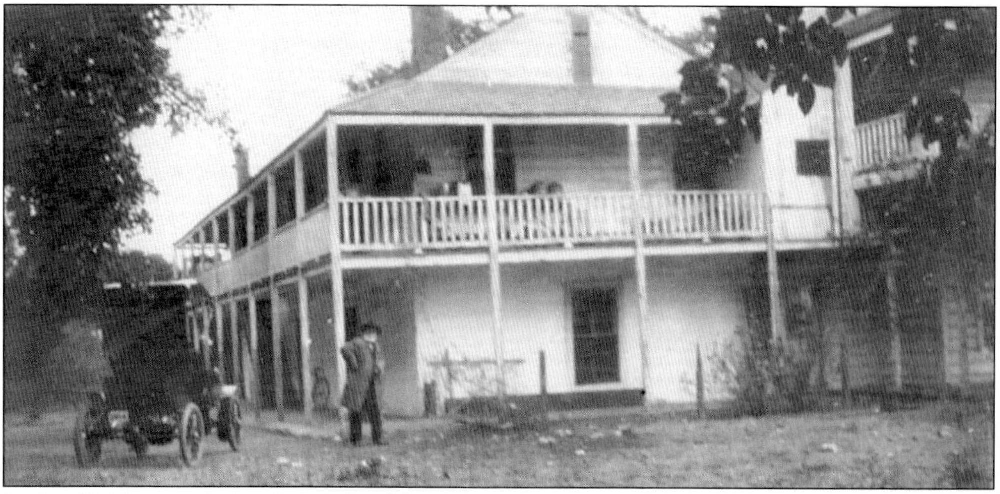

Luther H. Titus settled in San Gabriel from New York and in 1869 established a citrus ranch and horse-breeding farm. The Horseshoe Ranch, including a residence, was located in close proximity to L.J. Rose Ranch on the north side of Huntington Drive, east of San Gabriel Boulevard. Along with managing his ranch, Titus was known for developing ways to make concrete pipe for irrigation lines, moveable picking ladders, hand shears for cutting and picking fruit, and portable spraying apparatus. (Huntington Library.)

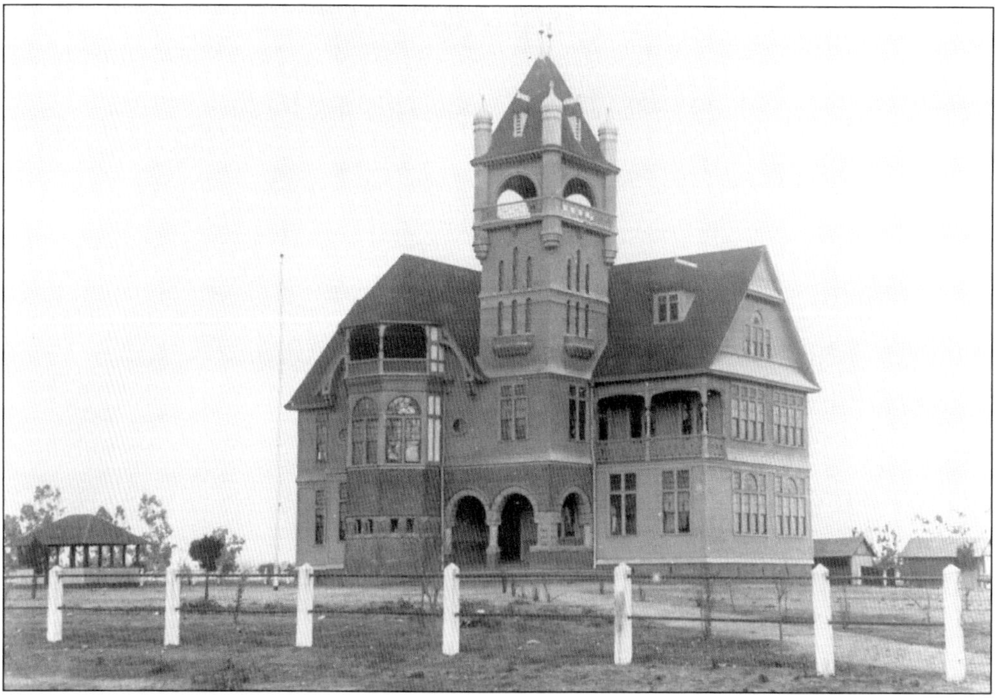

Washington School, located at the northeast corner of San Marino Avenue and Hermosa Drive, was built in 1888. Constructed of brick, red sandstone, and redwood, the new schoolhouse won national honors for being the best-designed school in the United States. The four-story building, which included a basement and attic, had two floors of classrooms. A permanent slide-type fire escape was a big hit with the children, who looked forward to fire drills. (San Gabriel Historical Association.)

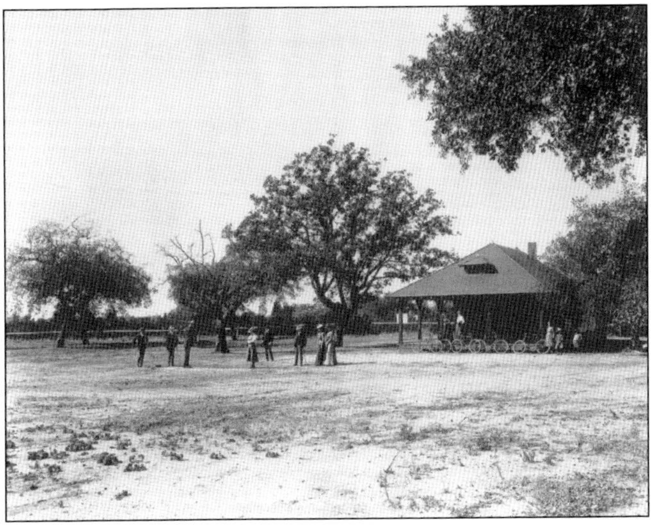

The San Gabriel Valley Country Club was formed on April 23, 1904, following the purchase of 50 acres from the San Gabriel Mission holdings at a cost of $12,500. The original greens were oiled sand that required leveling before and after putting. It was not until the 1920s that grass greens became successful after the introduction of better irrigation methods. The first clubhouse (pictured) was built in 1905. (Security Pacific National Bank Collection, Los Angeles Public Library.)

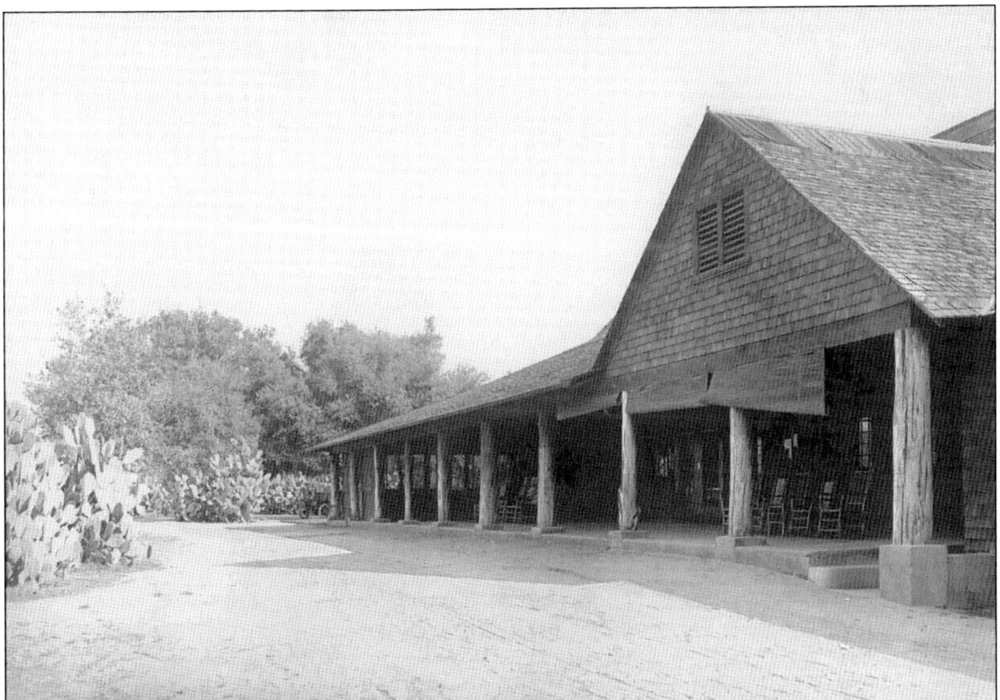

The original San Gabriel Valley Country Club clubhouse is pictured here in 1912. The original nine-hole course, which ran along the Rubio Wash above Las Tunas Drive, was expanded to 18 holes in 1911 following the purchase of an additional 87 acres. On December 4, 1933, a fire totally destroyed the clubhouse, and LeGrand Betts, an 83-year-old cashier for the club, was killed while attempting to save the organization's records. The clubhouse was rebuilt in 1934 and closely resembles the current structure. (Richard Arnold Collection.)

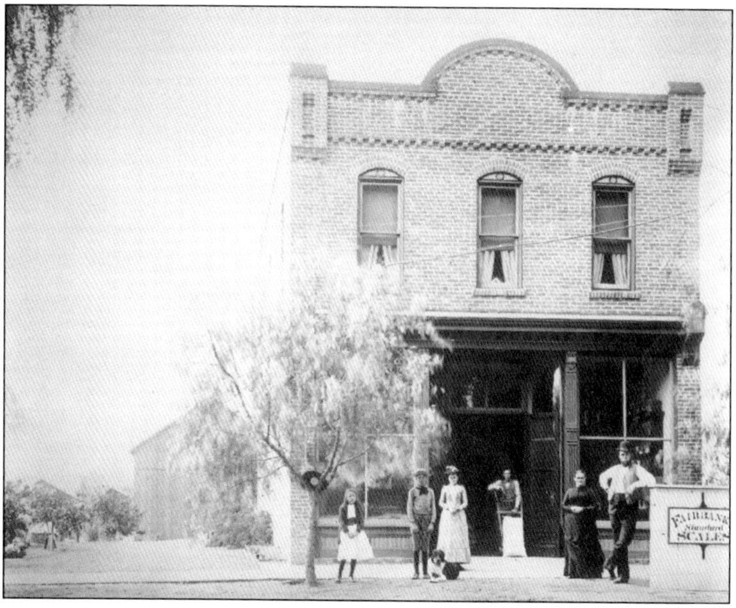

J.S. Harris (far right), proprietor of the Harris Feed Store located at 409 South San Gabriel Boulevard, poses in front of the family store along with his wife and children. Described as being the first two-story brick building in San Gabriel when this photograph was taken in 1901, the Harris Feed Store was the only business along San Gabriel Boulevard. (Huntington Library.)

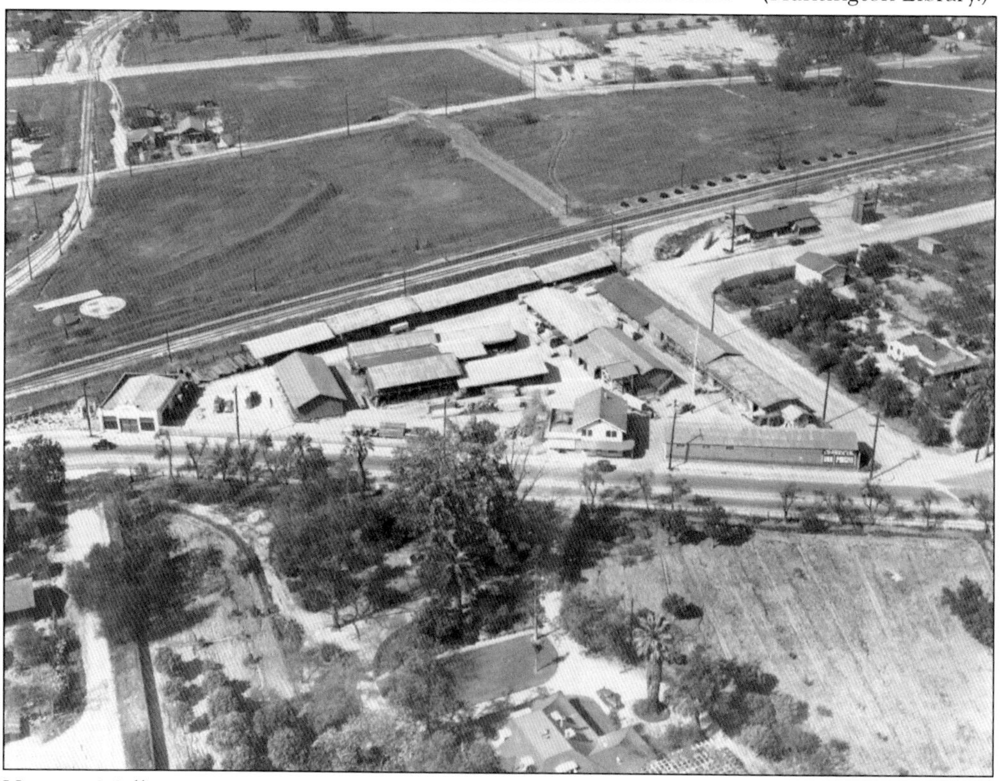

Herman Muller came to San Gabriel from Colmar, France, in 1884 and opened a lumberyard on Mission Drive opposite the Las Tunas adobe. Business was poor for a lumber company, so he moved to San Pedro in 1898. After 16 years in San Pedro, Muller returned and reopened the San Gabriel Valley Lumber Company, pictured here in the late 1930s. The lumberyard was approximately five acres in size and included a mill in the back of the yard to trim wood brought in on the Southern Pacific Railroad. (Lawrence Arnold Collection.)

Sheriff's deputy George Wilson of San Gabriel was shot by a Mexican desperado, Pedro Morales, whom he had arrested near Monrovia on December 6, 1896. Wilson allowed the arrested to dress, and Morales pulled a .45-caliber Colt revolver from his overcoat pocket and shot at Wilson. Wilson would subsequently die of his wound on January 8, 1897. Morales fled but was apprehended five years later and tried for the crime. (Richard Arnold Collection.)

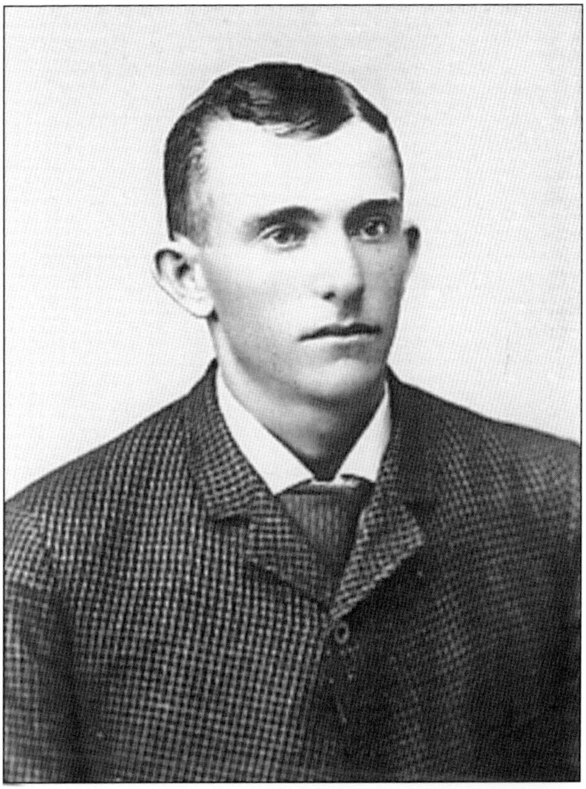

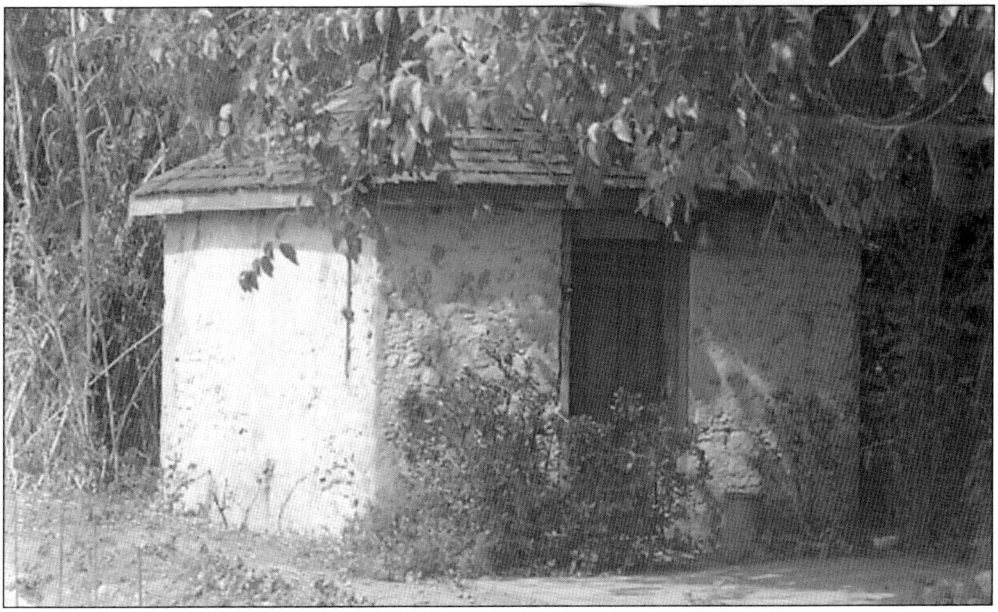

This stone milk house was located in the backyard of the home at 245 South Pine Street, which belonged to Milton Scott Wilson and his wife, Mary. Wilson was the justice of the peace for San Gabriel Township, and his son George Wilson, the local deputy sheriff for the Los Angeles County Sheriff's Department, would occasionally use the milk house to house prisoners he had arrested until they could be transported to Los Angeles. (Richard Arnold Collection.)

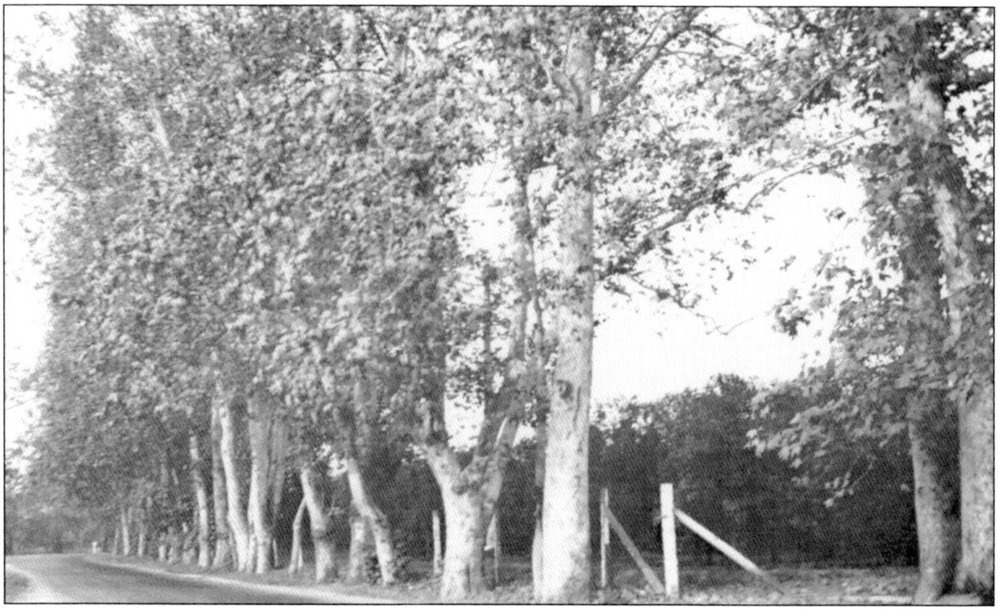

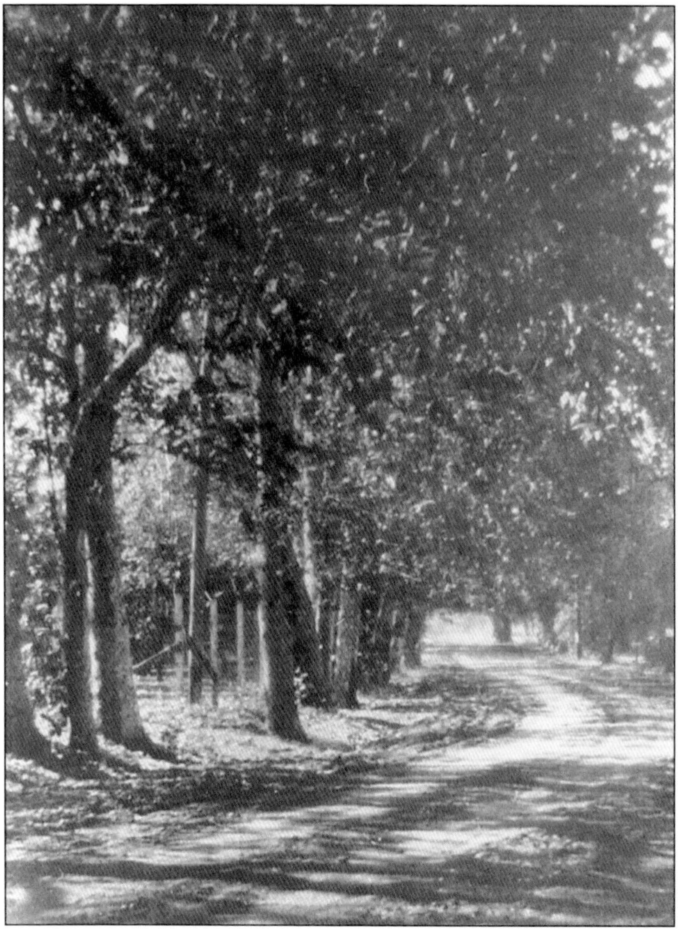

Mission Drive was one of the main routes north out of the city when this photograph was taken looking north from Las Tunas Drive around 1930. (Richard Arnold Collection.)

A view of Mission Drive looking south from Hermosa Drive is seen in this photograph taken in 1935. (San Gabriel Historical Association.)

Hermosa Drive was still a dirt road when then c. 1900 photograph was taken looking west from Del Mar Avenue. (San Gabriel Historical Association.)

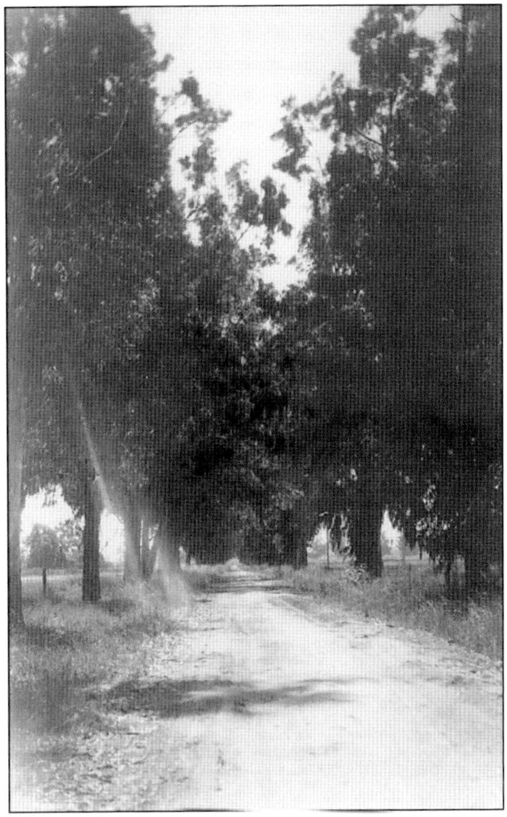

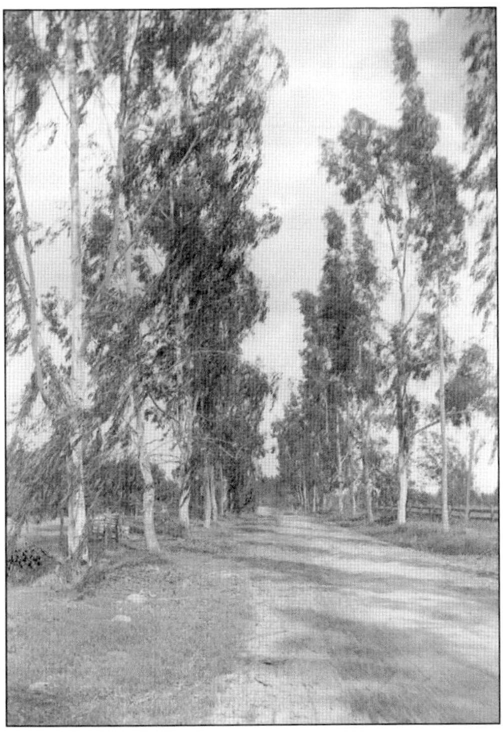

This scenic view of San Gabriel Boulevard was taken in the early 1900s when the tall eucalyptus trees still lined both sides of the boulevard north of the Southern Pacific Railroad tracks. Images similar to this were often used on postcards. The trees would be removed and replaced with businesses that formed the business district known as East San Gabriel. (San Gabriel Historical Association.)

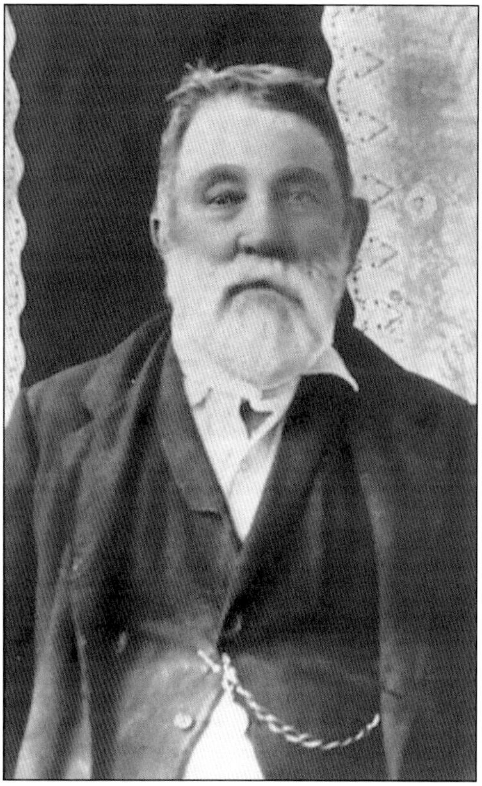

This photograph of Roy Bean, brother to Joshua Bean, who inherited the Headquarters Saloon after Joshua was mortally wounded, was taken during the later years of his life, long after his ownership of the San Gabriel saloon. Maj. Horace Bell, a founding member of the Los Angeles Rangers and author of two books that documented the early Wild West days in California, visited with Roy Bean at the Headquarters Saloon in 1852, shortly after Joshua's murder. Upon his arrival at the Headquarters Saloon, Bell was met by Bean, whom he described as a very handsome black-bearded young man dressed in elegant Mexican costume with a pair of revolvers in his belt and a bowie knife sheathed in his "red-topped" boots. A vast difference from the Bean shown in this photograph. Bean would operate the saloon for only a short period of time before being run out of town. (Richard Arnold Collection.)

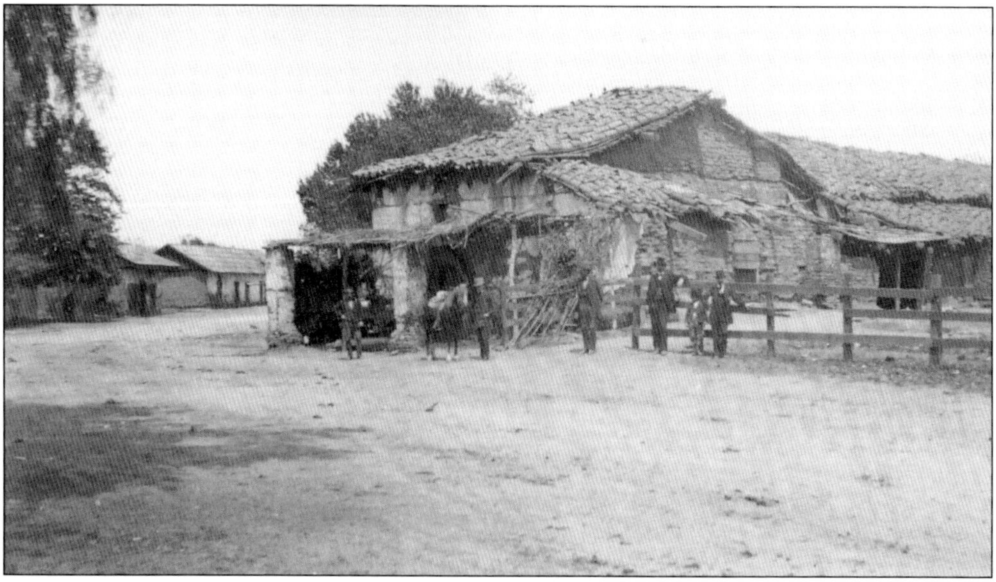

The Headquarters Saloon, the largest and most popular of the town's saloons, was located in what is believed to be the former military quarters of the San Gabriel Mission, part of the original quadrangle. Early accounts of the infamous "grog-shop" describe this as being the location, situated at the southwest corner of the mission building. The corner was consistently occupied by saloons, including the Billiard Saloon, for several years after Roy Bean was run out of town. (Constance L. Rothstein Collection.)

Four

East San Gabriel Hotel

With the driving of the Golden Spike at Promontory, Utah, in 1869, the nation was united by bands of steel rails. The end result was the great migration to Southern California that engendered the land boom of the 1880s.

As hordes of tourists and prospective landowners flocked to Los Angeles by train, housing of any type quickly became a scarce and costly item. In order to take full advantage of this crisis, savvy businesspeople quickly organized land speculating and development companies. Hotels of grand and elegant design, like the East San Gabriel Hotel, were built to attract customers, and while enjoying the comforts of a fine hotel, salesmen went to work on prospective landowners.

Although older towns, including San Gabriel, reaped a harvest from the increase in property values, this area was not to be blessed with a rise in overall development. Ironically, the hotel of East San Gabriel was just opening its doors for the first time when the land boom began its decline in the spring of 1888. Local support kept the hotel active for a few more years, but its doors finally closed in 1898, as it was unable to fill its 130 rooms and profitably operate without the support of the tourist trade.

The once glamorous hotel became known as the Southern California Sanitarium, housing those with diseased lungs, and the hotel was later used to house those with mental problems. The Southern California Masonic Home Association purchased the grand old hotel in April 1905. In time, the old hotel building began to age and became hard to maintain. On October 14, 1915, the owners decided to close the home in San Gabriel and build a new facility in Covina.

In 1919, the San Gabriel Film Company took over the building and grounds with plans to use the structure as a film studio, but the business was never successful, so it closed. The former East San Gabriel Hotel fell victim to time and progress in November 1925 when James A. Rook purchased the property, tore down the old hotel, and subdivided the vast grounds.

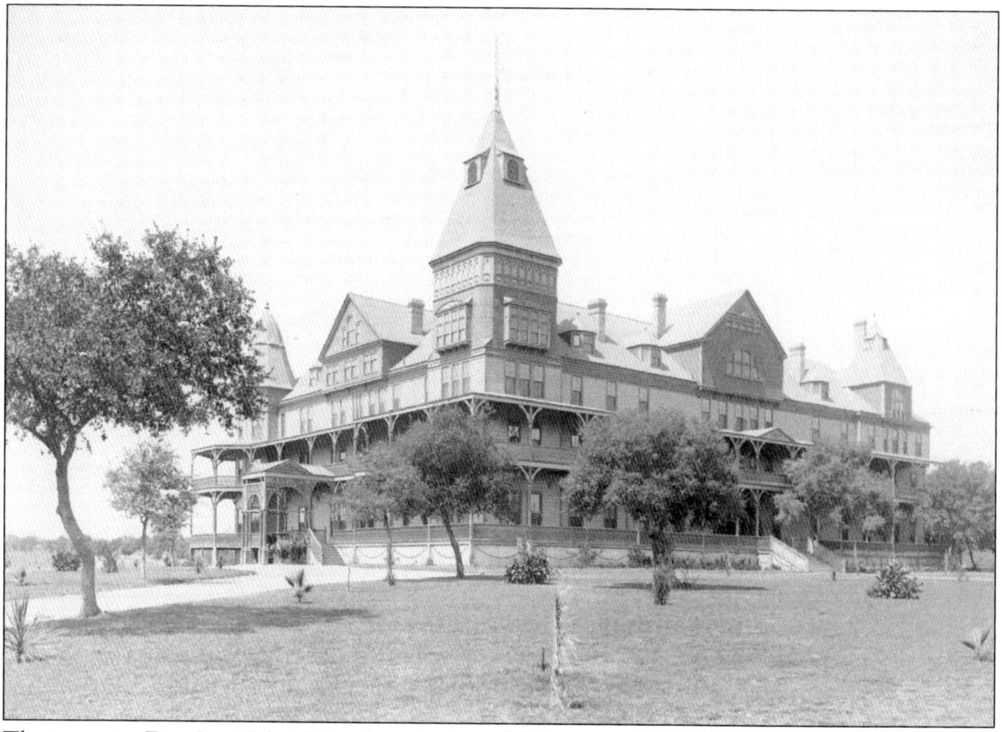

The imposing East San Gabriel Hotel was built in 1887 by the San Gabriel Land & Water Company, a local land developer. Intermingled in the acreage were palm trees, a two-acre vineyard, and beautiful orchards. It was hard to beat this setting on the southwest corner of Las Tunas Drive and San Gabriel Boulevard. (Huntington Library.)

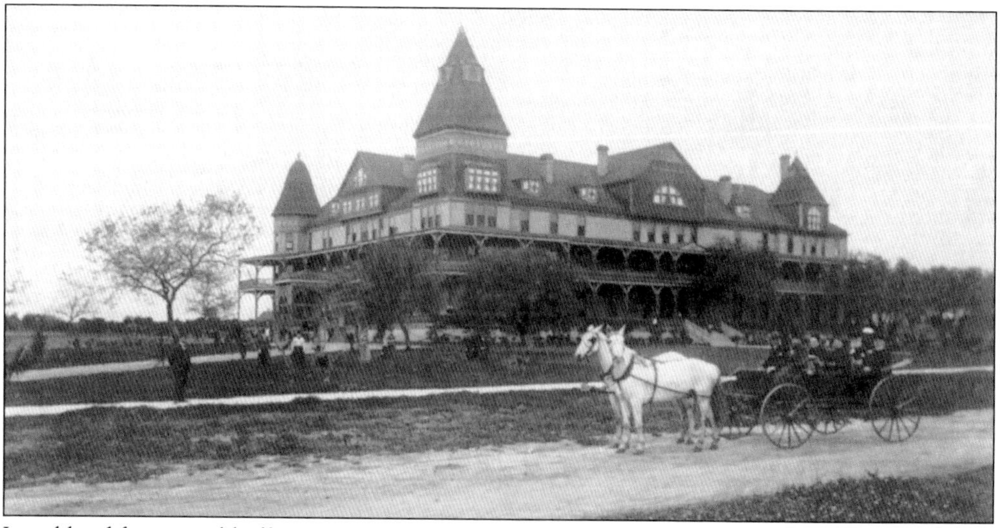

Local land firms would offer carriage rides to tourist attractions, then conveniently swing by real estate that was for sale. One fashionable excursion was the "Grand Round," which took hotel guests for scenic drives from Los Angeles to the Raymond Hotel in Pasadena. After a quick stop, the excursion continued on to the Sierra Madre Villa for lunch and a magnificent view. After a good meal, it was on to Lucky Baldwin's famous Santa Anita Rancho. The tour was not complete without a stop at the historic San Gabriel Mission. (Huntington Library.)

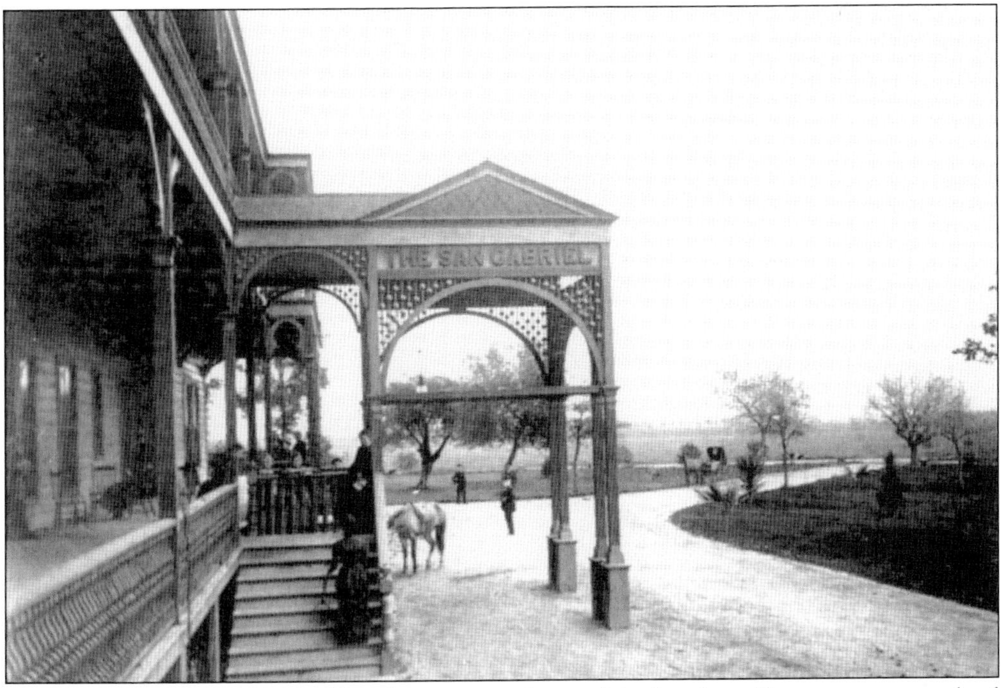

Many a carriage or coach would make a stop in front of the hotel to allow passengers to load or disembark at this grand entrance. At one time, the Southern Pacific brought a constant flow of tourists to San Gabriel aboard its local trains running between Los Angeles, San Bernardino, and Colton. The traffic was so brisk that San Gabriel had two Southern Pacific depots. (Huntington Library.)

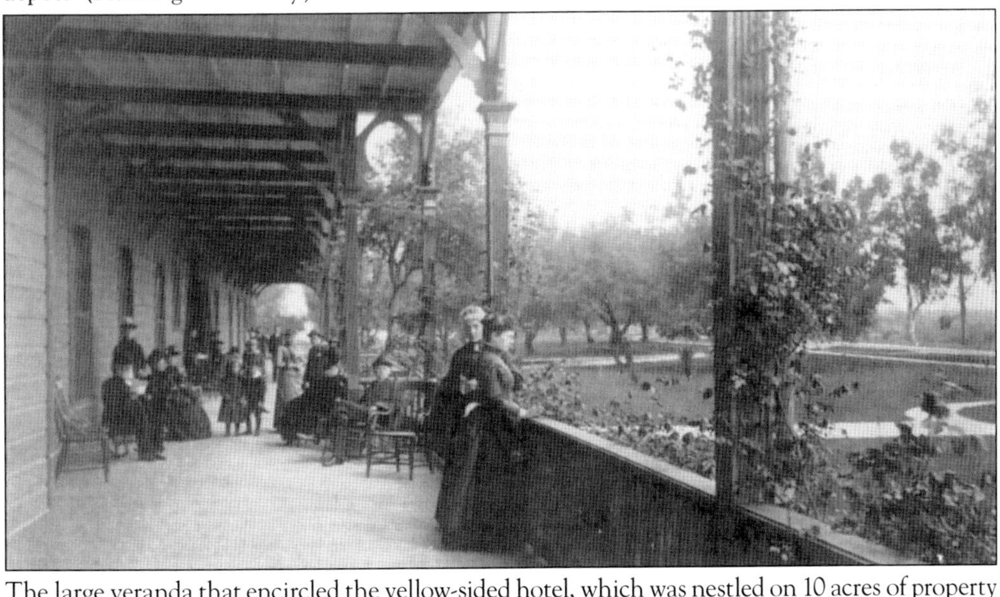
The large veranda that encircled the yellow-sided hotel, which was nestled on 10 acres of property with giant live oaks and lush lawns, was the perfect place to spend the afternoon relaxing. The hotel became famous as a summer resort for tourists and land speculators. On Tuesday, May 30, 1905, after the hotel closed, guests were treated to a band playing on the veranda as they toured the new Masonic home. (Huntington Library.)

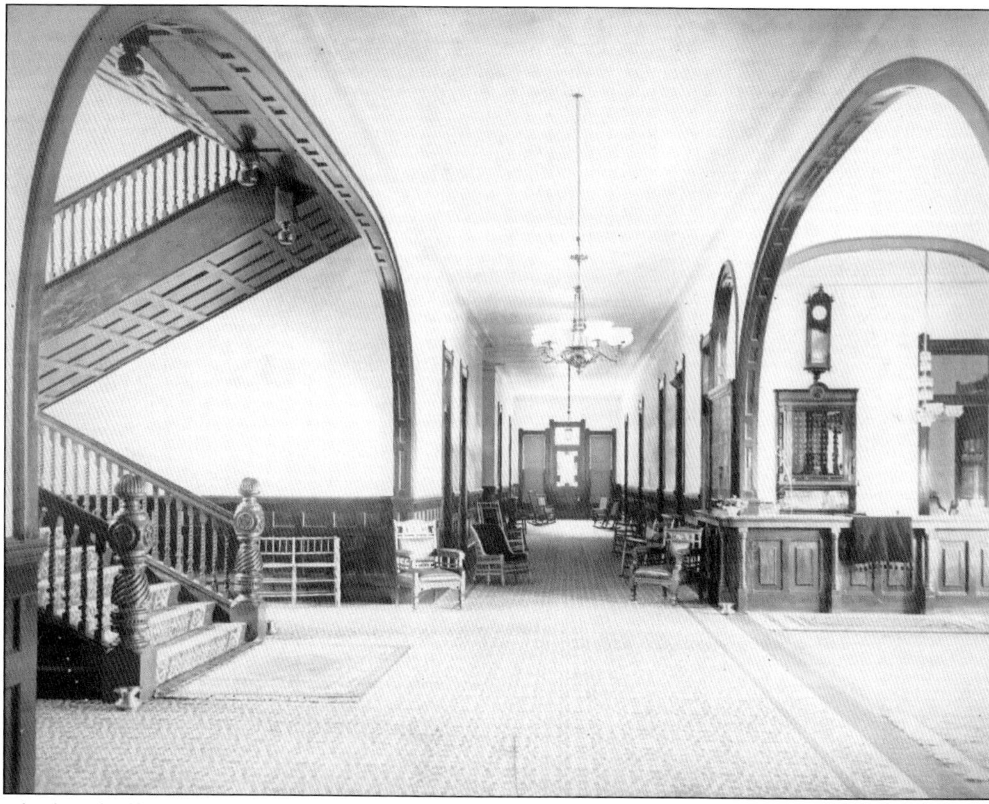

The hotel officially opened on June 1, 1888, under the able management of J.J. Martin, formerly of the Hotel Palmyra of Orange. The first registrant, according to the original hotel register, was J.M. Rustin, but his place of origin was not required on the hotel register at the time. During its short-lived success, the magnificent East San Gabriel Hotel catered to many prominent local members of society. The hotel's register includes names like Mr. and Mrs. George S. Patton Sr., Mr. and Mrs. William Banning, Mr. and Mrs. Hancock, O.W. Longden, A.L. Burbank, T.M. Van Nuys, and Marco Hellman. (Huntington Library.)

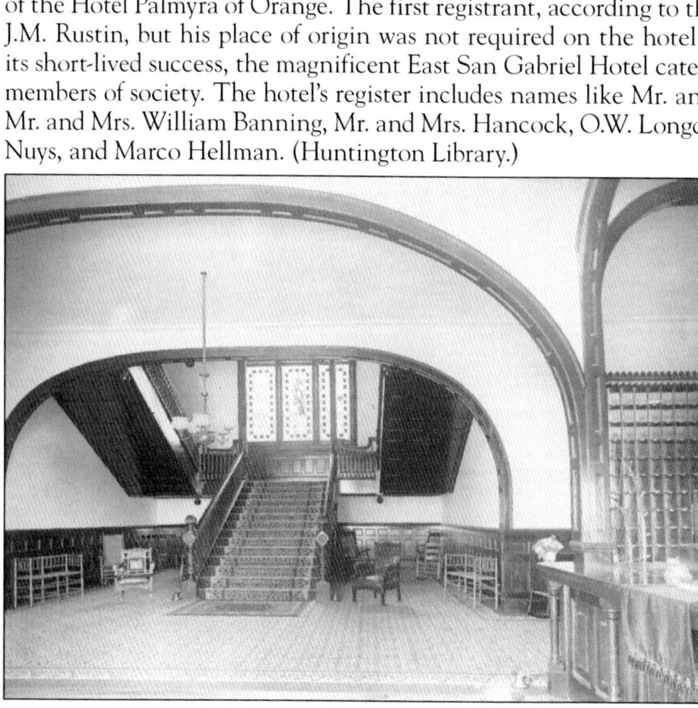

The spacious hotel contained 130 large rooms, each with a view, that were well lit and ventilated. According to one newspaper account, there was not a single "dark room" in the entire hotel. The wide hallways and broad staircases led hotel guests into the many private rooms, including a private dining room, convention hall, dance hall, barbershop, music room, and bridal chamber. (Huntington Library.)

Many guests arriving back at the hotel after a long day of sightseeing would freshen up in their respective rooms, then spend some time in the sitting room or adjoining music room before dining. (Huntington Library.)

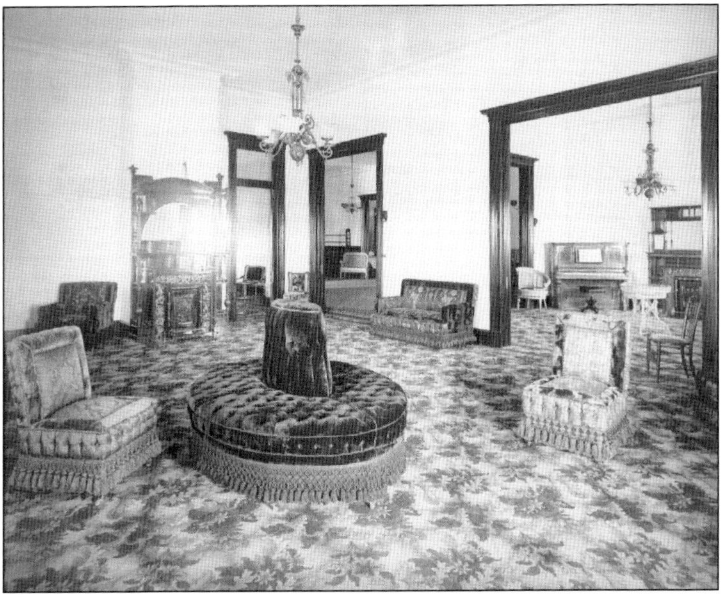

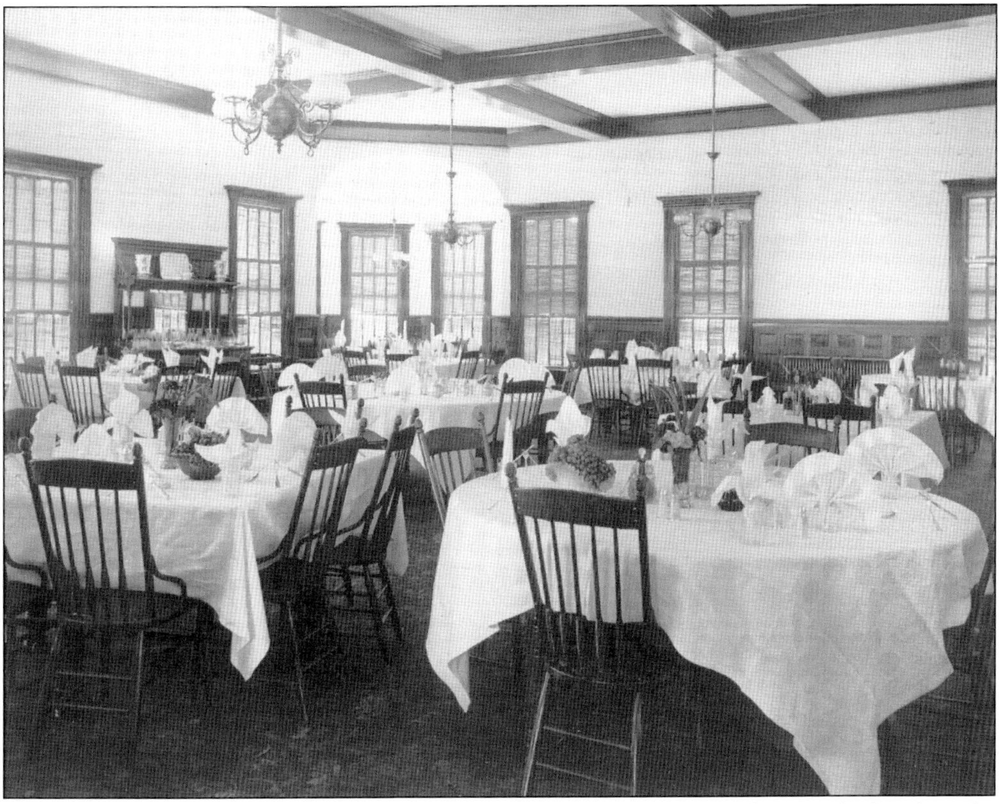

The hotel, while best known as a summer resort, soon became a popular spot for locals and a pleasant place to dine. Thanksgiving and New Year's festivities often brought out locals who filled the dining room to capacity. Once, after a five-mile cross-country race, more than 25 members of the Pasadena Athletic Club and 34 members of the Valley Hunt Club chose the hotel for dinner following the race. (Huntington Library.)

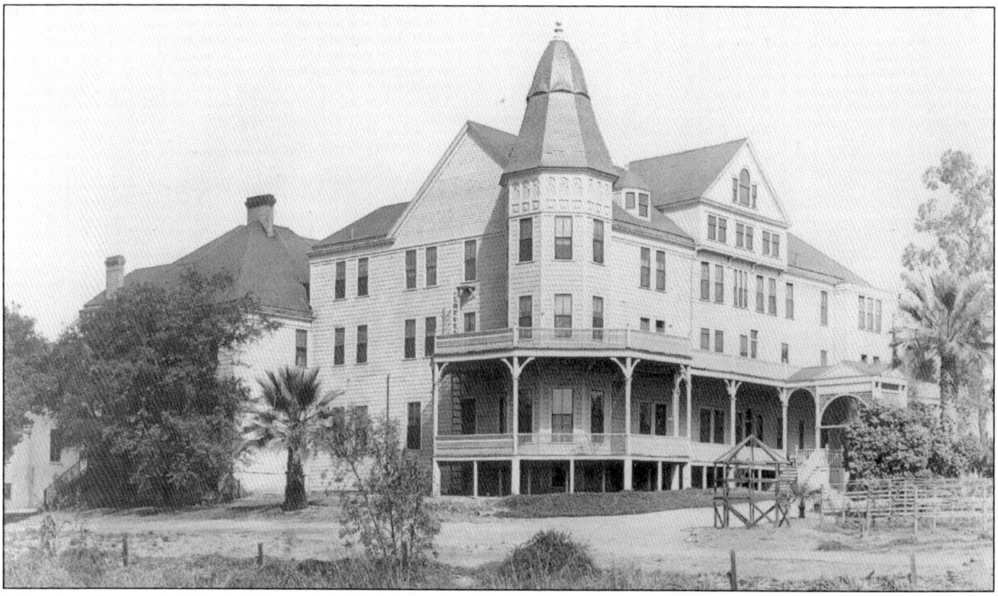

The Southern California Masonic Home Association purchased the grand old hotel in April 1905 for $18,500. The purchase price included all the furnishings, the household linen, and 13,000 pieces of silver tableware. The facility officially opened on Tuesday, May 30, 1905, and throughout the day, special Pacific Electric trains brought guests from various regions of Southern California. (Huntington Library.)

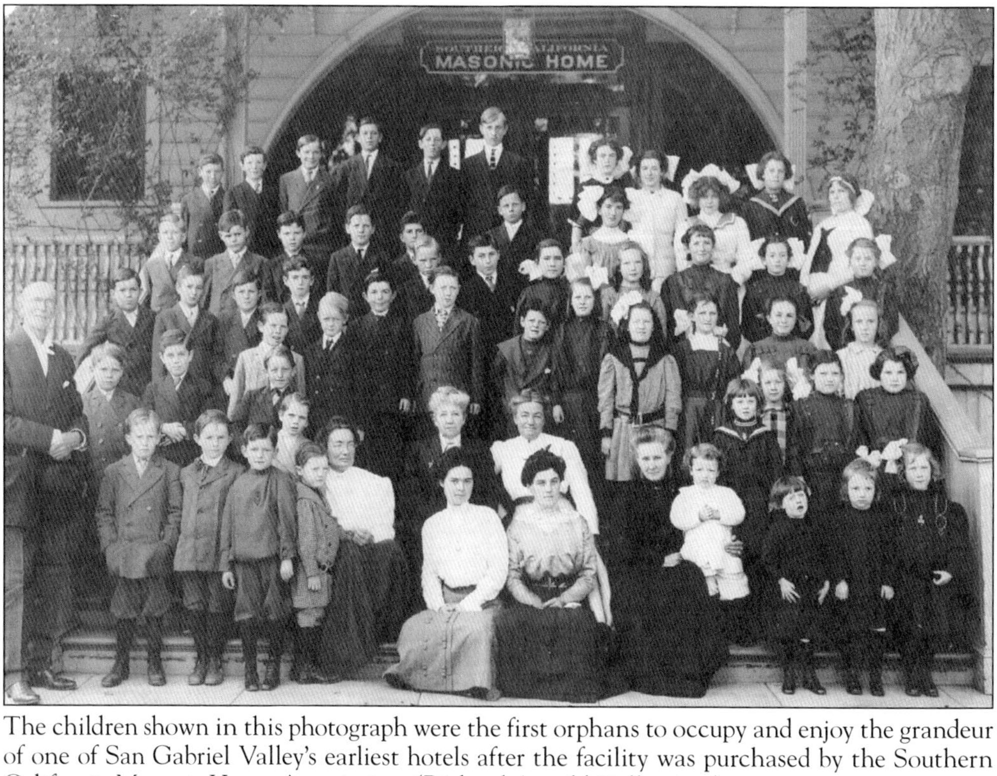

The children shown in this photograph were the first orphans to occupy and enjoy the grandeur of one of San Gabriel Valley's earliest hotels after the facility was purchased by the Southern California Masonic Home Association. (Richard Arnold Collection.)

Five

City with a Mission

As with other communities during this period, the residents of San Gabriel were becoming more and more frustrated with outside influences and the lack of adequate services from Los Angeles County. At the same time, having to contract with cities such as Alhambra for fire protection was becoming a burden. There was also the ongoing threat from the Alhambra citizens who were pushing to annex San Gabriel into their city. Residents upset with the prospects took to the streets, collecting signatures to have the incorporation issue put to the voters. With 306 ballots, the decision was won in favor of incorporation by 49 votes. The official date of incorporation as a city was on April 24, 1913.

The first meeting of the trustees was held at the home of Alex J. Cuneo on May 2, 1913. At this time, members of the council were referred to as trustees instead of councilmen, and Cuneo was elected president of the board of trustees. Justice of the peace W.M. Northrup was present at the first meeting and swore in the following trustees: Cuneo, Godfrey Dakin, Edwin Hayes, August Johnson, William C. Mulock, Claude Elmer Slack (treasurer), and Ira H. Stouffer (city clerk). Arthur E. Manzer was appointed the first city marshal on May 13, 1913, for a salary of $75 per month. Manzer was required to furnish and maintain his own car.

Meetings of the trustees were held in the library of Lincoln School, but during the September 29, 1913, meeting, it was decided that larger quarters were required, so an agreement was made to rent office space in the two-story building owned by William T. Slack on the southwest corner of Mission Drive and Carmelita Drive. After revisions were made to the facility, the first meeting at San Gabriel's city hall occurred on November 11, 1913.

One of the first ordinances adopted by the trustees on June 3, 1913, was Ordinance No. 39, which was related to "peace and order" and made certain offenses against the peace and good order of the city of San Gabriel a crime punishable by law.

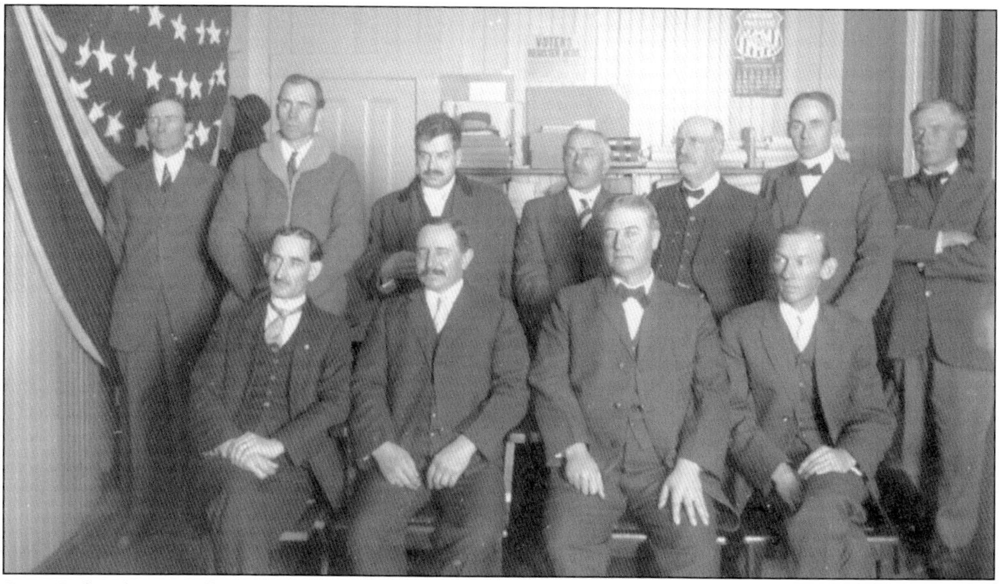

San Gabriel city officials are shown in this 1914 photograph, one year after San Gabriel was incorporated. From left to right are (sitting) Ira A. Stouffer, city clerk; A. J. Cunio, first mayor; Gilbert May, trustee; and C.E. Slack, first city treasurer; (standing) Edwin Hayes, former trustee; Arthur E. Manzer, city marshal; B.N. Jefferson, former trustee; Gottfried Daken, former mayor; E.A. Wright, former city engineer; Earl F. Wakeman, former city attorney; and John C. Stockberger, editor of record. (Richard Arnold Collection.)

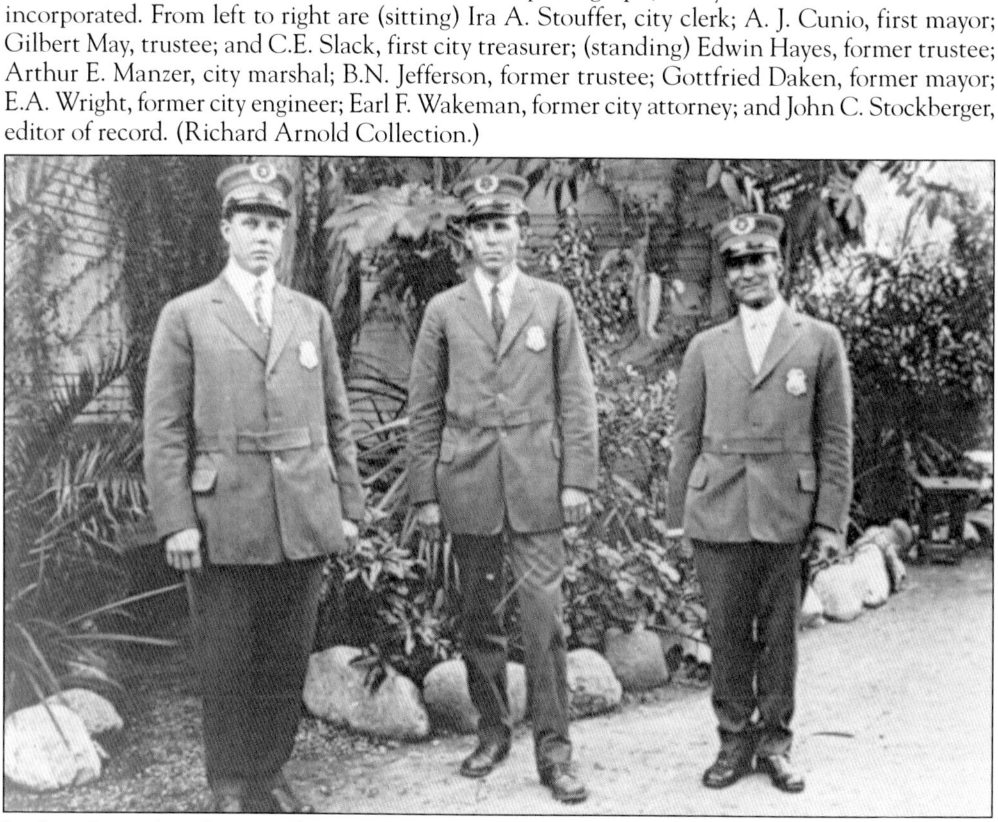

In this, the earliest known photograph of San Gabriel Police Department personnel, employees pose in front of the original Mission Playhouse in 1914. Pictured here are, from left to right, officer C.L. Atkinson, Marshal Arthur E. Manzer, and officer Manuel Salazar. (Richard Arnold Collection.)

Police chief Arthur E. Manzer (right) and officer Eddy Norwine are pictured with one of the department's Harley-Davidson motorcycles that was outfitted with a sawed-off repeating shotgun on the handlebars. Chief Manzer designed and patented the equipment with a concern that a "newly installed" network of call boxes throughout the city placed motor officers in such quick contact with the scene of a crime that something more than a service revolver might be needed. The pivot/sling design allowed for the officer to easily remove the gun. The magazine of each shotgun held six shells, and instead of small buckshot, each was loaded with special shells containing 12 pellets or slugs. (Richard Arnold Collection.)

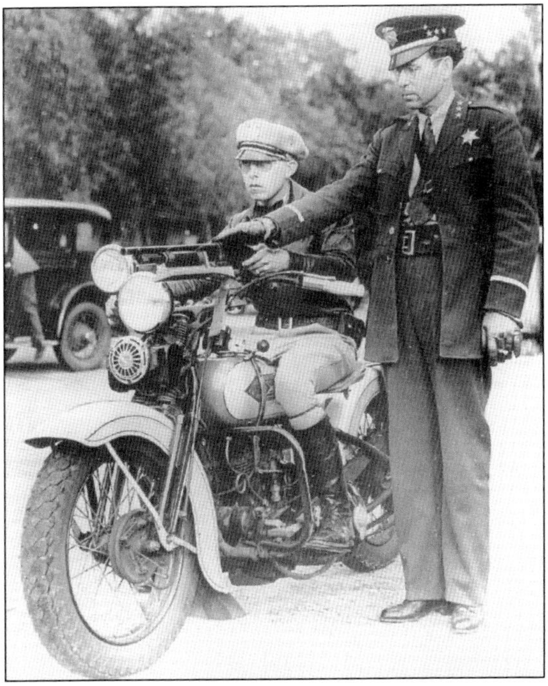

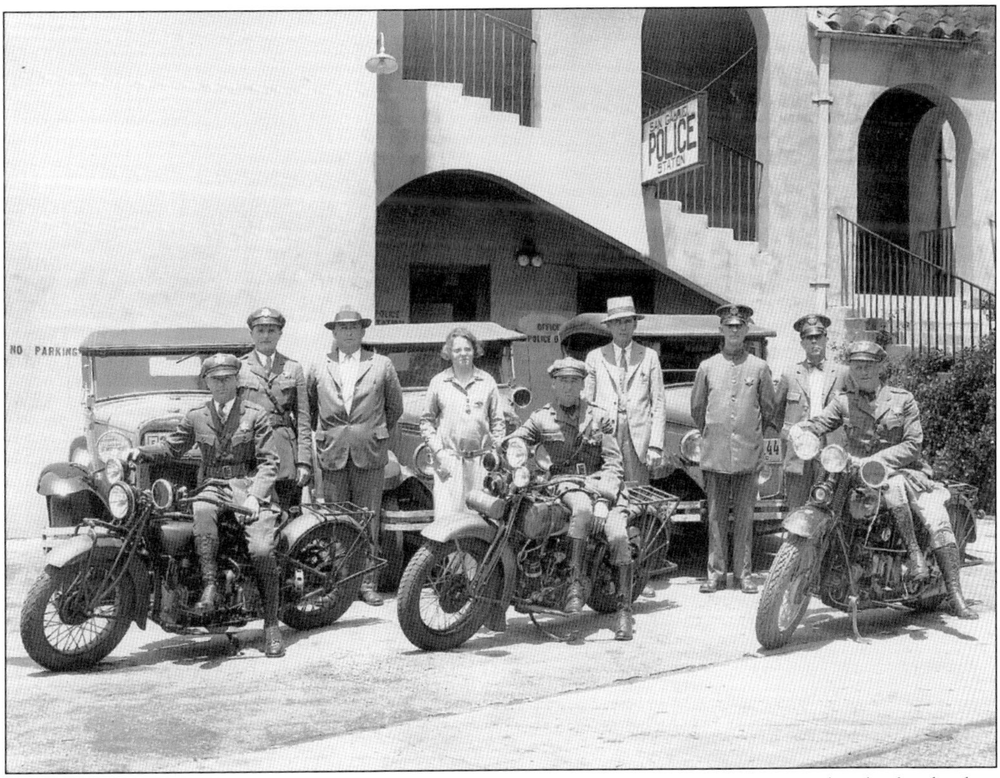

This April 1930 image shows members of the San Gabriel Police Department, under the leadership of Chief Arthur E. Manzer, posing in front of the San Gabriel Police Station. The police station was located at city hall, with an entrance off Ramona Street. (Richard Arnold Collection.)

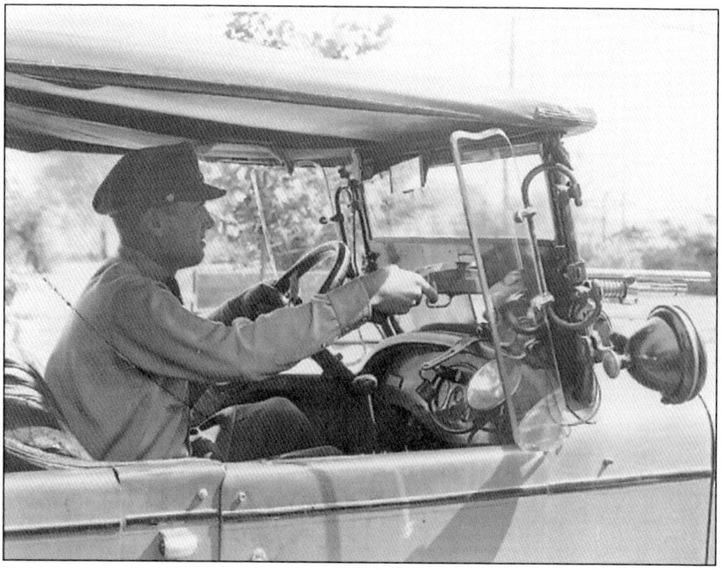

Officer Jesse L. Howell demonstrates a "slight" modification made to this 1926 Chrysler Model 60 touring car—a 12-gauge shotgun mounted on the dashboard below the windshield with the barrel protruding through a quarter-inch-thick steel plate. A locking device was included in the installation to prevent thieves from stealing the shotgun. (Richard Arnold Collection.)

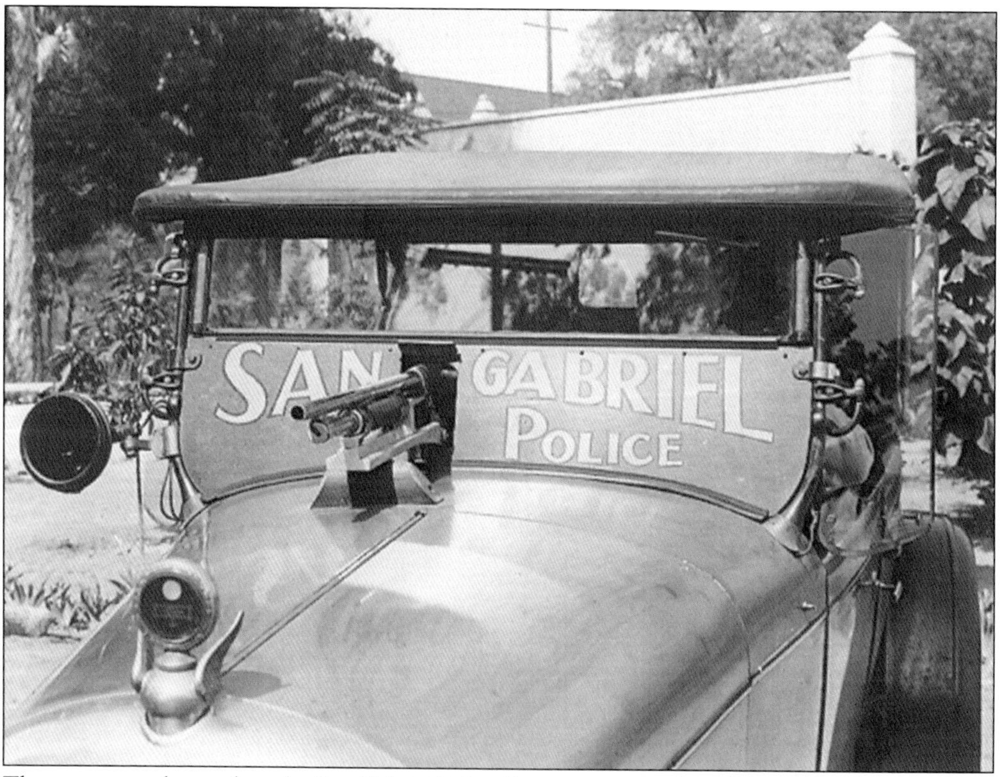

There was great hype when the San Gabriel Police Department purchased this 1926 Chrysler Model 60 touring car. Chief Arthur Manzer announced to the press that the police were determined to give lawbreakers a "run for their money" with the purchase of the vehicle. The 60 is a phaeton model, quick on the getaway, and can go 60 miles per hour or more when necessity demands. By November 1931, shotguns were also added to the department's fleet of motorcycles . Chief Manzer designed and built the units on the motorcycles and on the 1926 Chrysler Model 60. (Richard Arnold Collection.)

Officer Alvin W. Haynes was killed while conducting a traffic stop at the intersection of Valley Boulevard and San Gabriel Boulevard on September 6, 1933, when a drunk driver crashed into the back of the truck Haynes had stopped. Haynes was pinned between the two vehicles, causing massive injuries. He died while en route to the hospital. (Richard Arnold Collection.)

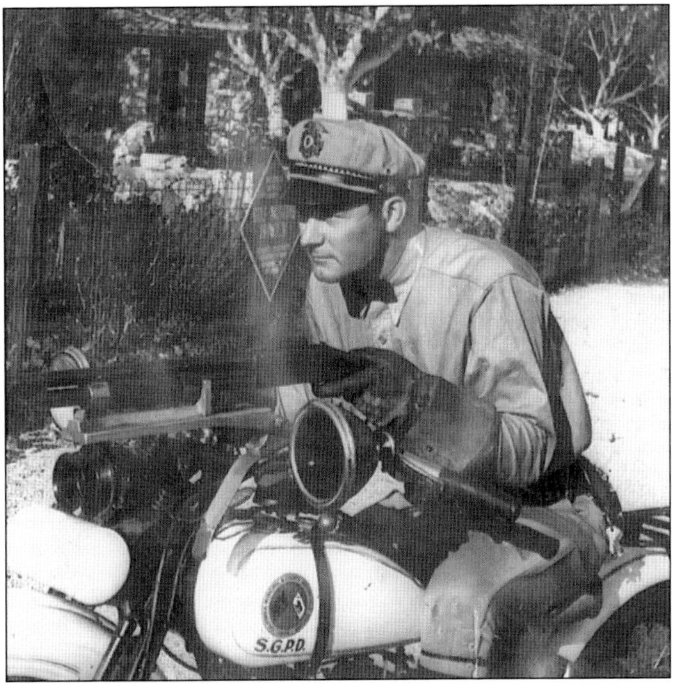

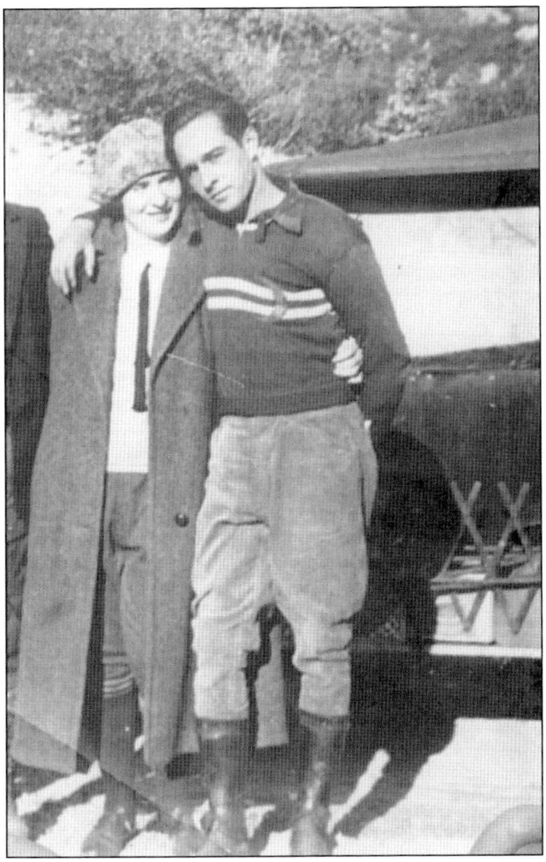

Officer Elmer H. Griffin, pictured with his girlfriend, was a 12-month veteran of the police department when he was killed while stopping a car loaded with "booze-runners," which he observed speeding through town. After inspecting the vehicle and its occupants for weapons, Griffin jumped on the running board of the vehicle and ordered them to drive to the police station. While en route, one of the suspects fired a .38 revolver toward Griffin, knocking him off the vehicle and onto the ground, where he was able to fire three rounds before he died. (Richard Arnold Collection.)

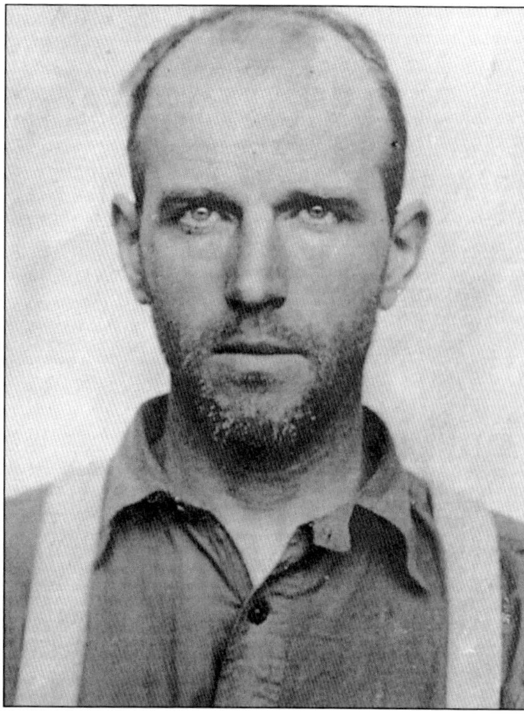

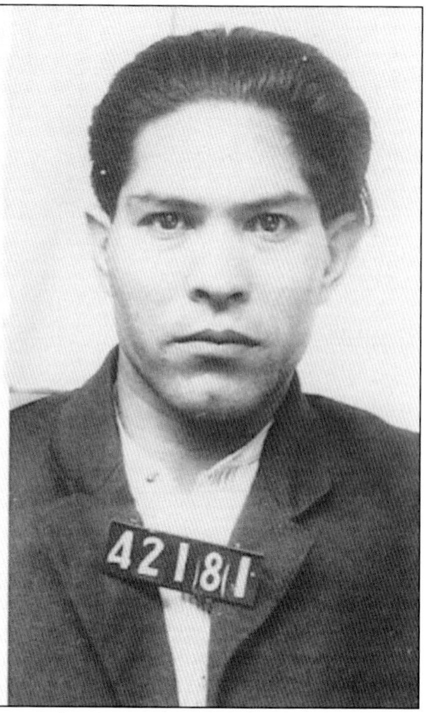

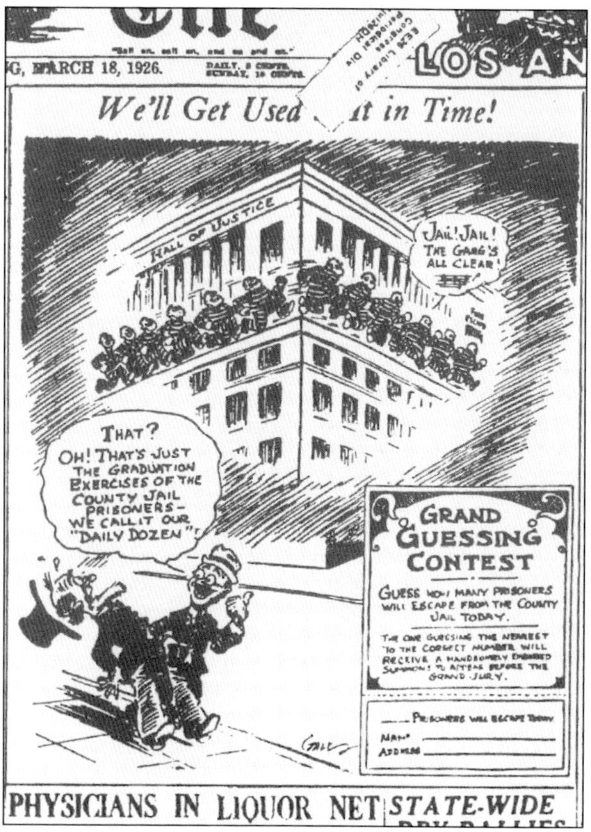

Charles Fitzgerald (above, left) was 40 years old when he was sent to Folsom State Prison for the murder of officer Elmer Griffin. On December 10, 1971, after serving 40 years behind bars, he was granted parole because of poor health. At 85, he had been the oldest inmate in California's correctional system. Antonio Rojo (above, right) was 41 years old when he was paroled after spending 23 years in Folsom. He was deported to Mexico. (Richard Arnold Collection.)

While awaiting trial for the murder of Elmer Griffin, one of the suspects implicated in the crime, Charles Fitzgerald, managed to break out of the jail on the top floor of the newly completed Los Angeles County Jail along with five other prisoners who were being held in the 10th-floor jail cell. The March 18, 1926, edition of the *Los Angeles Times* poked fun at the escape of Fitzgerald with this satirical cartoon. (Richard Arnold Collection.)

The 27-year-old Forest Ray Colson, tagged the "Man From Mars" by police for wearing this attire, staged holdups of local supermarkets for six months—netting more than $55,000—before his luck ran out on Thursday, October 12, 1951. Colson entered Boy's Market at 120 East Valley Boulevard and forced the cashier to empty the evening receipts, which totaled $13,675. Officer Harry Stone, responding to the robbery call, fired one round from his revolver, striking Colson in the head; he died two hours later. The crime spree was documented in a weekly television show *Gang Busters: The Man From Mars*, written and produced by Phillips H. Lord. At right, an actor is wearing the outfit used by Colson in this publicity shot for the show that aired on March 20, 1952, on NBC. (Richard Arnold Collection.)

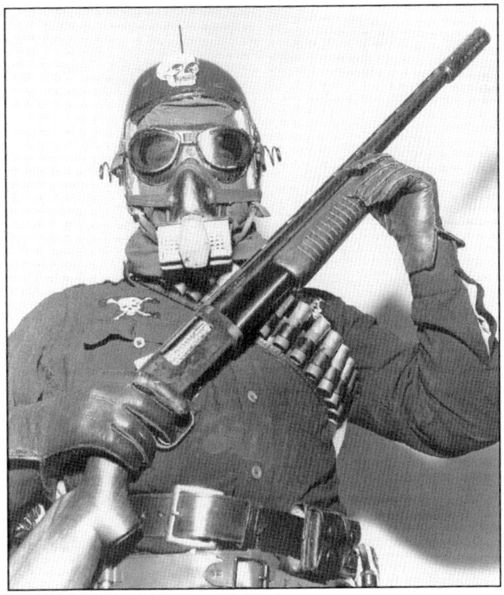

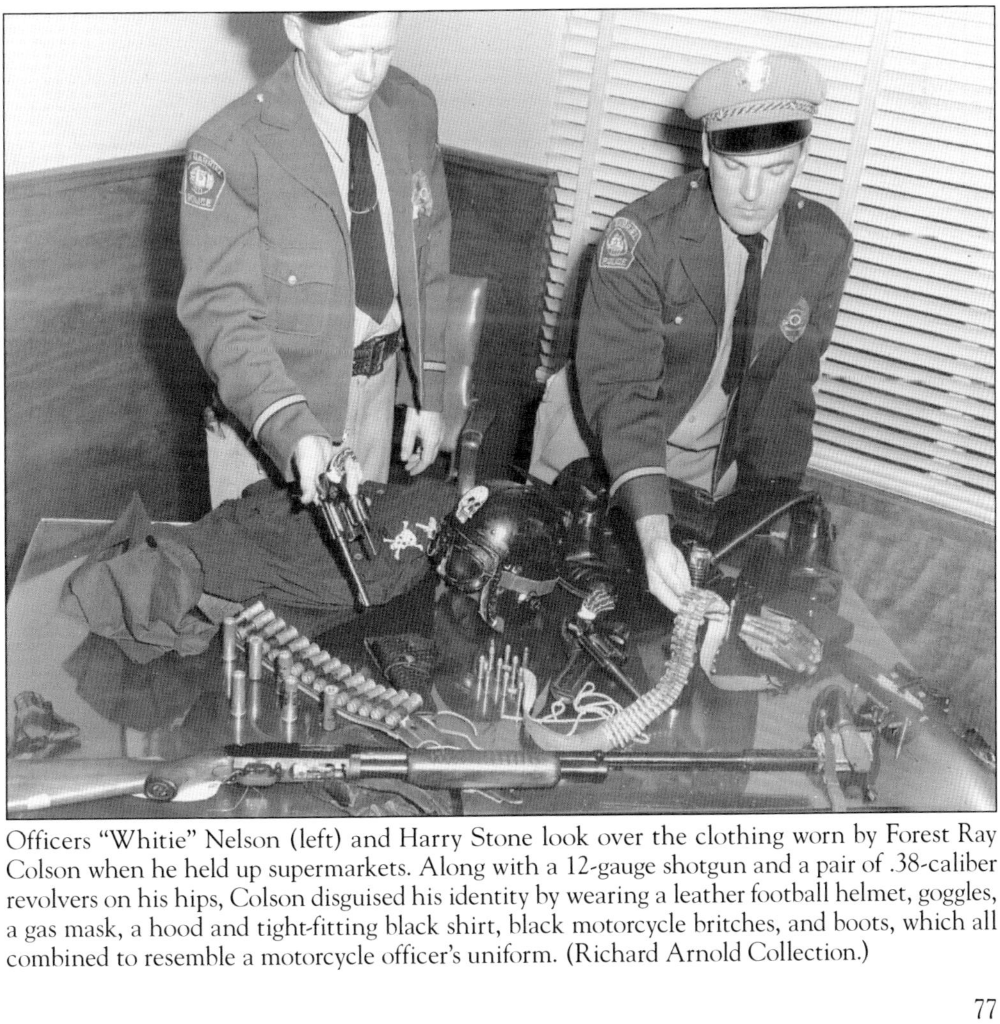

Officers "Whitie" Nelson (left) and Harry Stone look over the clothing worn by Forest Ray Colson when he held up supermarkets. Along with a 12-gauge shotgun and a pair of .38-caliber revolvers on his hips, Colson disguised his identity by wearing a leather football helmet, goggles, a gas mask, a hood and tight-fitting black shirt, black motorcycle britches, and boots, which all combined to resemble a motorcycle officer's uniform. (Richard Arnold Collection.)

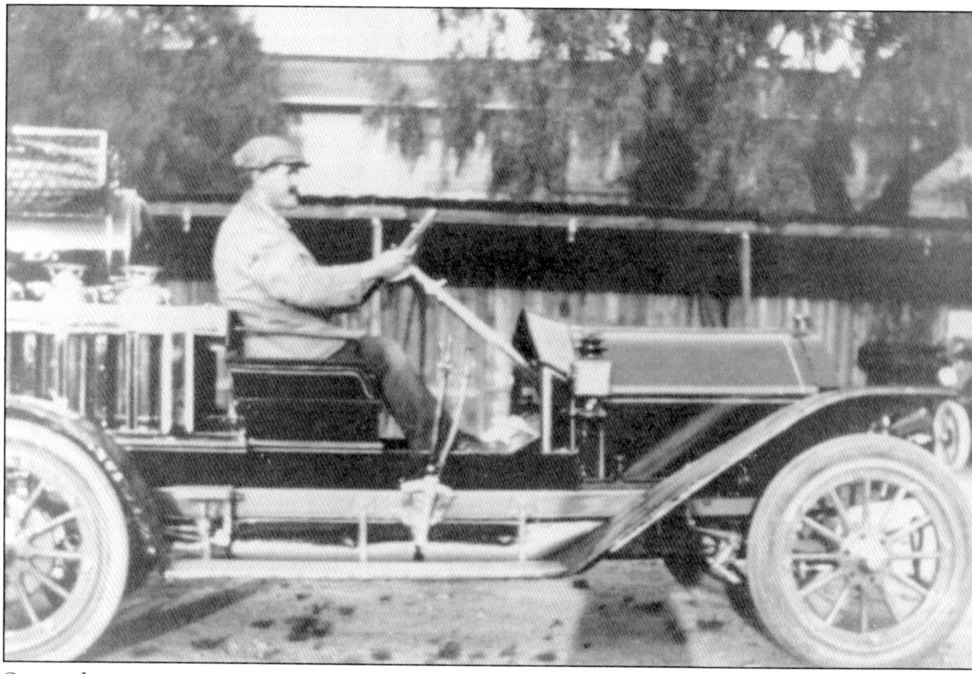

Soon after it was incorporated as a city on April 24, 1913, San Gabriel decided to contract with the Alhambra Fire Department for firefighting services. By December 1914, however, the city council decided to form their own department and requested bids for a chemical apparatus to be placed on an automobile chassis of 40 horsepower to be used for firefighting. Only one bid was received, in January 1915, from A.W. Roe and Leo Davis of the Mission Garage for $925. The bid was received, and by March 17, 1915, Roe was appointed fire chief with the authorization to form a volunteer fire department. In this photograph, Chief Roe takes the recently delivered chemical wagon for a test drive. (San Gabriel Historical Association.)

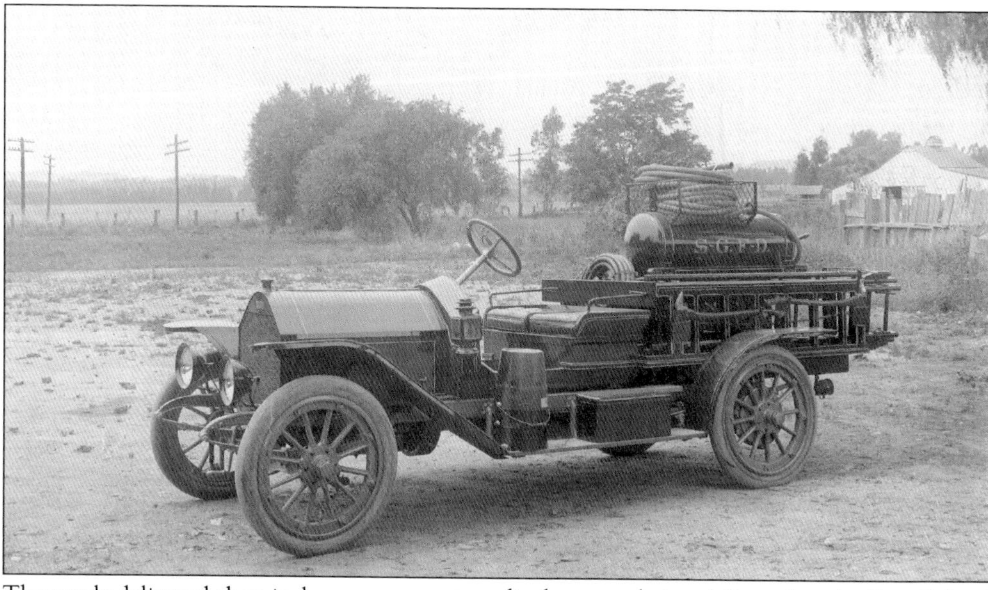

The newly delivered chemical wagon was put on display upon being delivered to the San Gabriel Fire Department in 1915. (San Gabriel Historical Association.)

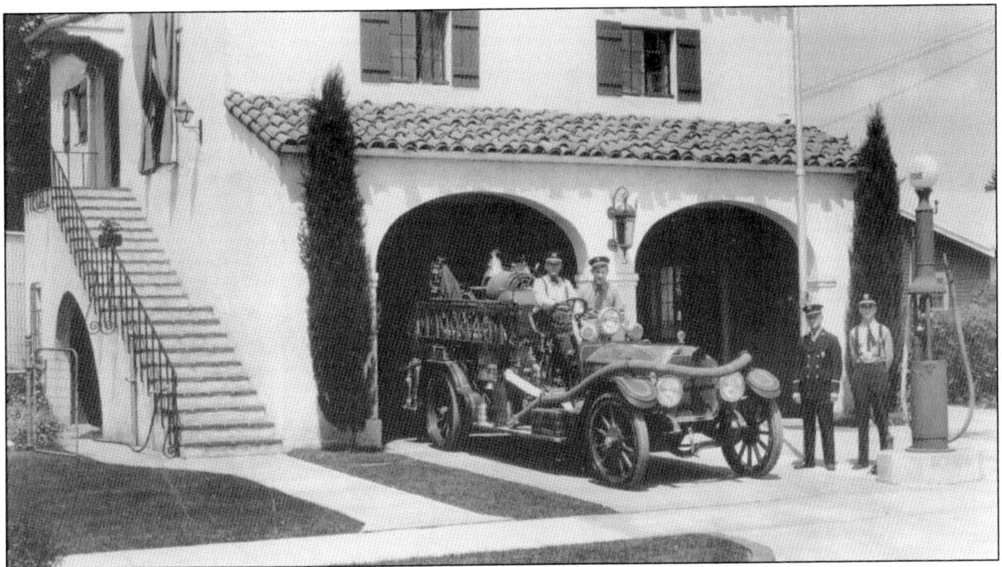

Members of the San Gabriel Fire Department, from left to right, Capt. Bob Elder, unidentified fireman, Chief Glen Stokes, and fireman Homer D. Mann pose in front of the fire station with their 1917 America La France pumper. The two-story Spanish style station, built in 1926 and located at 605 South Del Mar Avenue, was designed by architects Quintin & Kerr, Alhambra and was built by Steed Brothers Construction, Alhambra. (Richard Arnold Collection.)

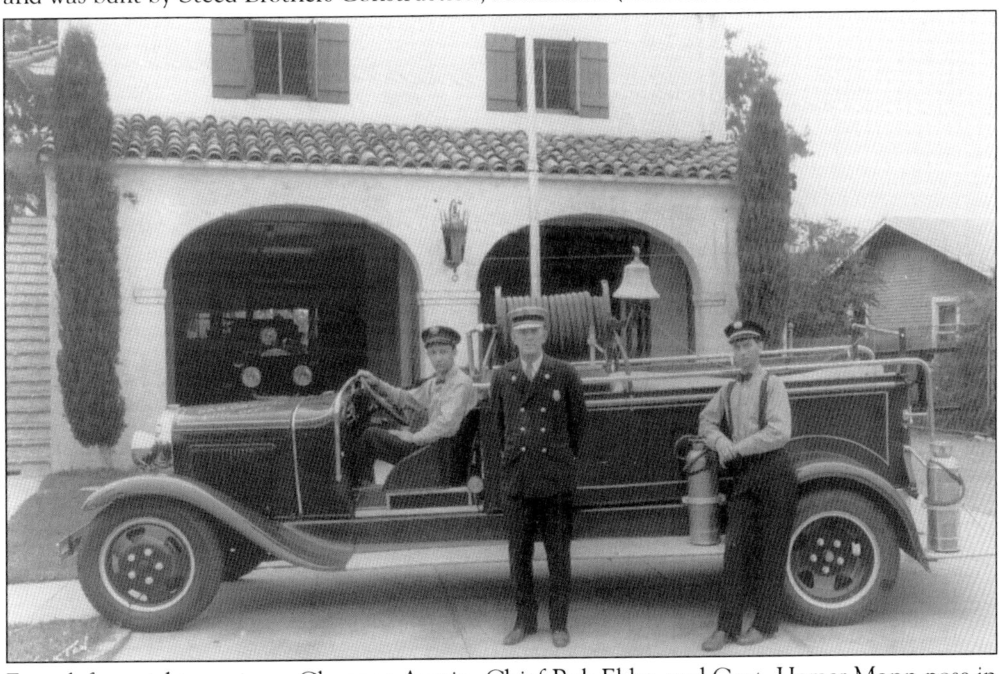

From left to right, engineer Clarence Austin, Chief Bob Elder, and Capt. Homer Mann pose in front of the San Gabriel Fire Station on September 5, 1933. The three converted the 1933 Ford truck chassis into a usable piece of fire equipment for a total cost of $800. Finished in bright red with gold lettering and chrome plating, the engine was equipped with a 160-gallon water tank, 100-gallon Viking pump, 1,000 feet of fire hose, a first aid kit, a ladder, and fire extinguishers. (Richard Arnold Collection.)

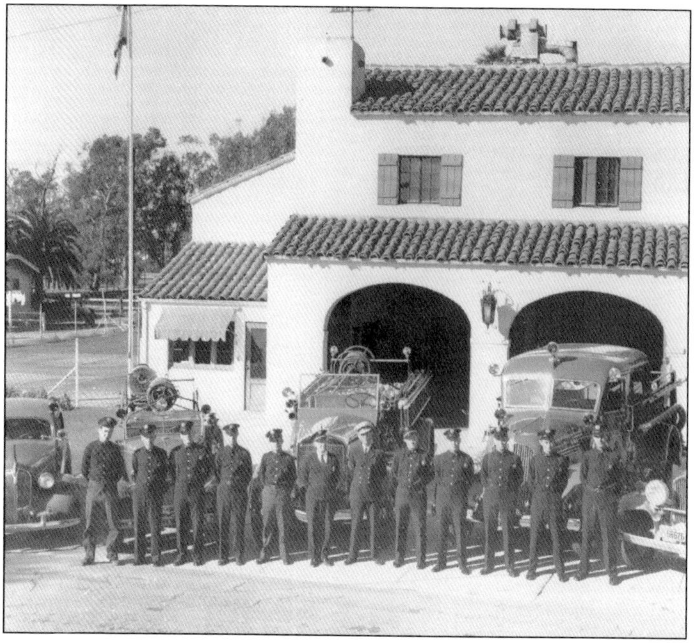

Members of the San Gabriel Fire Department pose in front of the fire station, located at 605 South Del Mar Avenue, in this c. 1938 photograph. Chief Homer Mann, shown with the white dress cap, started with the department in November 1930 and became the fire chief in September 1941. In 1960, the 34-year-old Spanish-designed facility was replaced by a modern fire headquarters at 1303 South Del Mar Avenue. In its place a new police facility was built and dedicated in 1962. (Lynn C. Youngs Collection.)

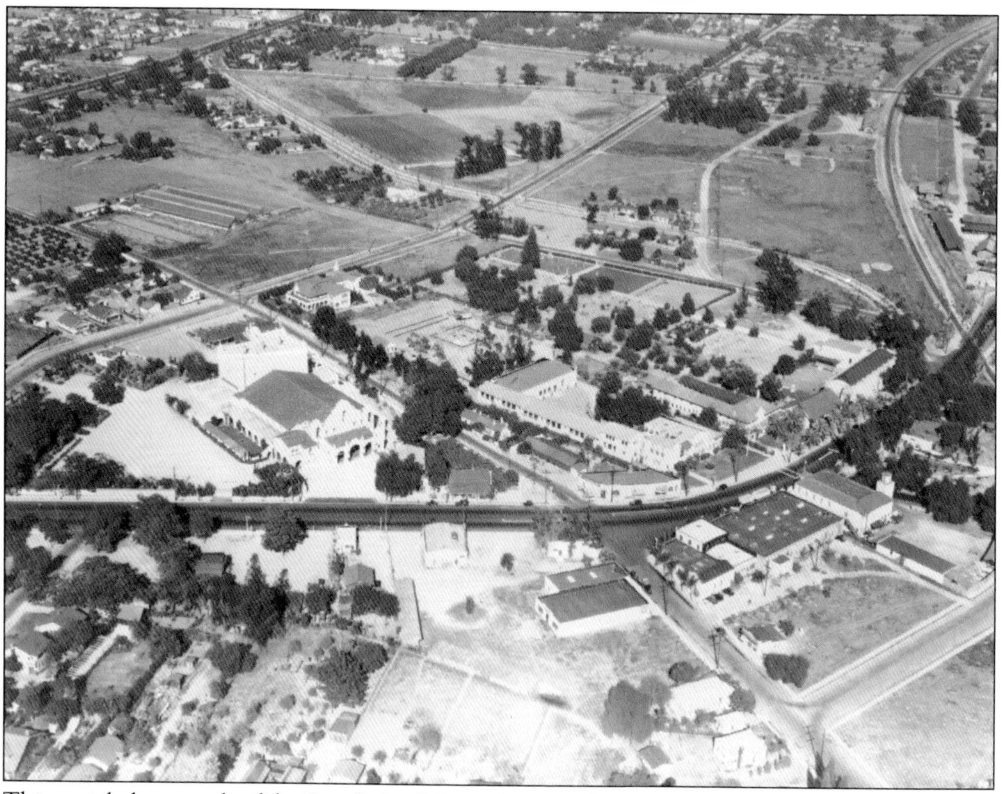

This aerial photograph of the San Gabriel Civic Center taken in 1927 provides a good perspective of the many landmarks that surround the San Gabriel Mission. It also provides a look at the many pieces of property to the east of the mission that have yet to be developed. (Lawrence Arnold Collection.)

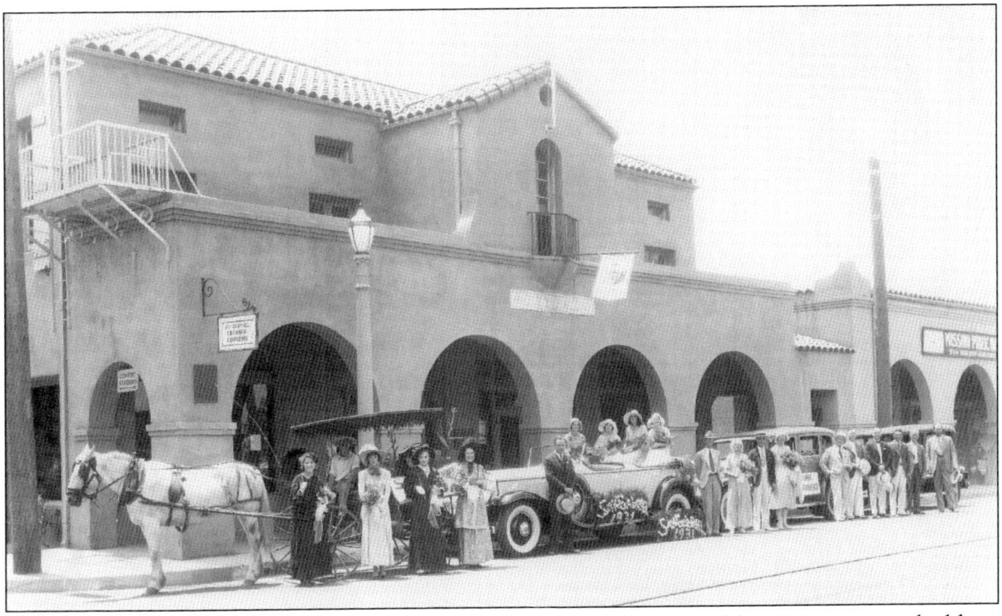

In this 1931 photograph, the queen of the San Gabriel Fiesta and her princesses—holding their bouquets—line up in front of city hall along with city officials. (San Gabriel Historical Association.)

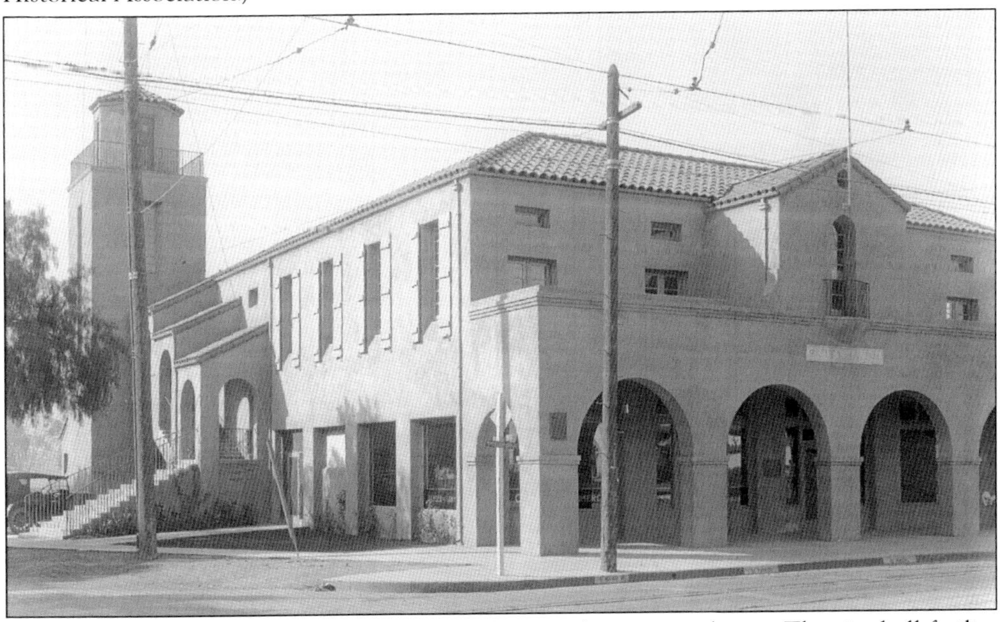

San Gabriel City Hall is pictured here in 1923 soon after its completion. The city hall facility also housed the police department, council chambers, the San Gabriel Justice Court, and the San Gabriel Chamber of Commerce on the northeast corner of the building. The top portion of the tower was damaged as a result of the 1932 earthquake and needed to be rebuilt to remove the top ornate portion. In January 1994, the 50-foot tower was once again damaged as a result of an earthquake and needed to be taken down, since the unreinforced brick tower had numerous cracks, making the structure unsafe. The tower was subsequently rebuilt as part of a project to retrofit the entire city hall. (Richard Arnold Collection.)

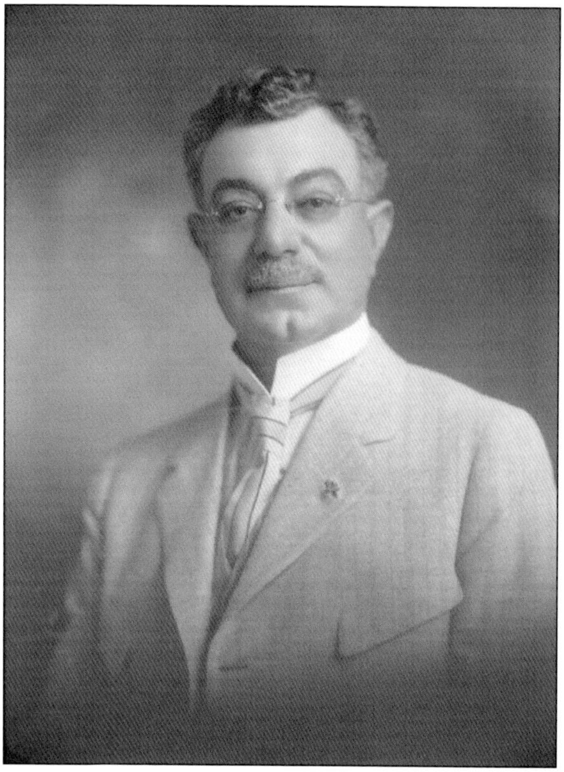

Walter P. Temple, son of Francis Pliny Fisk Temple (an early settler of the southland) and Antonia Margarita Workman (whose father, William Workman, was also an early settler), founded Temple City in 1922 in a wish to perpetuate the family name. In 1922, Temple also donated the property on which San Gabriel could build their new city hall. Temple rose from moderate circumstances to wealth through the discovery, by his son Thomas, of oil on the family property. This resulted in the establishment of the famous Montebello oil fields. (Workman and Temple Family Homestead Museum.)

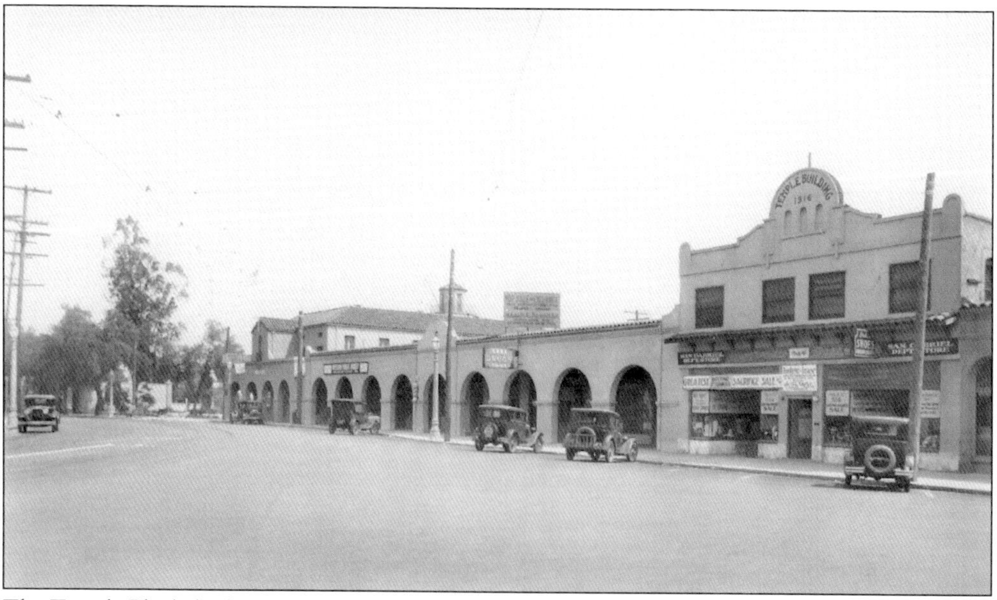

The Temple Block, built in 1922 by Walter P. Temple, was located at the southwest corner of Mission Drive and Santa Anita Avenue and contained a variety of businesses, including the San Gabriel Department Store, San Gabriel Public Market, a barbershop, and a drugstore. The building was designed by Los Angeles architects Albert Walker and Percy Eisen. Local photographer Burton Frasher photographed the complex in 1930. It is unknown why Temple marked the front facade "1916" when the building was erected in 1922. (Richard Arnold Collection.)

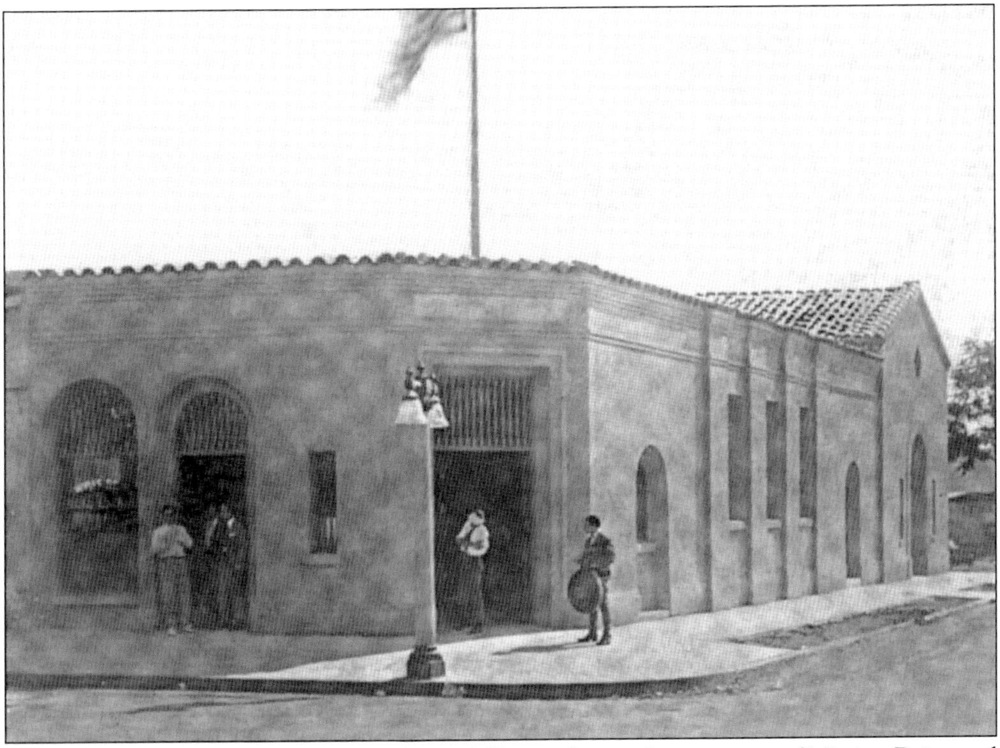

Walter P. Temple built the San Gabriel Post Office at the southeast corner of Mission Drive and Santa Anita Avenue in 1922. The building was designed by Los Angeles architects Albert Walker and Percy Eisen. The corner building has been home to the John L. Raya Insurance Group since 1980. (Richard Arnold Collection.)

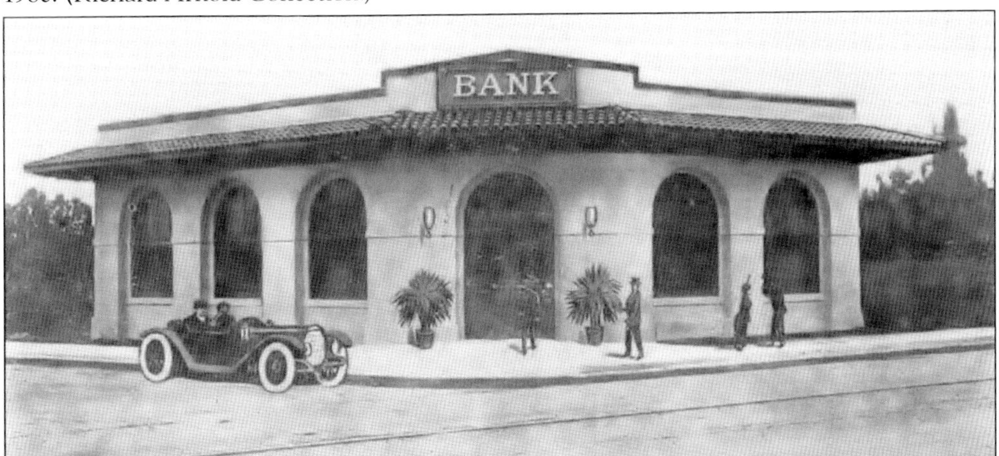

The Bank of San Gabriel, located at 343 South Mission Drive, formed on September 26, 1914, and moved into this facility the following year with William R. Fee serving as the bank's first president. The bank expanded by 1923, opening another branch in east San Gabriel at the southwest corner of San Gabriel Boulevard and Broadway. In 1925, the bank was purchased by the California Bank, later known as United California Bank. In May 1930, both branches were consolidated and moved to a new facility at 641 West Las Tunas Drive. The building was purchased by the City of San Gabriel on January 31, 1969. (San Gabriel Historical Association.)

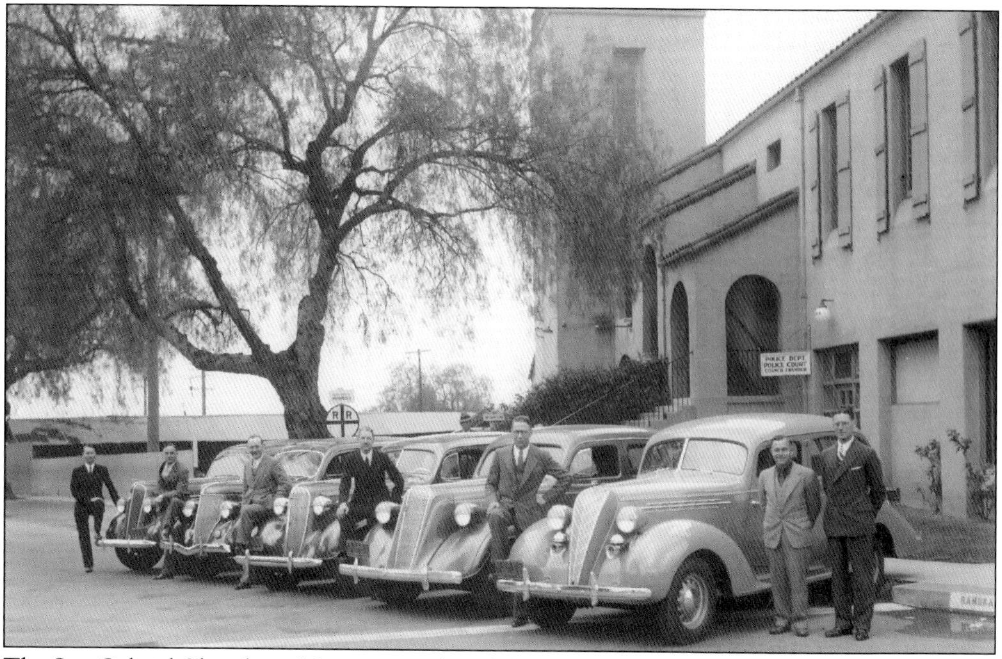

The San Gabriel Chamber of Commerce, founded in 1926, had its first offices in the front corner space of the new city hall facility. In this 1936 photograph, San Gabriel automobile dealers parked their respective wares in front of the chamber of commerce for this photo opportunity. The automobiles are, from left to right, Plymouth, Ford, Chevrolet, Nash, and Terraplane. (Richard Arnold Collection.)

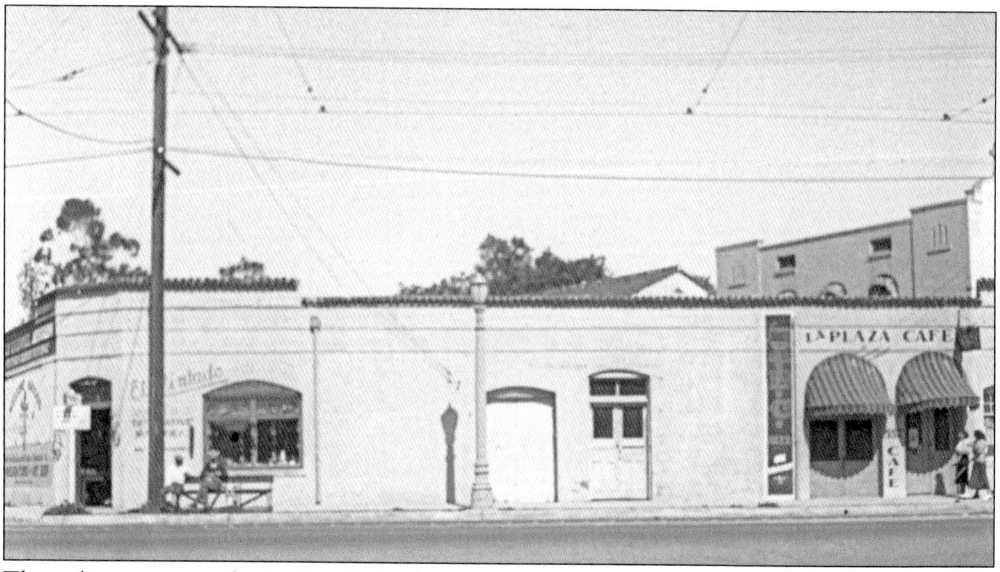

The military quarters for the San Gabriel Mission once occupied this corner (northeast corner of Santa Anita Avenue and Mission Drive), which was later home to Headquarters Saloon, owned by Joshua Bean in 1854. The wood-frame Billiard Saloon was built around the late 1860s to replace the adobe structure, and this brick structure was constructed in the 1890s to replace the Billiard Saloon. From 1915 to 1923, one portion of the building was used as the San Gabriel Post Office. (Richard Arnold Collection.)

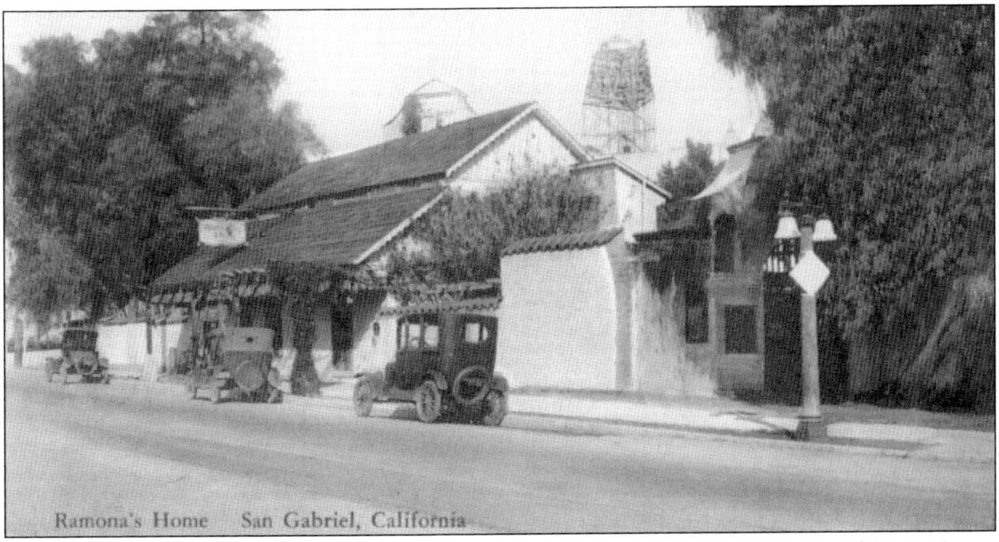

The two-story wood-frame grocery store that once graced the northwest corner of Santa Anita Avenue and Mission Drive was demolished in the early 1900s and replaced by the Spanish-style archway that became another entrance to the grapevine arbor behind the old adobe San Gabriel Hotel. The hotel changed ownership several times, becoming Bailey's Hotel and Ramona's Home before being purchased by the City of San Gabriel in August 1945. The adobe fell into disrepair and was demolished by the city in 1951. (Richard Arnold Collection.)

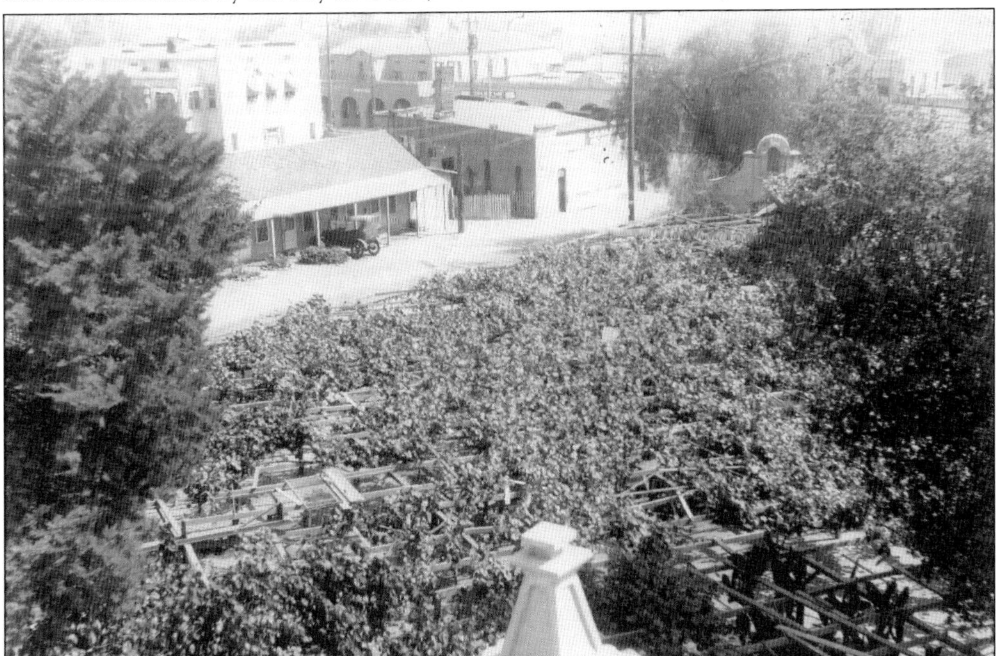

The massive size of the grapevine behind the San Gabriel Hotel becomes apparent in this overhead photograph of the vine taken in the early 1930s. The adobe, which faced Mission Drive, was a popular gathering site for visitors who came to town by carriage or Pacific Electric streetcars to visit the historic San Gabriel Mission. (Security Pacific National Bank Collection, Los Angeles Public Library.)

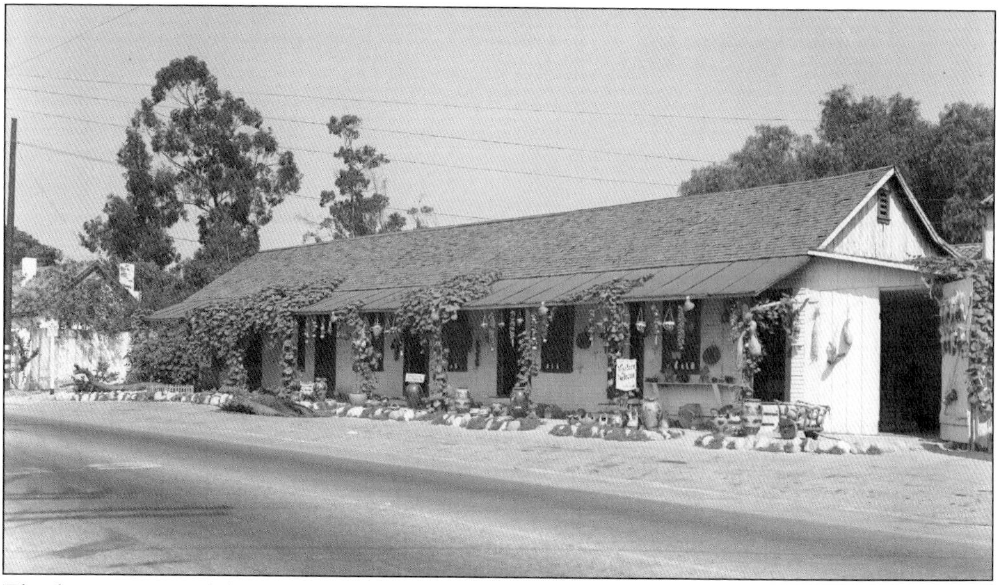

This long, narrow adobe once stood on Santa Anita Avenue just north of Mission Drive between the Lopez de Lowther adobe and the military quarters. All three adobes were part of the original mission quadrangle. (Security Pacific National Bank Collection, Los Angeles Public Library.)

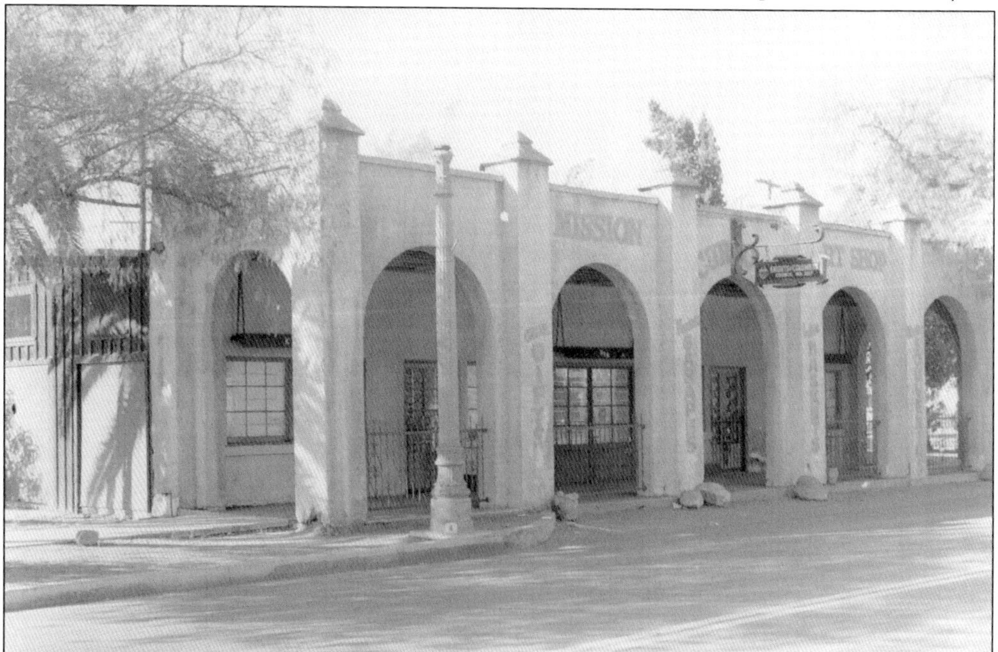

The original site of the Mission Curio and Gift Shop was directly across from the San Gabriel Mission and to the east of the first playhouse, the present-day site of Plaza Park. The Mission Curio and Gift Shop moved to a new location in front of the Mission Playhouse in 1929, and this building was abandoned. When this photograph was taken, the building was being used by the Knights of Columbus No. 3517. (San Gabriel Historical Association.)

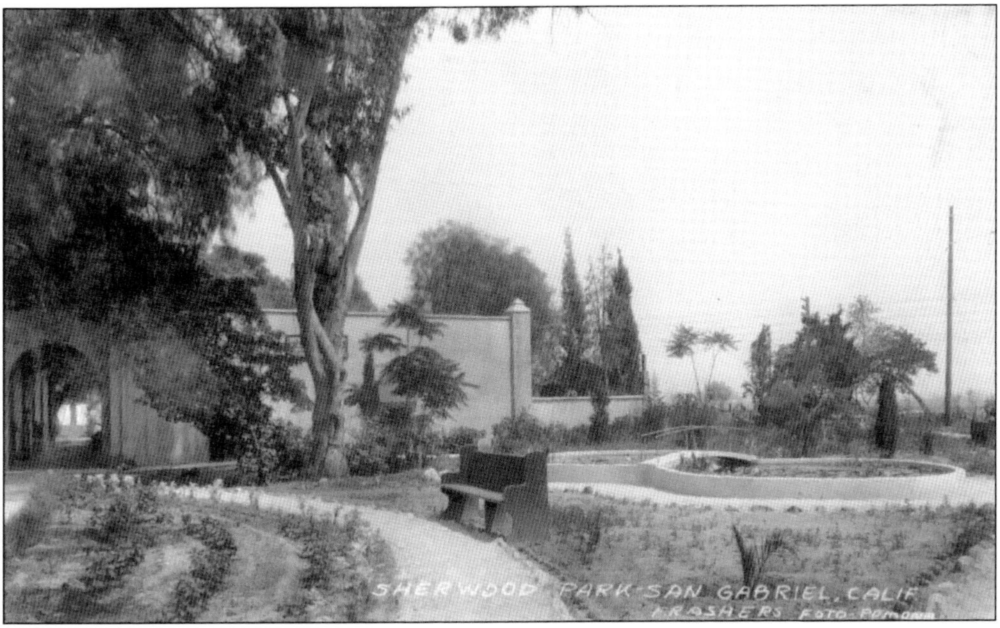

On January 16, 1931, the San Gabriel Women's Club dedicated the property where the original Mission Playhouse once stood for use as a city park. The park was named Sherwood Park in honor of Mrs. Howard U. Sherwood, president of the Los Angeles District Federation of Women's Clubs. During the 1976 bicentennial celebration, the park was renamed Plaza Park. (Richard Arnold Collection.)

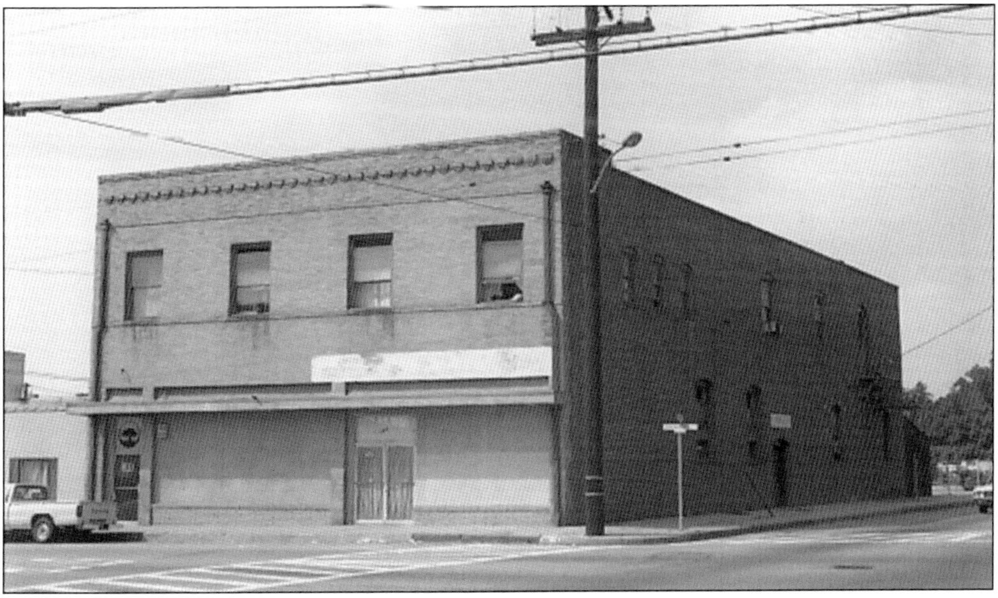

Johnson Hall, located at the southwest corner of San Marino Avenue and Broadway, was built in 1912 by Robert K. Johnson and was the original "meeting place" for many organizations, including the San Gabriel Woman's Club, which was founded on October 23, 1913. The earthquake on February 12, 1987, caused extensive damage to the brick building, so the second story was removed. Johnson became the ninth postmaster of San Gabriel on November 25, 1903, and operated the general store on Shorb Road. (Richard Arnold Collection.)

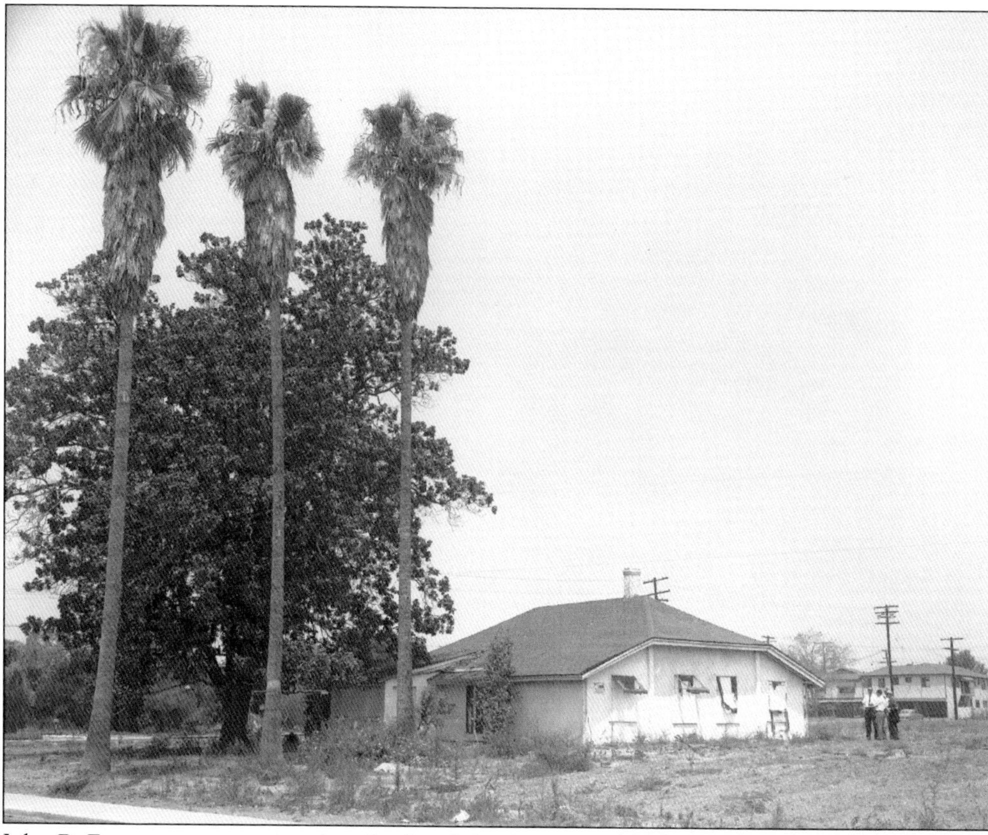

John R. Evertsen was appointed as the first federal census taker for Los Angeles County in 1850. For five months, he rode on horseback gathering statistics and jotting them down in pencil. He counted 518 families and a total of 3,035 residents. His original document was found in May 1915 by Cecil B. DeMille in an old barn being used as a set behind an adobe near the San Fernando Mission. DeMille glanced in a box of papers and old clothing set aside to be burned and located the document. Evertsen and his wife, Laura, built this adobe home (torn down in April 1961) on a 10-acre site that later became 725 Carmelita Drive. (Regional History Center, Special Collections Department, University of Southern California.)

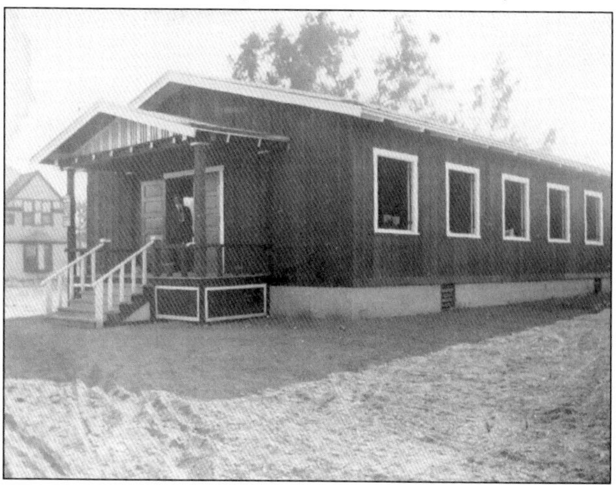

The Methodist Episcopal Church of San Gabriel, officially recognized on June 24, 1913, began construction of their first church building in 1916, located at the northwest corner of Myrtle and Pine Street. Prior to building this facility, church members met at fellow parishioners homes and eventually met at the Johnson Hall, located at the southwest corner of Broadway and San Marino Avenue. (First United Methodist Church of San Gabriel.)

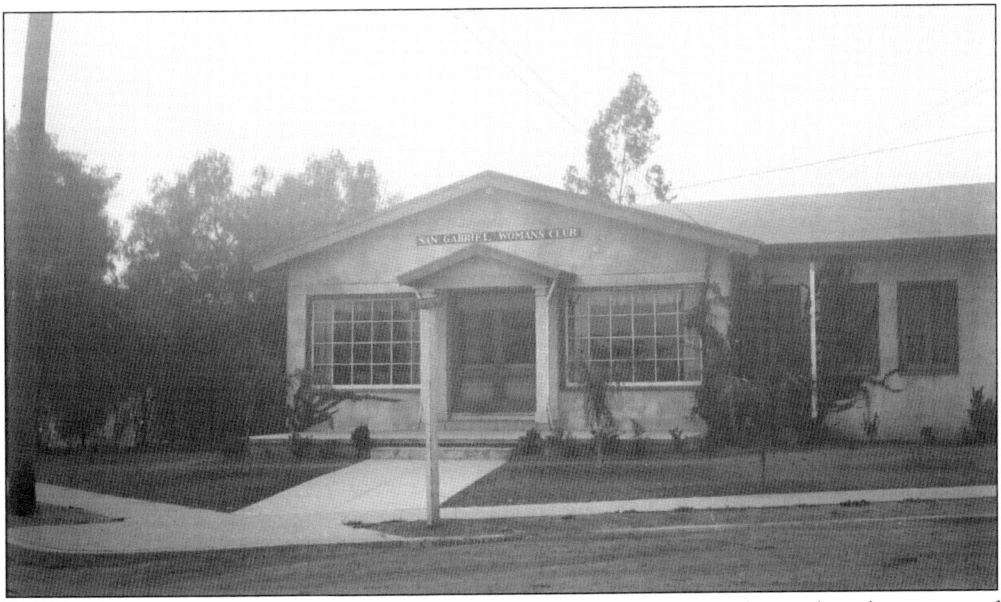

The San Gabriel Woman's Club, founded on October 23, 1913, was located at the corner of Junipero Serra Street and Shorb Road (present-day San Marino Avenue). Mr. and Mrs. William Orr donated their house with the stipulation that the club pay for the house to be moved from its original location in Alhambra to San Gabriel. (Richard Arnold Collection.)

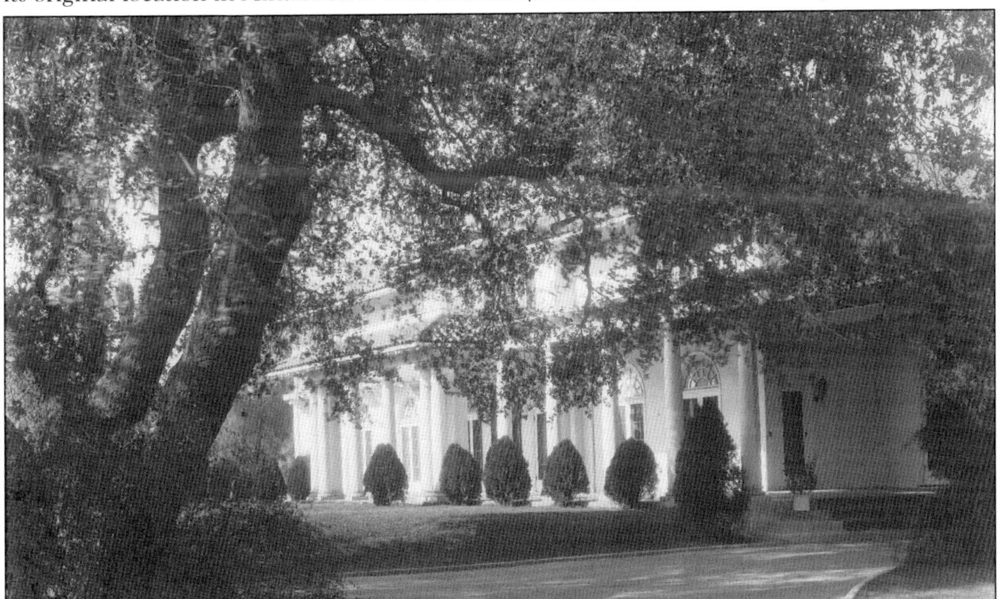

Charles H. Warner, coinventor (with his brother Arthur) of the automobile speedometer, built this 16-room mansion on a 10-acre site at 515 North San Marino Avenue in 1915 for $175,000. The mansion had imported hardwood floors, a huge ballroom, and a $35,000 pipe organ. The mansion appeared in many Hollywood movies, including *Gone With the Wind*, where it served as Ashley Wilkes's backyard for the outdoor party. The mansion was demolished in 1962, and the property was subdivided, but the two-story carriage house remains at 413 Warner Lane. (Richard Arnold Collection.)

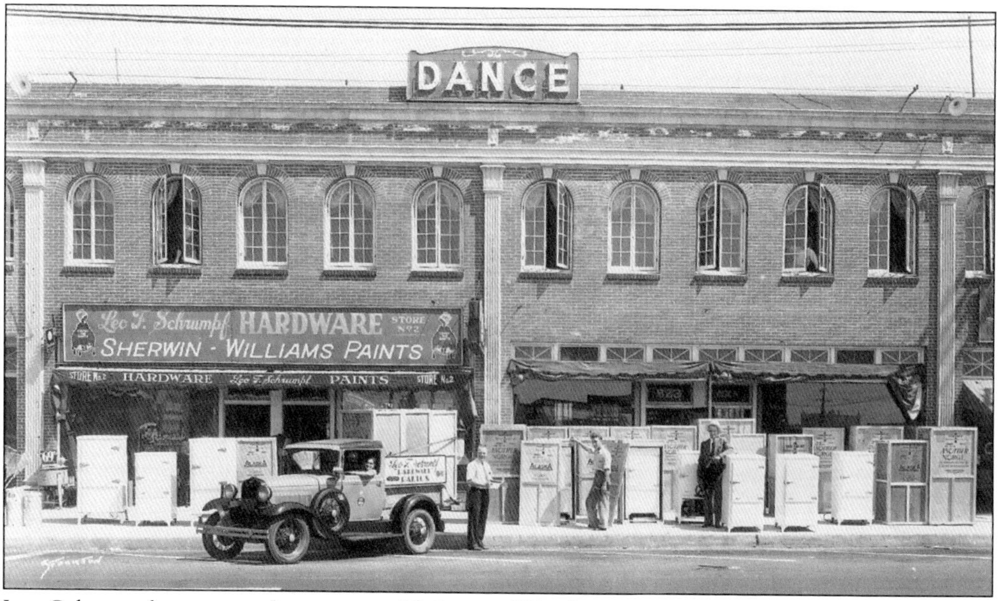

Leo Schrumpf, owner and operator of Schrumpf Hardware Store, 825 West Las Tunas Drive, poses in front of his store (to the right of the Model A Ford pickup truck in white shirt) with Ivan Manzer, store manager (wearing hat), and other unidentified people in this 1932 photograph. (Richard Arnold Collection.).

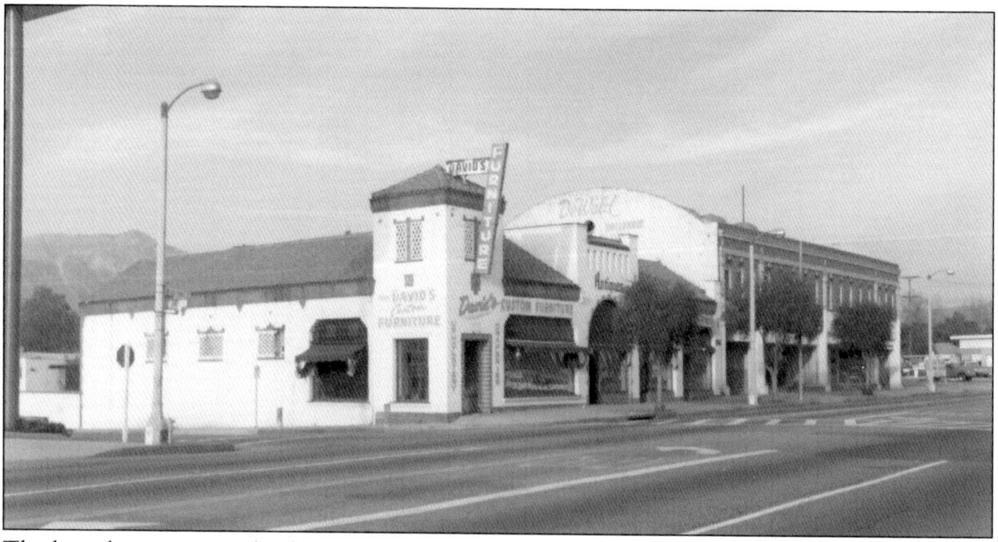

The large business complex located on the north side of Las Tunas Drive, between Bridge Street and Mission Drive, was once the home of the Stewart Sisters Ballroom, Leo Schrumpf's Hardware Store, Owl Dry Cleaners, and the NASH Motor Car dealership. The complex was built in 1926 by H.P. Buttress, a well-known San Gabriel contractor. During the 1930s and 1940s, the Stewart sisters provided local residents of San Gabriel with dance instruction twice a week. The ballroom took up the majority of the second floor above the hardware store. By the late 1940s, the sisters retired and the ballroom was turned over to Bonnie Lee. In the early 1950s, Gene DeWald discontinued use of the hall for public dances but used the facility for dance lessons. In March 1981, the building, along with all its memories, was razed and in its place came a corner shopping mall. (Lawrence Arnold Collection.)

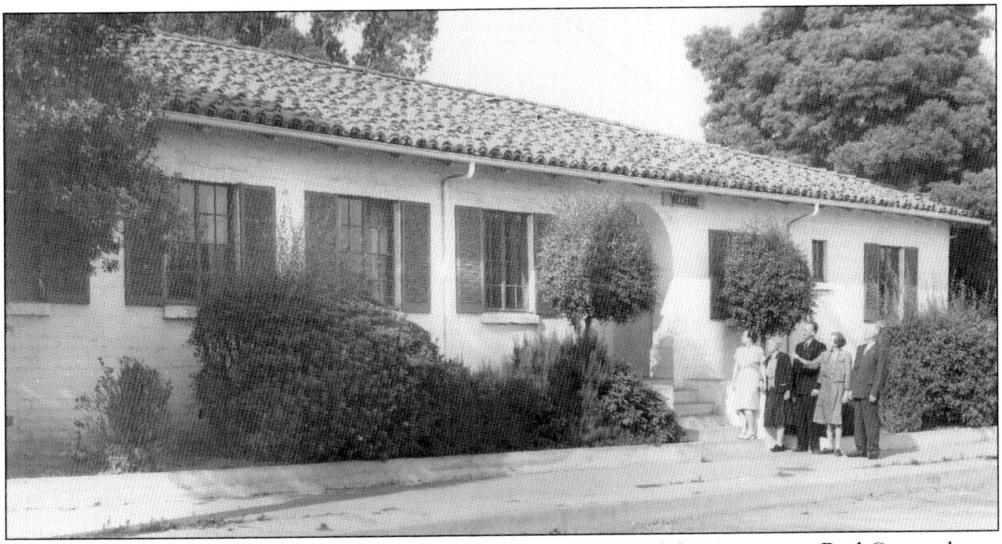

Charles Elgar (center), president of the San Gabriel Chapter of the American Red Cross, shows other board members the new Red Cross building in this photograph from July 24, 1946. The building, located at 203 East Mission Road, has had many uses over the years, including as a maternity hospital, a Welfare Association office, and the La Casa de San Gabriel Community Center, founded in 1946 and still using the space. Rev. Cesar Lizarraga, pastor of the Presbyterian Church, and his wife, Angelita, led a movement to purchase the former Red Cross facility to establish a youth recreation center. Today, La Casa continues to serve as a family resource center. (San Gabriel Historical Association.)

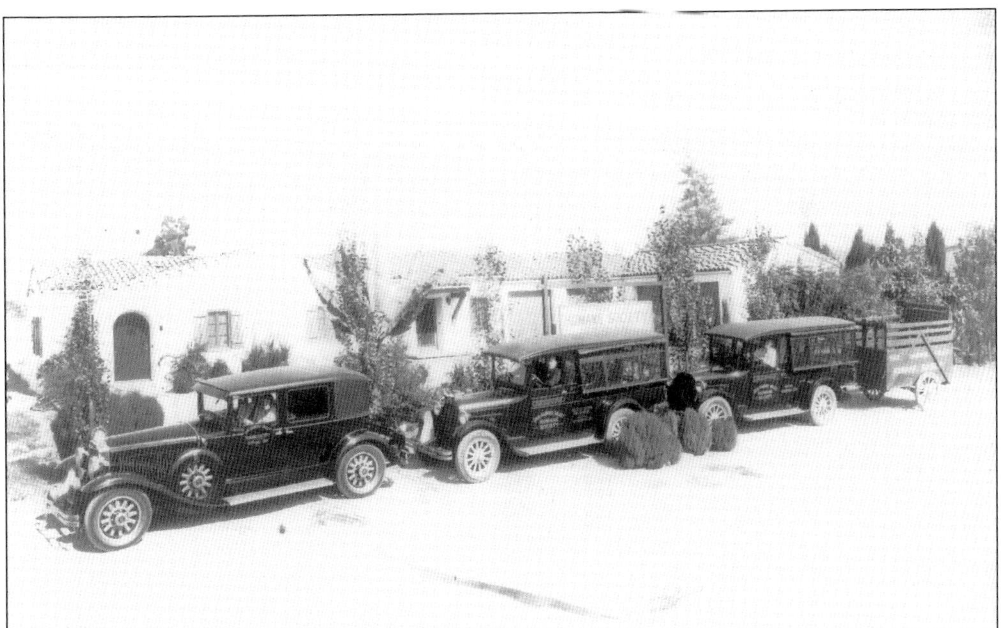

The San Gabriel Humane Society was founded in 1924 by Fannie Thompson Kessler, shown in the driver's seat of the first automobile, and her husband, John Kessler. The name was officially changed from Alhambra-San Gabriel Humane Society to the San Gabriel Humane Society in 1959. (San Gabriel Human Society.)

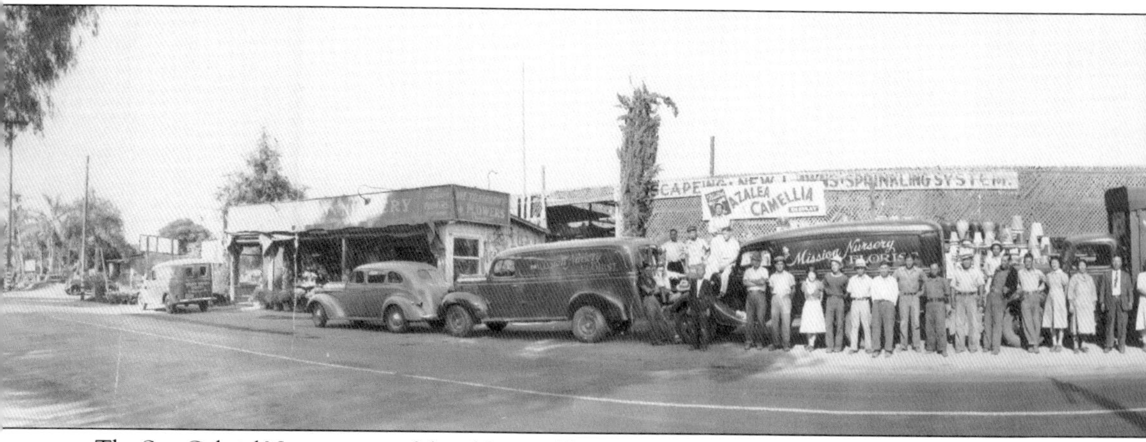

The San Gabriel Nursery, one of the oldest and largest nurseries and florists in Southern California, has served the community since 1923. Founded by Fred and Mitoko Yoshimura as the Mission Nursery, the facility was originally located at 735 South San Gabriel Boulevard, across from its

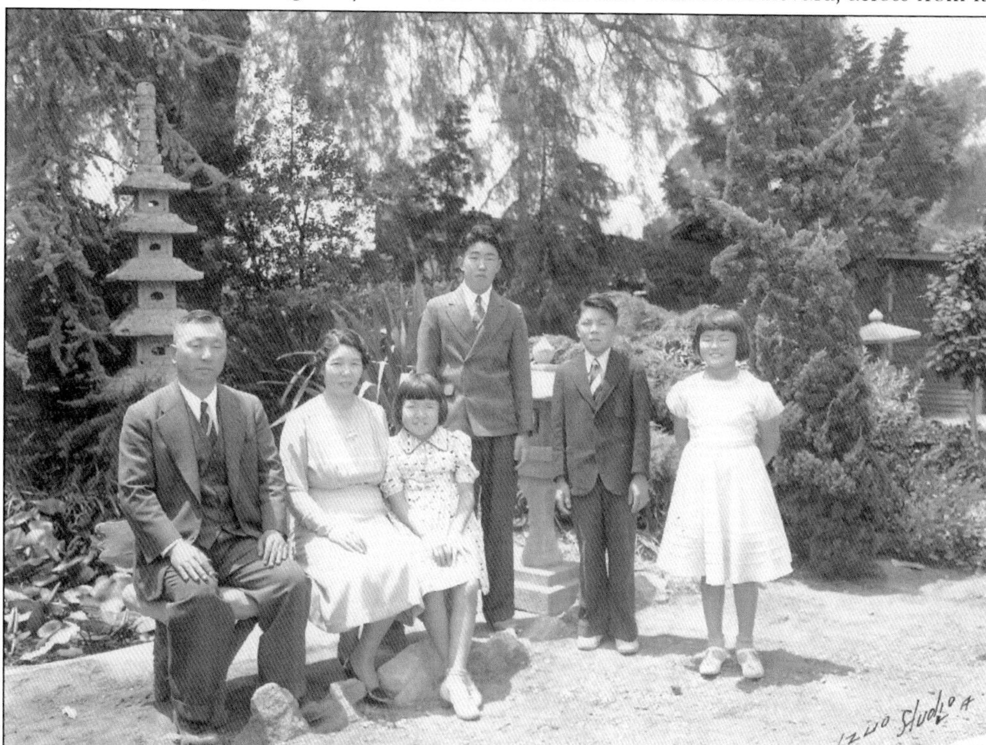

When World War II broke out, the Yoshimuras were forced to sell the business while the family was interned at a relocation camp. E. Manchester Boddy, publisher of the *Los Angeles Daily News*, who regularly visited the nursery to find plants for his La Canada estate, found out about their financial needs because of their internment and offered to buy the business. After the war ended, the Yoshimuras returned to San Gabriel and opened the San Gabriel Nursery and florist across the street. The Yoshimura family posed for this photograph in the gardens on the grounds of the San Gabriel Nursery. From left to right are Fred Waichi Yoshimura, Mitoko Yoshimura, Florence (Yoshimura) Ishihara, Hayao Yoshimura, Raymond Yoshimura, and Margie (Yoshimura). (San Gabriel Nursery.)

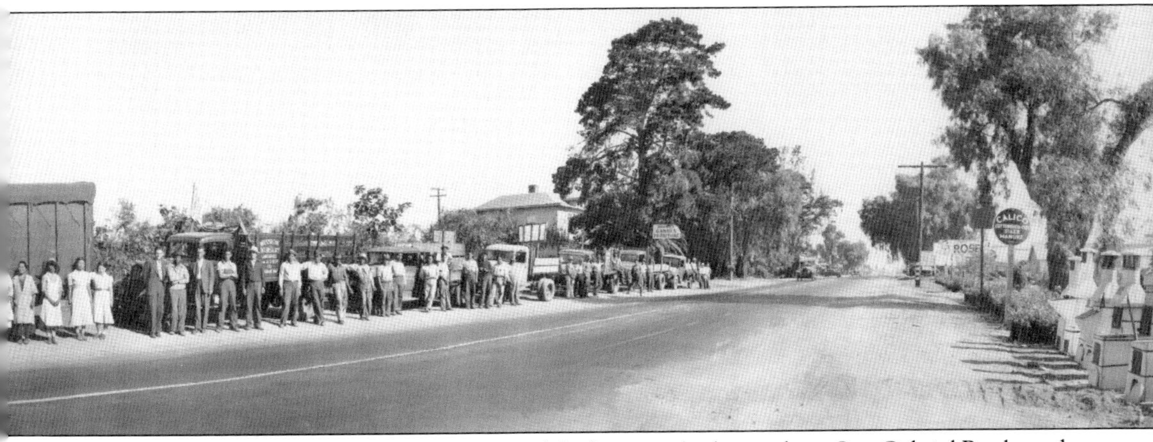

current location. This 1938 panoramic view of the business looks north on San Gabriel Boulevard. (San Gabriel Nursery.)

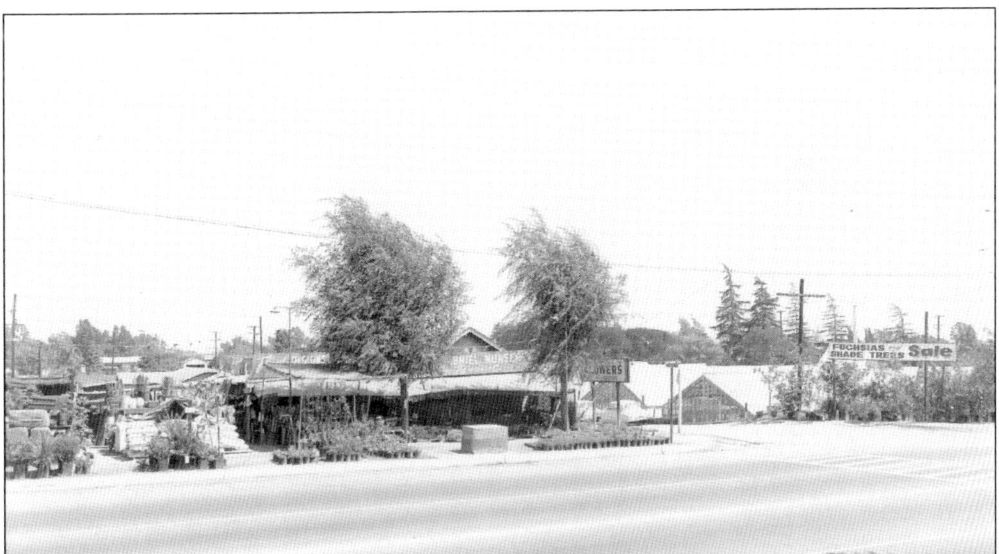

The San Gabriel Nursery and Florist, located at 632 South San Gabriel Boulevard, operated out of this retail store until 1969, when an arsonist set the building on fire. The store and everything inside was completely destroyed. The owners built a new retail store in 1970, and the business, still owned by the Yoshimura family, continues to provide quality service to the community. (San Gabriel Nursery.)

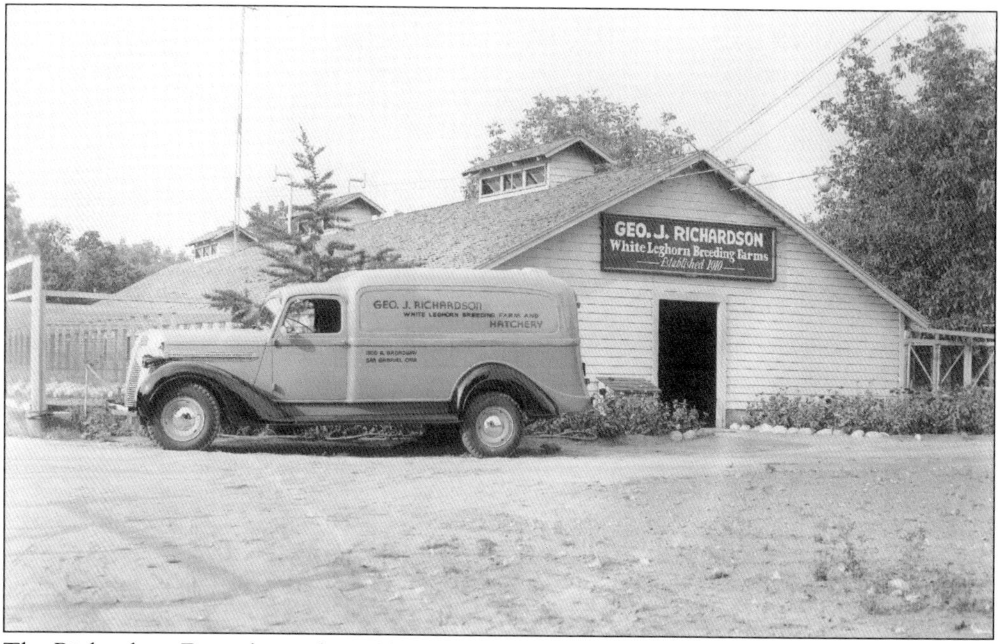

The Richardson Farm, located at 1300 East Broadway, was founded by George R. Richardson and his brother Fred in 1910. The 20-acre farm was widely known for its huge output; around 365,000 chicks were hatched yearly from eggs produced on the farm. The Richardson Farm bordered on both sides of Broadway. When the business closed, the San Gabriel School District was able to purchase a substantial portion of the former ranch property through a school bond, and Madison Elementary School (present-day Jefferson Intermediate School) opened in August 1952. (Constance L. Rothstein Collection.)

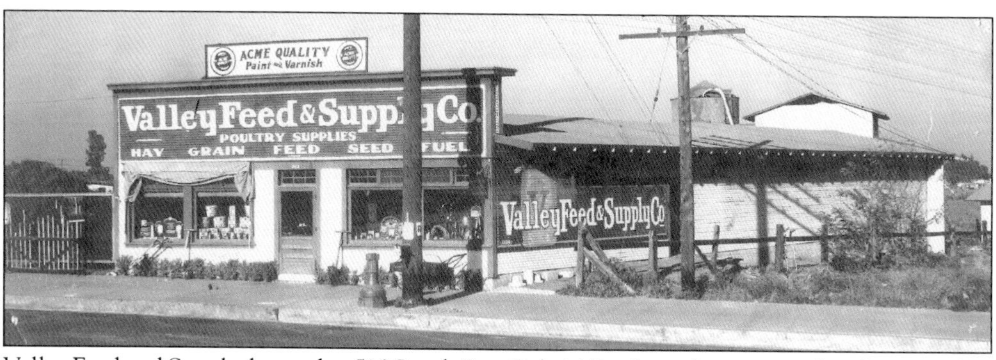

Valley Feed and Supply, located at 516 South San Gabriel Boulevard, was owned and operated by L.W. Barlow. The firm had a complete mill for the manufacturing of poultry and stock feeds. The store also carried flowers, grass, seeds, fertilizers, garden tools, incubators, paints, and varnishes. (Richard Arnold Collection.)

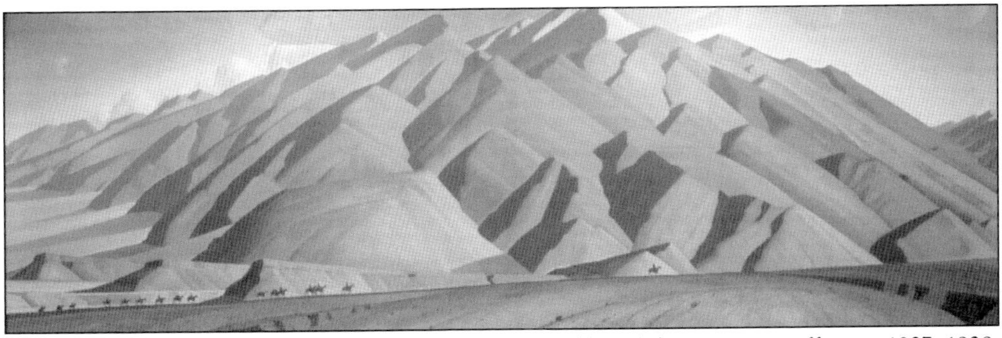

San Gabriel Country, painted by Ray Strong for the lobby of the new post office in 1937–1938, is shown in this photograph. The mural depicts Jedediah Smith and his band of scouts on their first historic trip to the San Gabriel Valley and their visit to the San Gabriel Mission in 1826. The party of men on horseback is struggling up the eastern slopes of the Sierras, heading for Cajon Pass. Strong received his commission to paint the mural as part of a fine arts competition. (Richard Arnold Collection.)

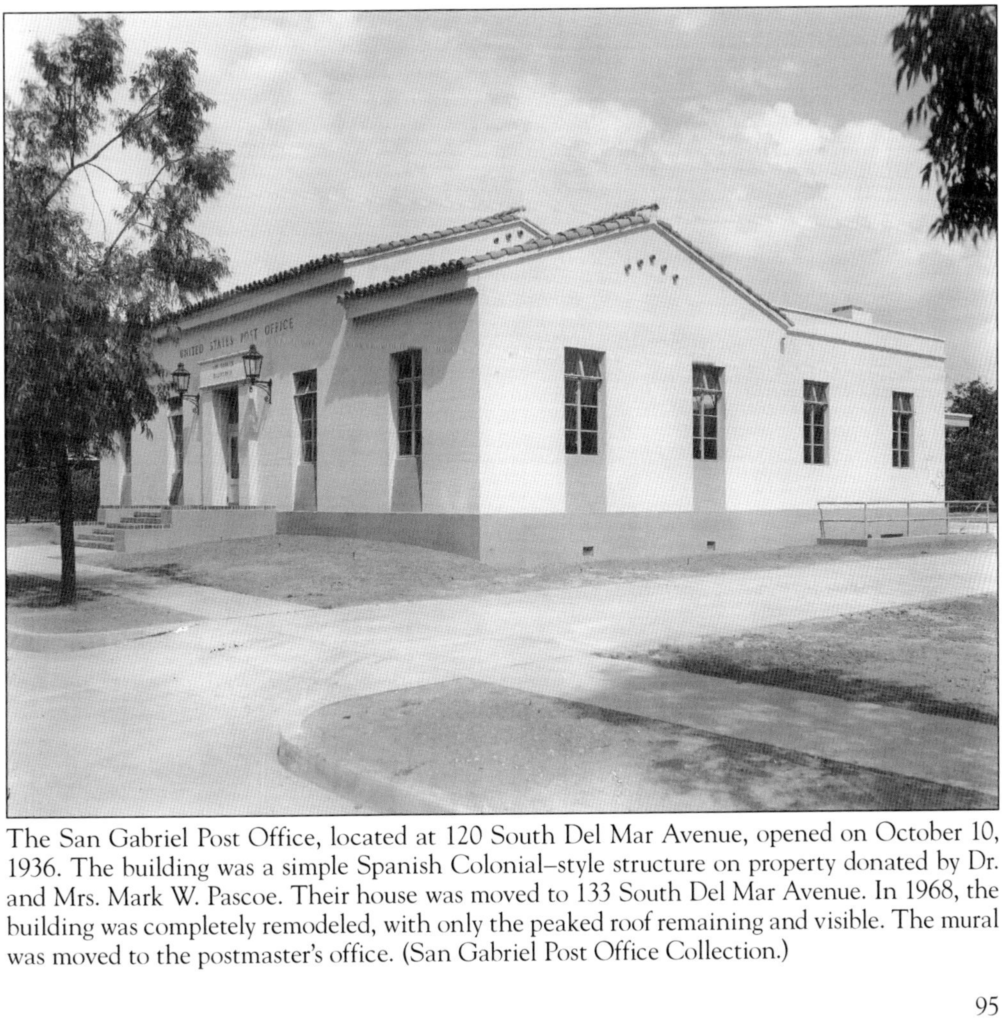

The San Gabriel Post Office, located at 120 South Del Mar Avenue, opened on October 10, 1936. The building was a simple Spanish Colonial–style structure on property donated by Dr. and Mrs. Mark W. Pascoe. Their house was moved to 133 South Del Mar Avenue. In 1968, the building was completely remodeled, with only the peaked roof remaining and visible. The mural was moved to the postmaster's office. (San Gabriel Post Office Collection.)

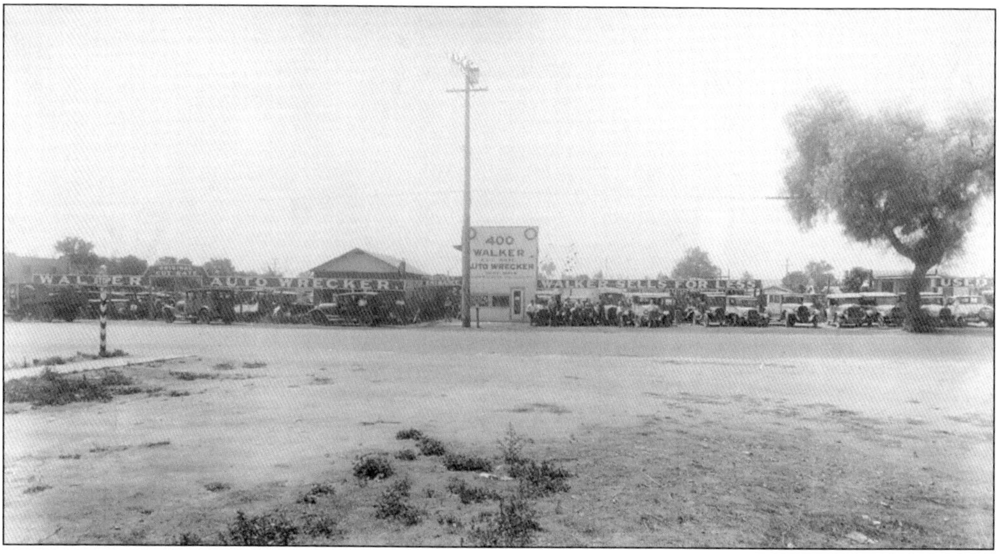

Walker 400 occupied the 400 block of West Valley Boulevard as a wrecking lot from 1928 until 2008. The family-owned and -operated lot was opened by Gary Walker and is now operated by a fourth-generation Gary Walker in the city of Rancho Cucamonga. (Richard Arnold Collection.)

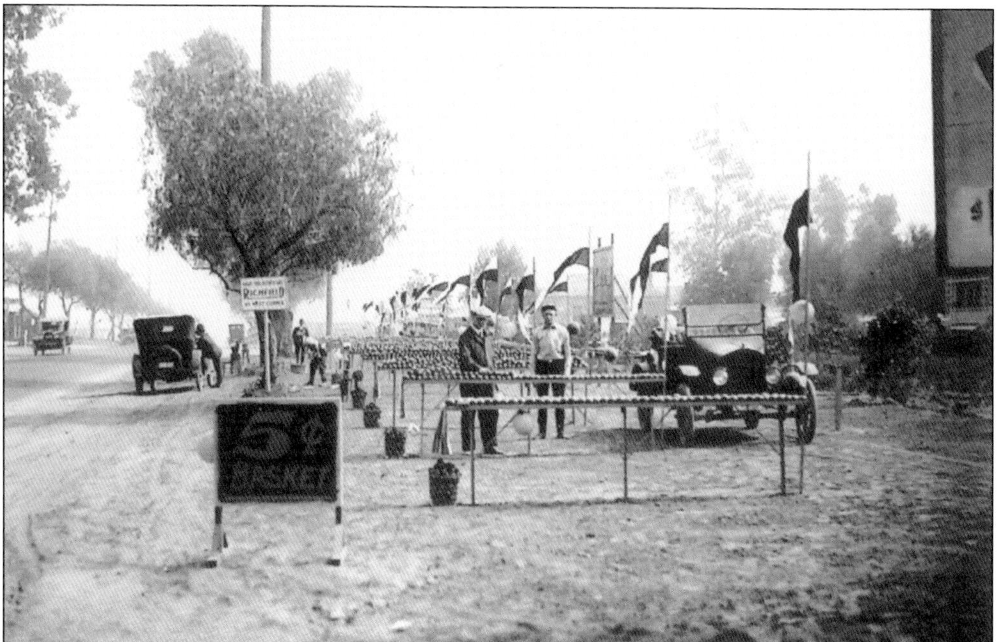

The Jedofsky Ranch, located at 100 West Valley Boulevard, occupied the corner of Del Mar Avenue and Valley Boulevard. This photograph of produce sales was taken looking south on Del Mar Avenue from Valley Boulevard. (San Gabriel Historical Association.)

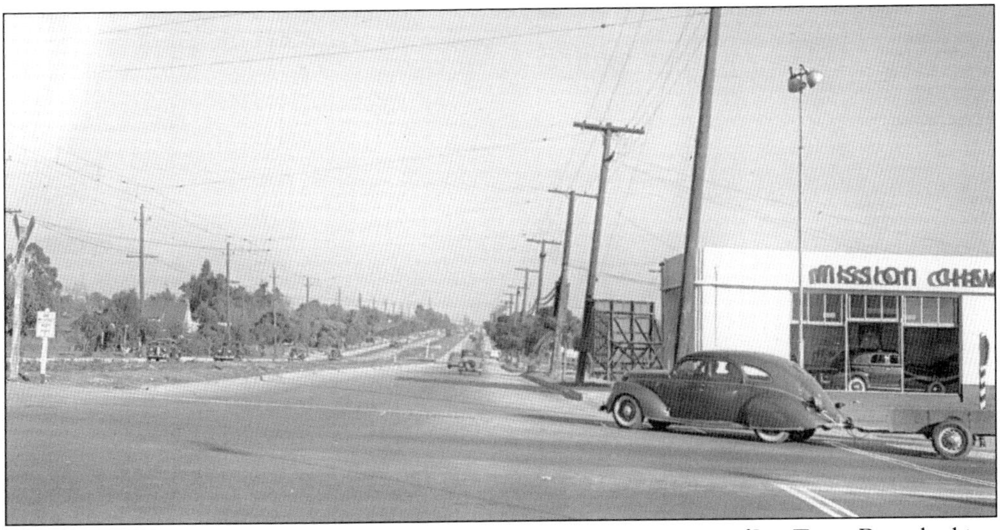

In the mid-1940s, railfan Harold Stewart photographed the intersection of Las Tunas Drive looking east from San Gabriel Boulevard and showing the Pacific Electric right-of-way down the center of the drive. Mission Chevrolet, located on the southeast corner, was founded in 1938 by John D. "Scotty" Stewart and Vern Harding. In 1989, Richard O'Donnell purchased Mission Chevrolet, combining it with his Buick dealership. (Harold Stewart Collection.)

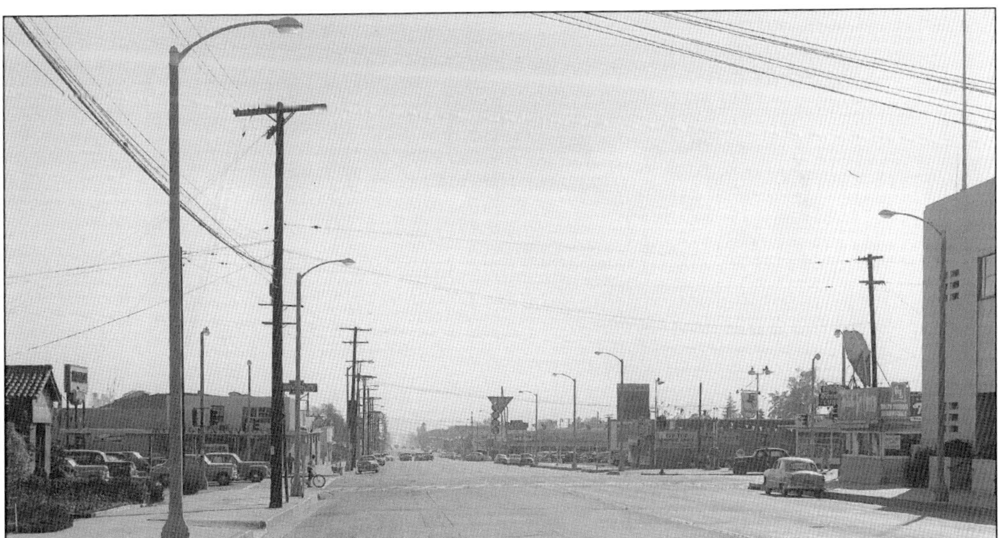

Looking south, the intersection of San Gabriel Boulevard and Las Tunas Drive is shown as it looked in 1954. In view is the new Pacific Telephone & Telegraph building (far right) that was constructed in 1947 to house central office switching equipment, Currie's Ice Cream on the northwest corner, Seward's Florist on the northeast corner, and Mission Chevrolet on the southeast corner. Visible on the right of the photograph are San Gabriel Bowling, Safeway grocery store, and the Mobil gas station on the southwest corner. (Huntington Library.)

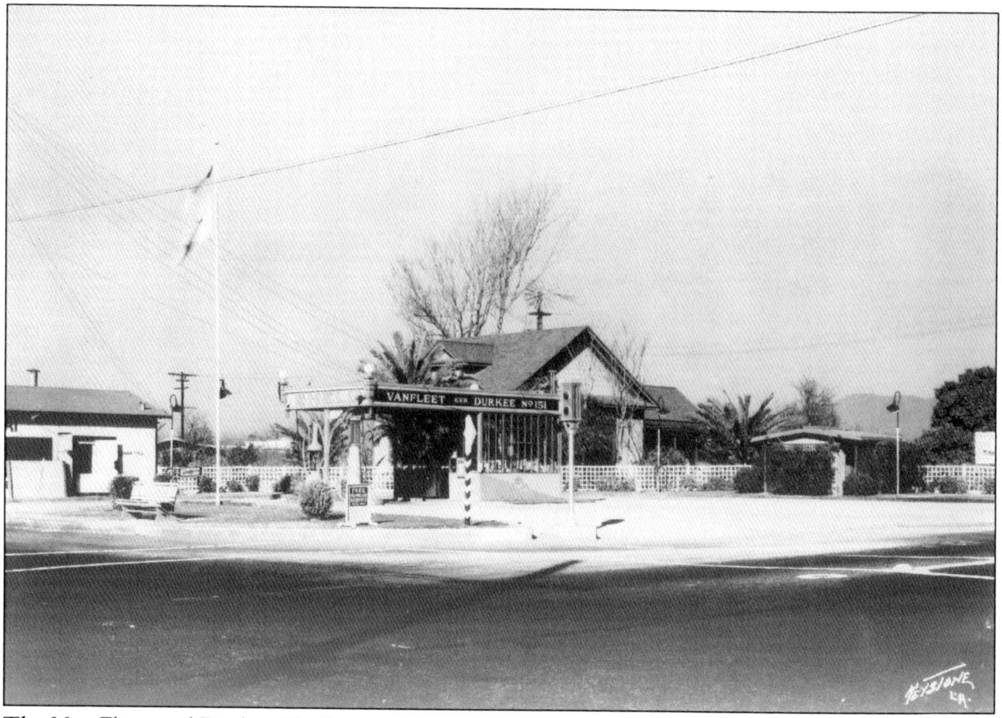

The Van Fleet and Durkee Shell gas station, seen here around 1930, was located at the northwest corner of San Gabriel and Valley Boulevards. (San Gabriel Historical Association.)

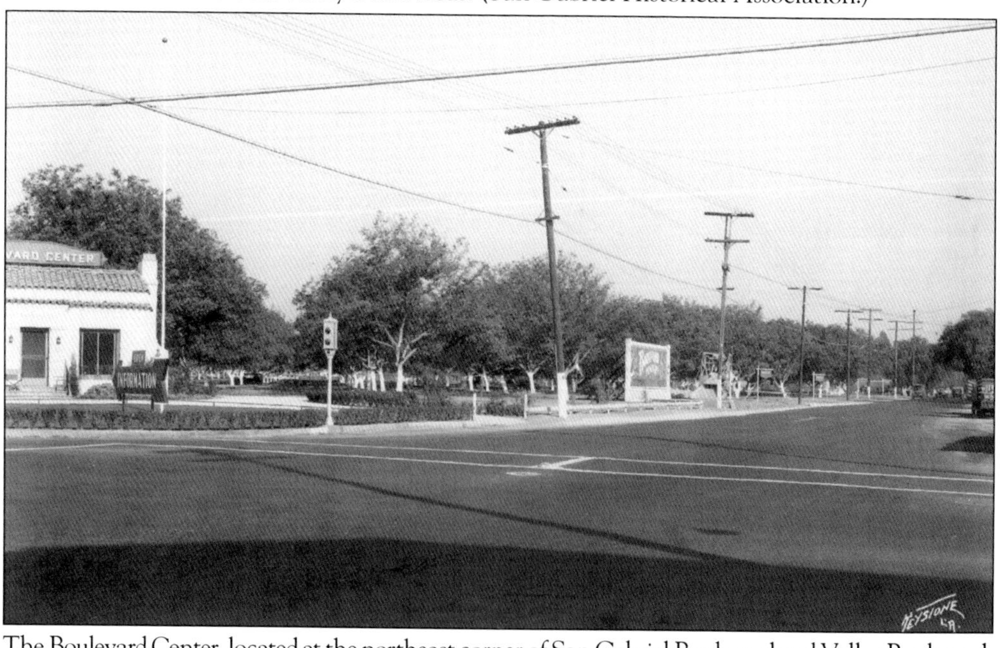

The Boulevard Center, located at the northeast corner of San Gabriel Boulevard and Valley Boulevard, was a model bungalow built by J.W. Weatherby as part of a subdivision planned for the walnut groves that occupied the acreage along Valley Boulevard to the northeast. Weatherby strived to build homes that people of moderate means could afford, allowing them a beautiful house amongst the fine old walnut trees. It is pictured here around 1930. (San Gabriel Historical Association.)

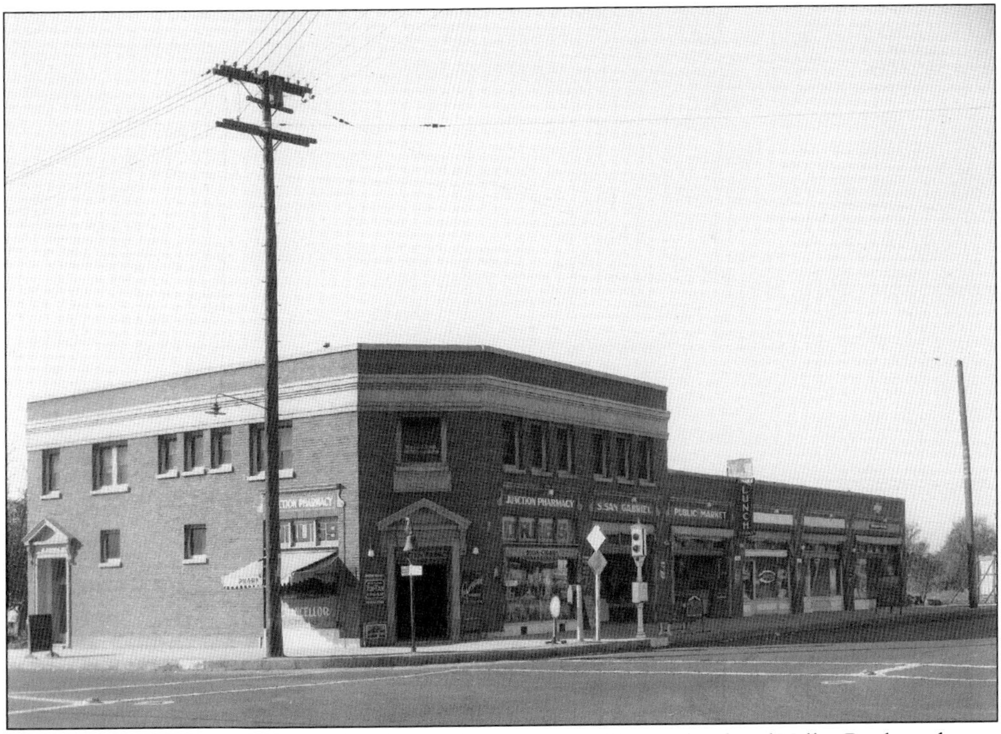

The J.D. McLeod Building, located at the southwest corner of San Gabriel and Valley Boulevards, was home to Junction Pharmacy and Public Market c. 1930. (San Gabriel Historical Association.)

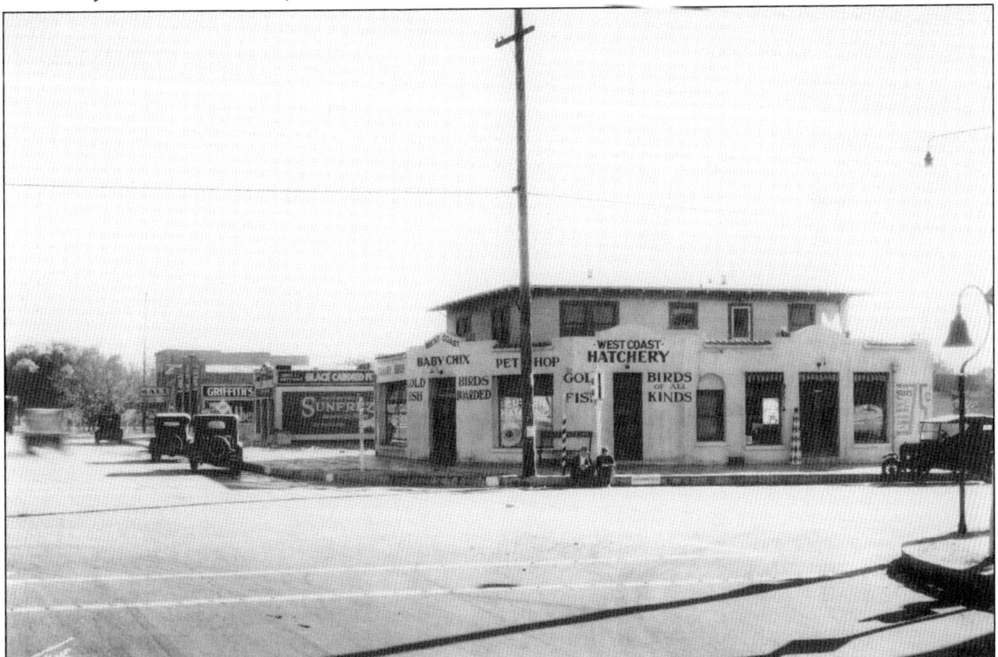

Pictured here around 1930, the West Coast Pet Shop and Hatchery, along with the Bestway Cleaners, was located at the southeast corner of San Gabriel and Valley Boulevards. The cleaners are advertising a special—75¢ for cleaning a man's suit. (San Gabriel Historical Association.)

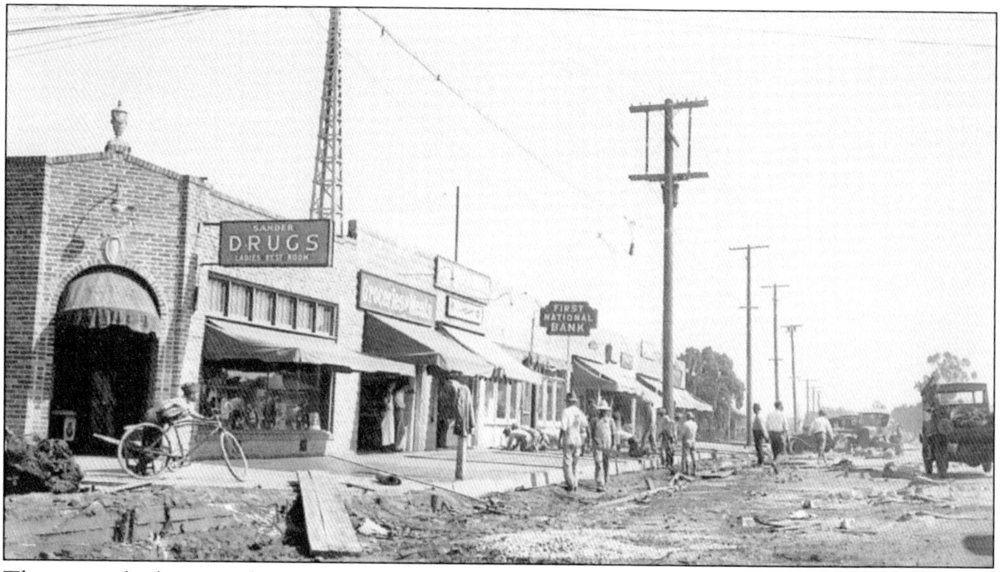

This image looking south on San Gabriel Boulevard from Broadway documents the major street-widening project that was completed in November 1925. The street-widening project widened San Gabriel Boulevard from Hermosa Drive south to the Southern Pacific Railroad tracks and improved the boulevard to a 72-foot wide street with 15 feet of sidewalks on either side. The entire cost of the project was $150,000, which was huge outlay of money for a small community. A big four-day event was held along the boulevard to celebrate its completion. (San Gabriel Historical Association.)

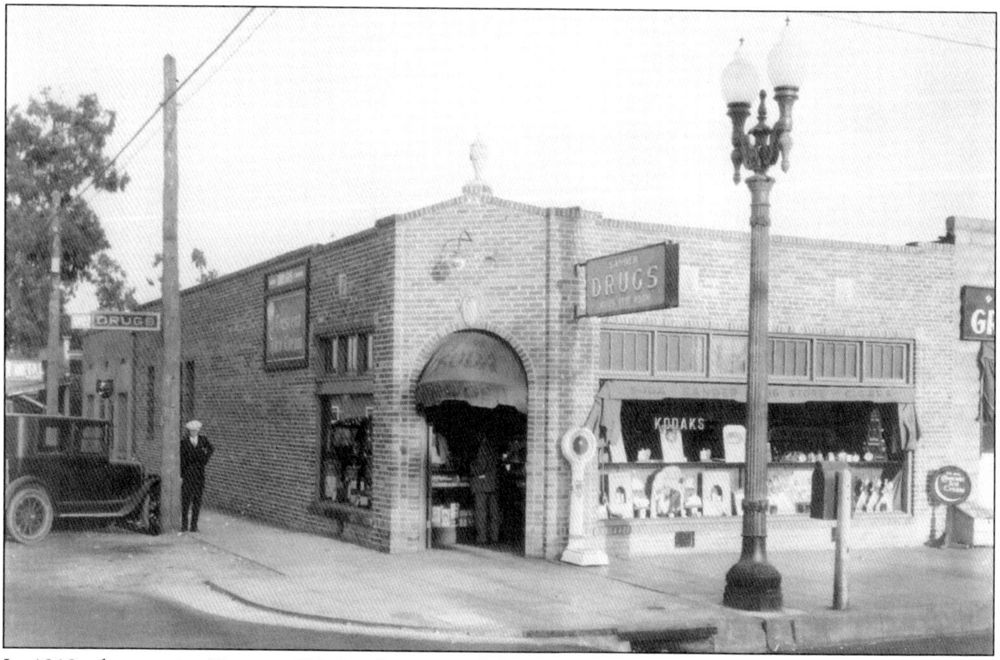

In 1919, pharmacist Herman W. Sander opened the Sander Drug Store at 300 South San Gabriel Boulevard. As the only drugstore in East San Gabriel, Sanders specialized in a full line of rubber goods, drugs, film, stationary, and sundries. The soda fountain and the candy counter were two features known to attract customers to the store. (San Gabriel Historical Association.)

The First National Bank, located at 308 South San Gabriel Boulevard, was established in June 1922 with C.C. Threlkeld as its first president. It quickly became competition for the San Gabriel Bank, located across the street at the southwest corner of San Gabriel Boulevard and Broadway. (San Gabriel Historical Association.)

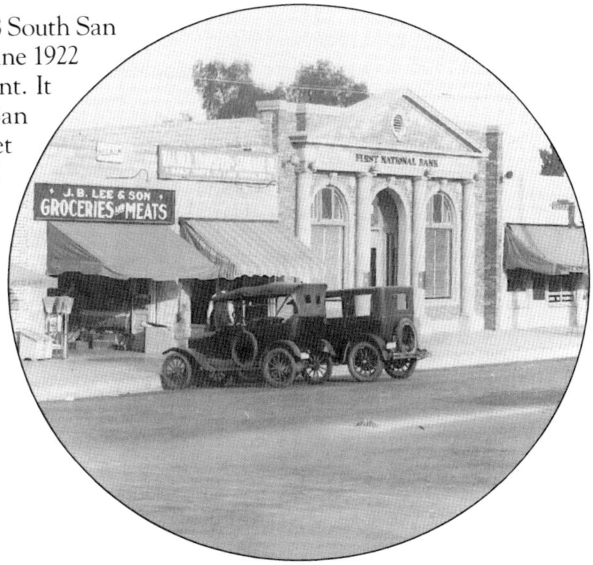

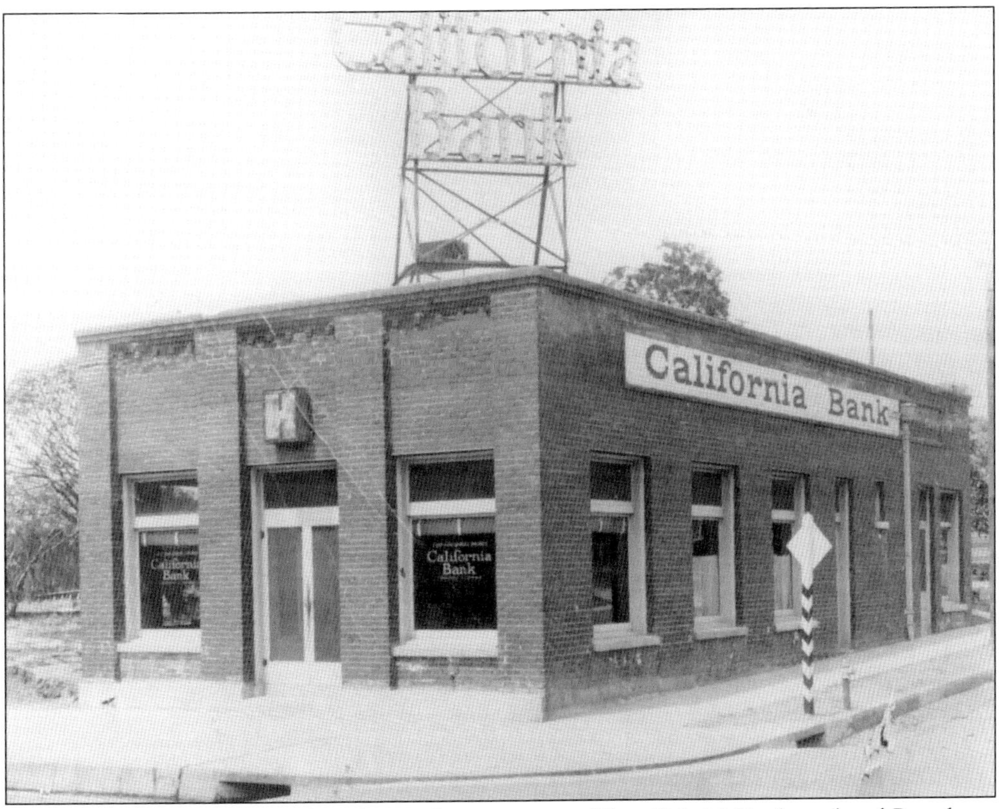

The California Bank, located at the southwest corner of San Gabriel Boulevard and Broadway, originally opened in 1923 as the East San Gabriel branch of the Bank of San Gabriel. The main office was located at 343 South Mission Drive. In 1925, both offices were purchased by the California Bank, which later became the United California Bank. In May 1930, the old San Gabriel branch and the East San Gabriel branch were consolidated and moved into a new facility located at 641 West Las Tunas Drive. (San Gabriel Historical Association.)

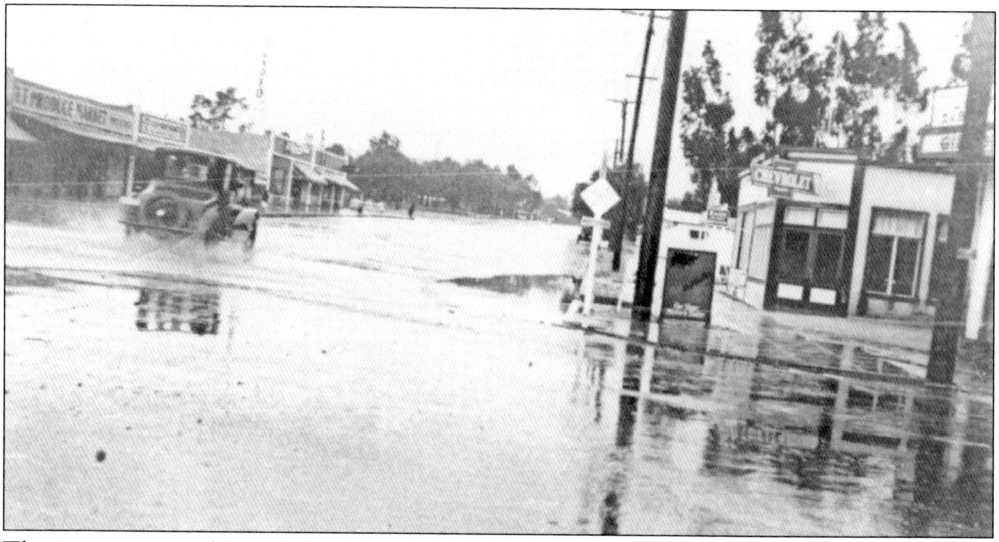

The intersection of San Gabriel Boulevard looking north from Broadway is shown in this photograph on a rainy day in the early 1930s. (San Gabriel Historical Association.)

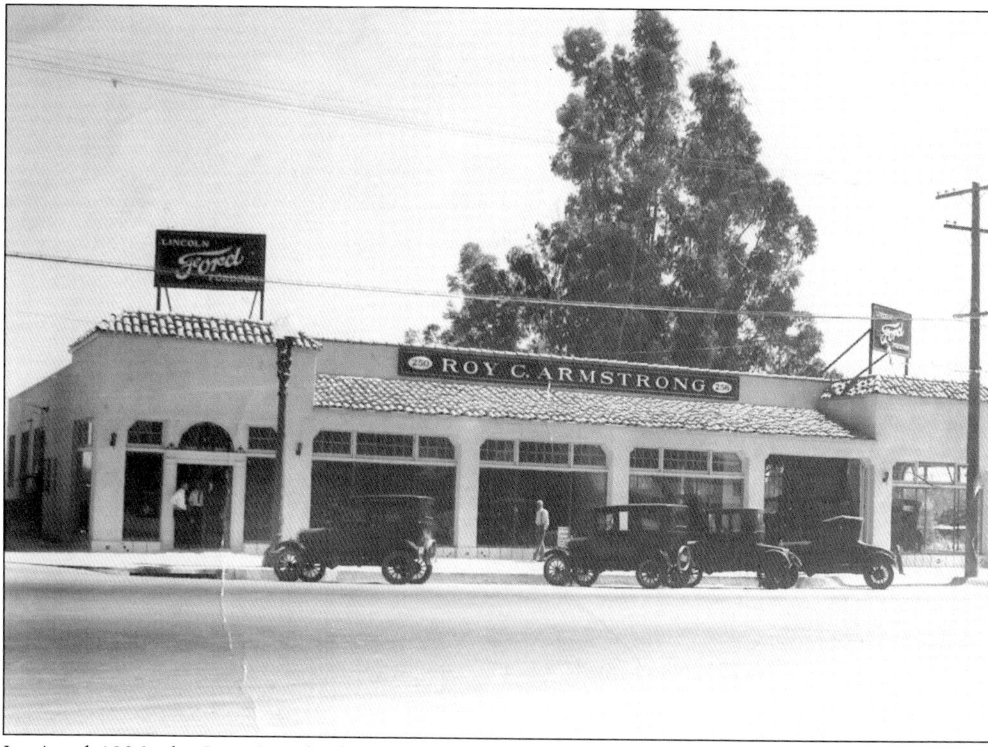

In April 1926, the Los Angeles branch of the Ford Motor Company announced that Roy C. Armstrong was appointed the dealer for San Gabriel. In January 1927, Armstrong opened the doors of the new facility (pictured) at 250 South San Gabriel Boulevard. Armstrong's name appeared in gold letters over the handsome structure designed specifically for an automobile dealership. The new building had ample space for displays, spacious offices, and a large, well-equipped service department. The showroom allowed for several automobiles to be displayed. (San Gabriel Historical Association.)

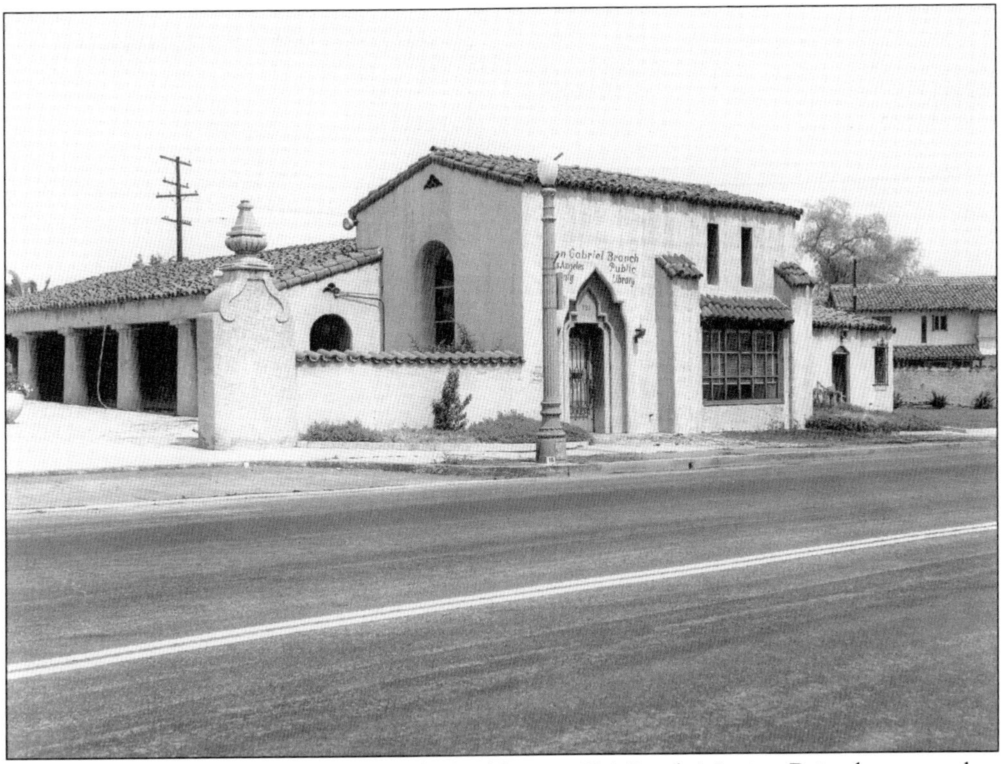

Constructed in 1929 as a curio shop, the building at 324 South Mission Drive became a law library in 1942, housing law books belonging to the late William J. Hunsaker, fourth mayor of San Diego and former district attorney. The city purchased the building in August 1945, along with the playhouse, and in 1946, it became the San Gabriel branch of the Los Angeles County Public Library. On December 13, 1956, the building became the Adult Recreation Center. (Richard Arnold Collection.)

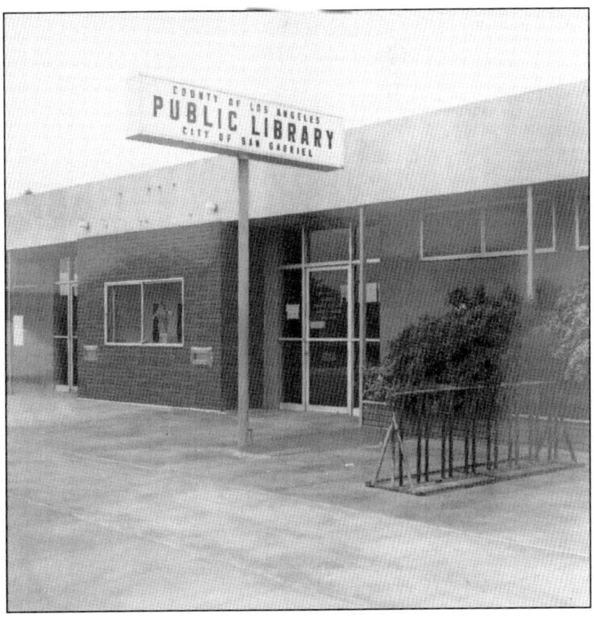

The first county library in San Gabriel was located next to the R.K. Johnson grocery store on Shorb Avenue and later moved to a storefront location at 103 North Del Mar Avenue, where it remained until moving to 324 South Mission Drive in 1946. The library was moved to this facility at 117 South Del Mar Avenue in the 1950s and remained here until a new library was opened at 500 South Del Mar Avenue in 1967. (San Gabriel Historical Association.)

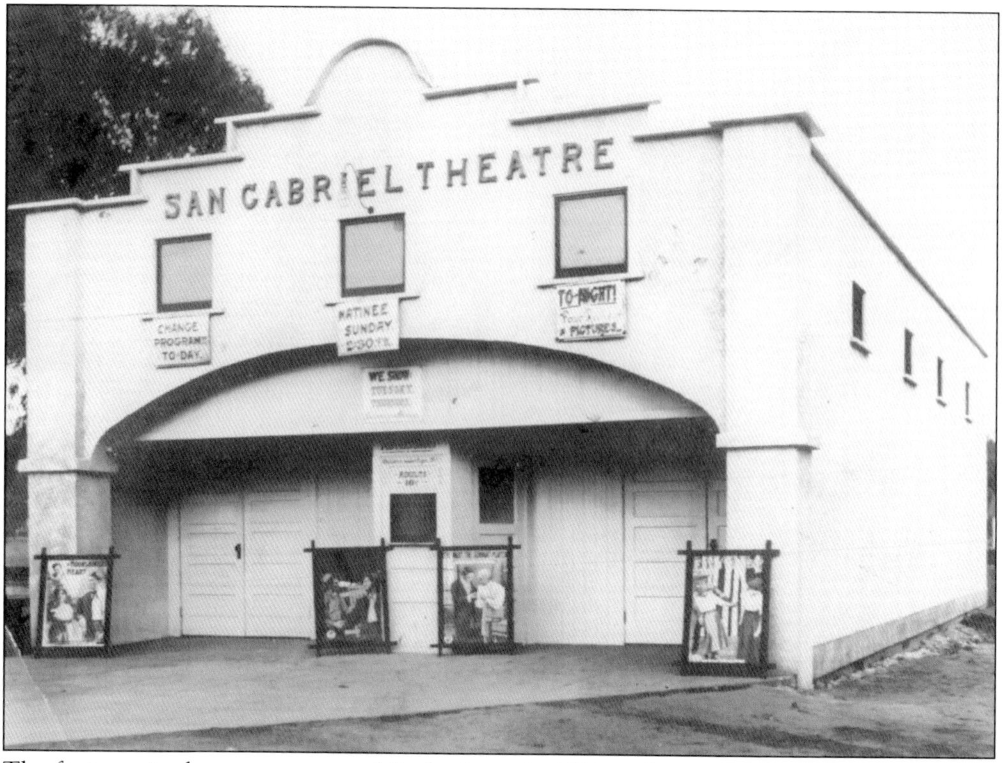

The first movie theater was opened for business in 1911 at the triangular-shaped property at Angelino Street and Mission Drive. The John Feldmiller family began showing silent movies on an Edison hand-cranked projector under a tent with folding chairs. A year later, construction was completed on the brick and stucco building with a mission-style facade. The small foyer served as a light lock, and a small balcony provided a few seats and a place for the projector. The theater accommodated 200 people and a piano player to the right of the screen. With the introduction of talkies, Arthur Caswell, an earlier pioneer in the development of HI-FI, installed one of the first theater sound systems. When the Mission Playhouse became a movie theater in 1930, the San Gabriel Theater lost business and closed the same year. (Constance L. Rothstein Collection.)

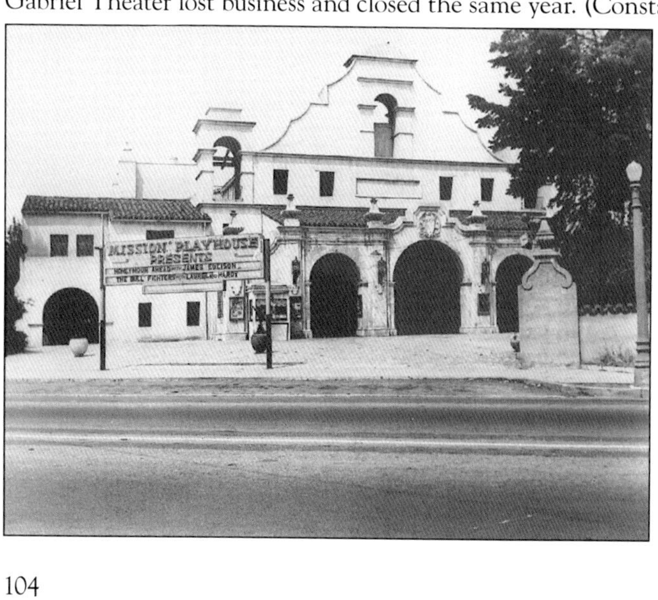

The Mission Playhouse became a motion picture theater on Sunday, August 28, 1932, when O.W. Lewis was given a 10-year lease on the building. (Richard Arnold Collection.)

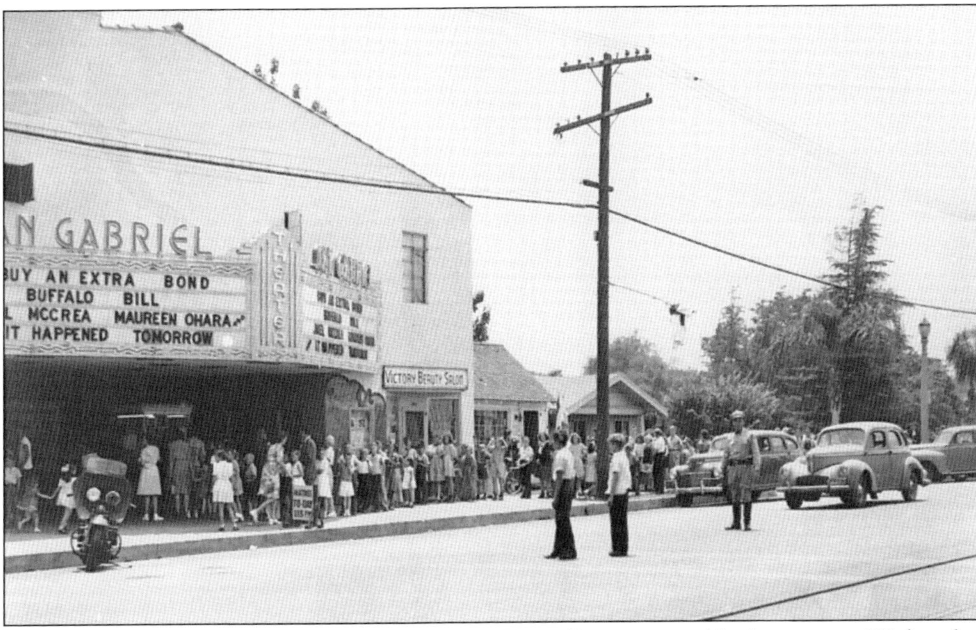

The San Gabriel Theater, located at 330 West Las Tunas Drive, opened for business on Wednesday, February 18, 1942. O.W. Lewis, who also managed the Mission Playhouse, built the new 750-seat theater for $75,000. The theater provided patrons with the latest developments—loge-type seats and an advanced RCA sound system. Edwards Perkins Theater Corporation purchased the facility in September 1957 and operated the theater as Edwards Century. Edwards sold the theater in the 1990s, and the new owners operated the facility as the Kuo Hwa Theater until it was torn down in 1997. (Richard Arnold Collection.)

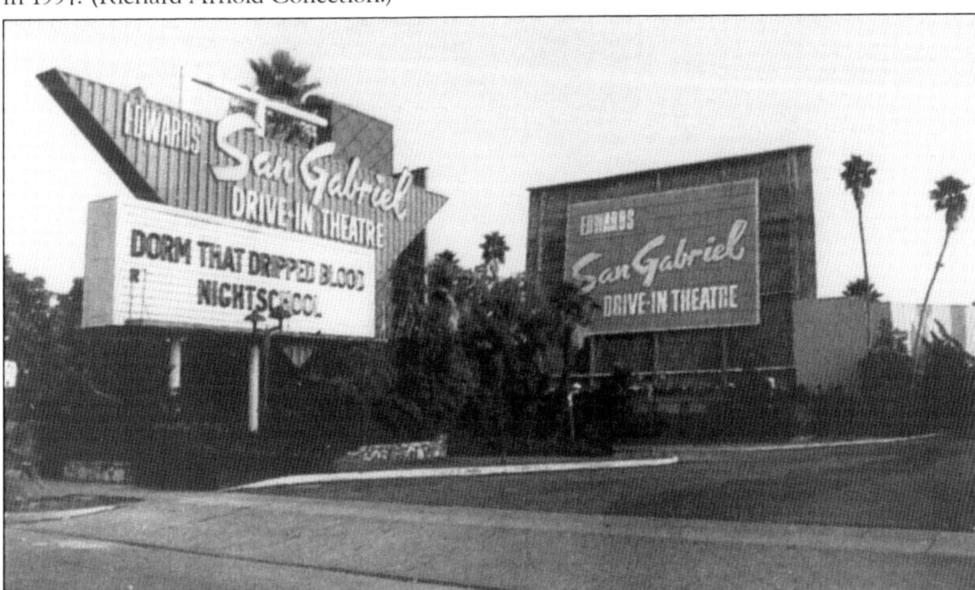

Edwards San Gabriel Drive-In Theater, located at 140 West Valley Boulevard, opened for business in 1955. The 1,100-car theater was designed by Arthur Drielsma and included a 2,400-square-foot building at the base of the screen tower that was designed as a business office for Edwards Theater Circuit. (Richard Arnold Collection.)

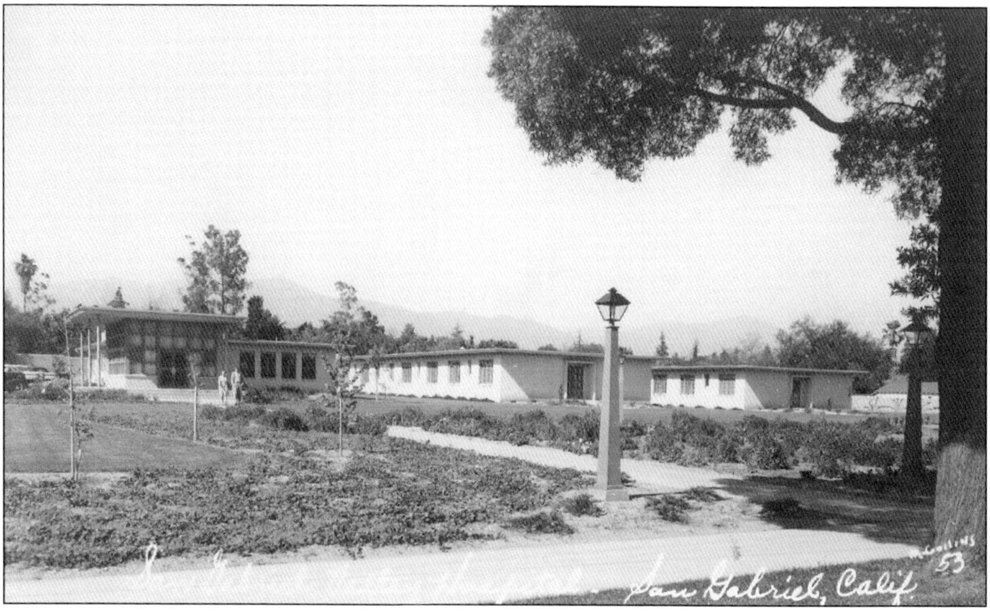

The San Gabriel Valley Hospital, located at 115 East Broadway, opened in 1947 with 48 beds and originally cost $350,00. In 1953, when this photograph was taken, a new wing had just been constructed at a cost of $170,000, which increased the hospital's capacity to 82 beds. The hospital changed names to Valley Vista Hospital before it closed in 1989. (Constance L. Rothstein Collection.)

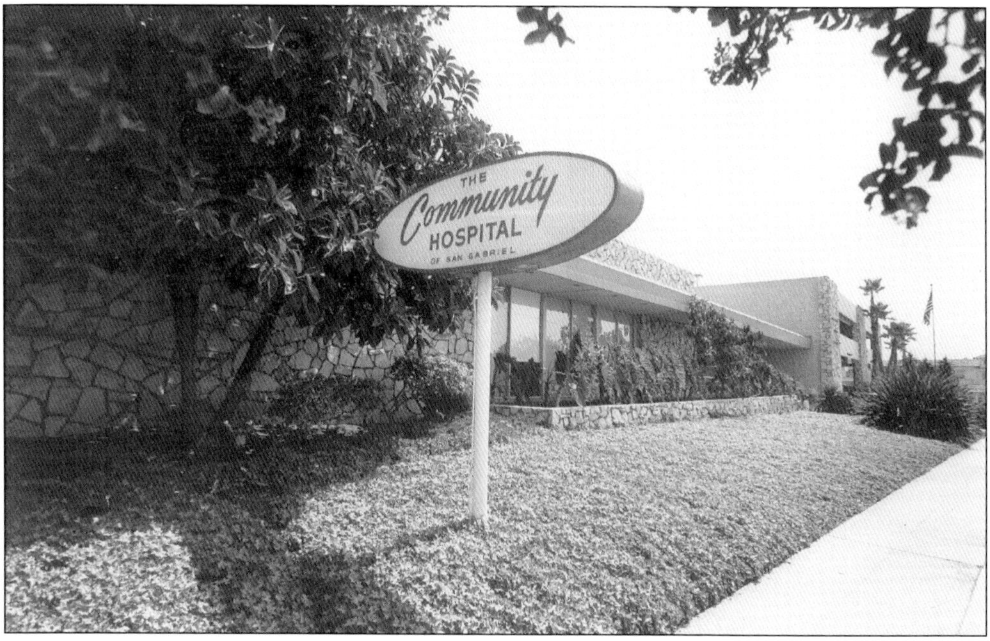

The Community Hospital of San Gabriel, located at 218 South Santa Anita Avenue, opened its doors in August 1960 as a 141-bed general hospital. In September 1985, the hospital name was changed to San Gabriel Valley Medical Center, which better reflected the spectrum of services provided. The facility underwent a $30 million rebuilding project, which included a five-story patient tower. The new facility was completed in 1987. (Richard Arnold Collection.)

Gen. George S. Patton Jr.; his wife, Beatrice (left); and sister Ruth (center) are departing the Church of Our Savior after attending church services on Sunday, June 10, 1945. The general spoke before the congregation and taught Sunday school to children on what would be his last visit to the church where he was baptized and confirmed as a boy. General Patton died on December 21, 1945, in Heidelberg, Germany, as a result of injuries sustained in a traffic collision. On December 30, 1945, family members and friends gathered at the church for a memorial service for the general, who was buried in Luxembourg American Cemetery alongside other wartime casualties of the Third Army, per his request to "be buried with my men." (Charles M. Province Collection, The George S. Patton, Jr. Historical Society.)

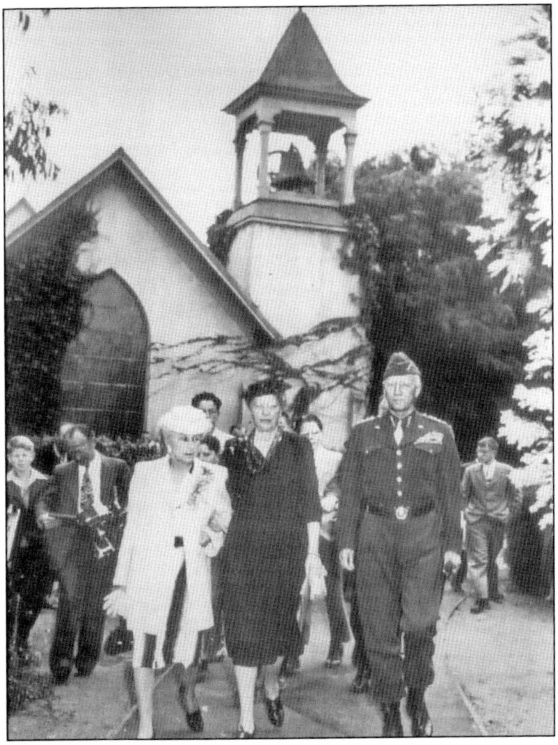

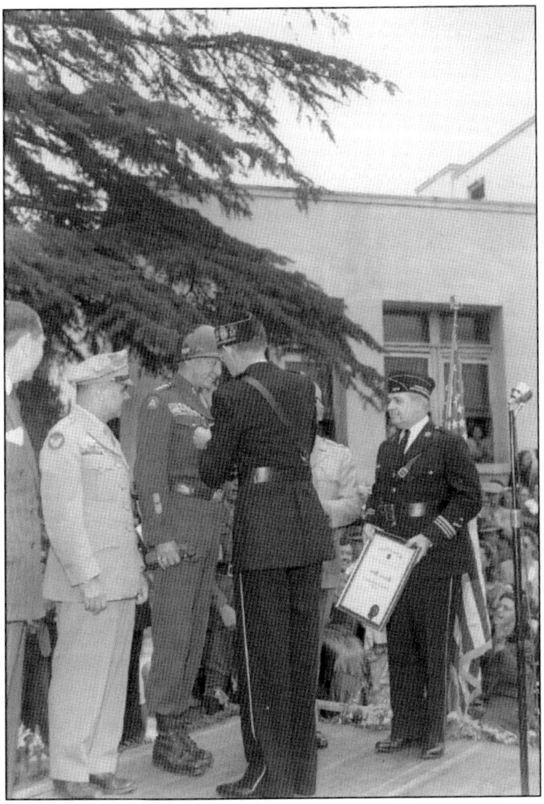

San Gabriel American Legion post commander Lou Bacon pins a Legion Medal of Merit in the name of San Gabriel on the uniform of Gen. George S. Patton Jr. as Charles Rhoads, county legion commander holds the citation that accompanied the medal. Lt. Gen. James H. Doolittle watches the presentation. As part of a "victory tour" upon returning home from Europe, General Patton and Lieutenant General Doolittle stopped in San Gabriel and Los Angeles. (San Gabriel Historical Association.)

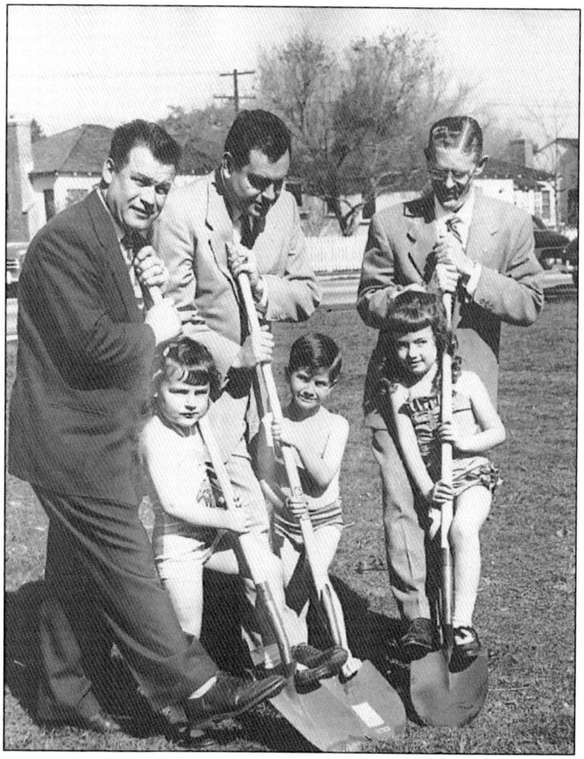

Ground-breaking ceremonies for the city's swimming pool in Smith Park took place on February 3, 1953, as shown in this photograph. The park was officially named after John F. Smith, former superintendent of San Gabriel School District in January 1931. Smith left $10,000 to the City of San Gabriel for the purchase of not more than two acres of land in the heart of San Gabriel with a stipulation that the site be not more than one-quarter of a mile from the mission. (Richard Arnold Collection.)

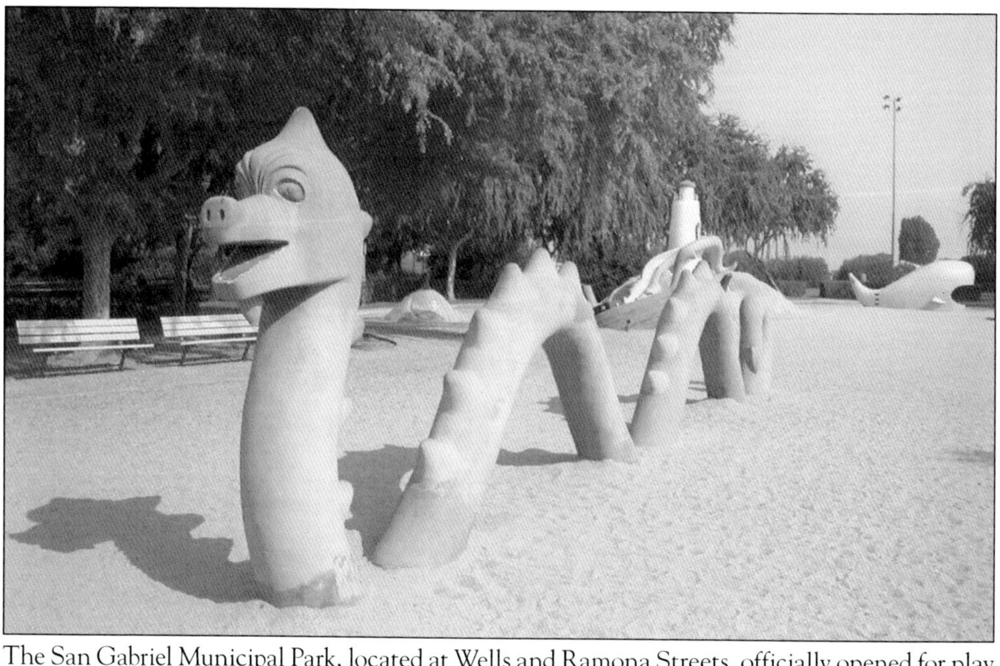

The San Gabriel Municipal Park, located at Wells and Ramona Streets, officially opened for play on May 16, 1965. The nine-acre site, home to the Laguna Play area, was renamed Vincent Lugo Park on October 22, 1988, in honor of former park supervisor Vincent Lugo. The park has been known by many names over the years, including Sea Serpent Park, Monster Park, and Dinosaur Park. (Richard Arnold Collection.)

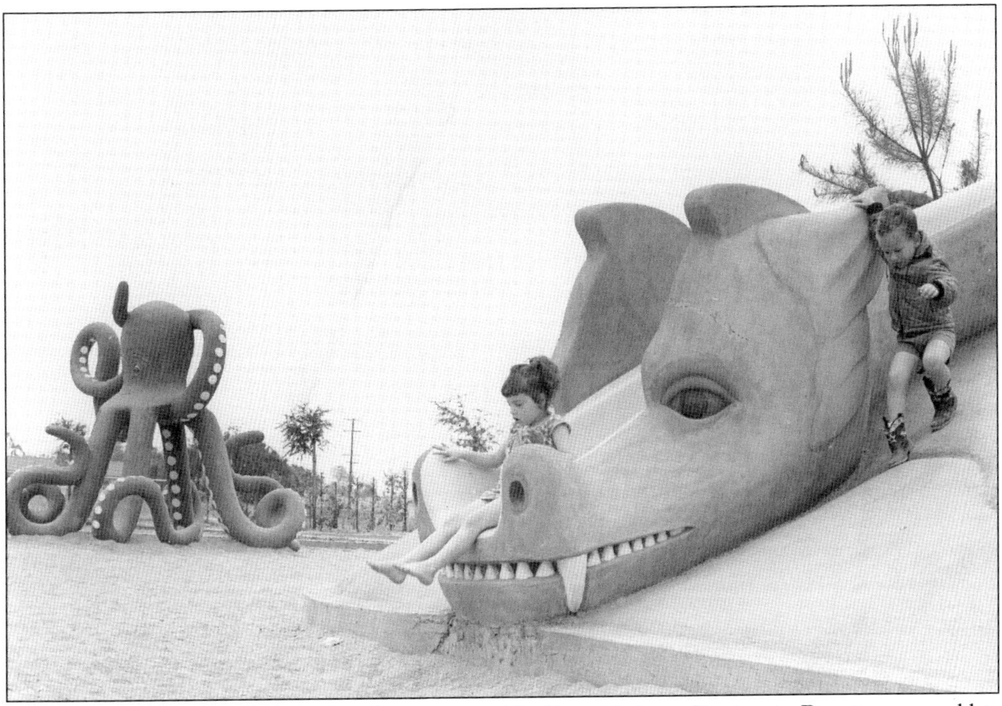

The Laguna Play area, designed and constructed by Spanish-born Benjamin Dominguez and his two sons in 1965, includes 14 concrete creatures, including an eight-foot-high snail, a 40-foot-long blue undulating serpent, and an octopus, all of which took over a year and a half to build. In 2006, a proposed new master redevelopment plan called for the demolition of the play structures, partially due to safety and accessibility issues. A preservation group made up of local community members and known as the Friends of la Laguna brought this fact to the attention of the public, and the Laguna playground area was saved and has been restored and preserved for future generations. (San Gabriel Parks and Recreation.)

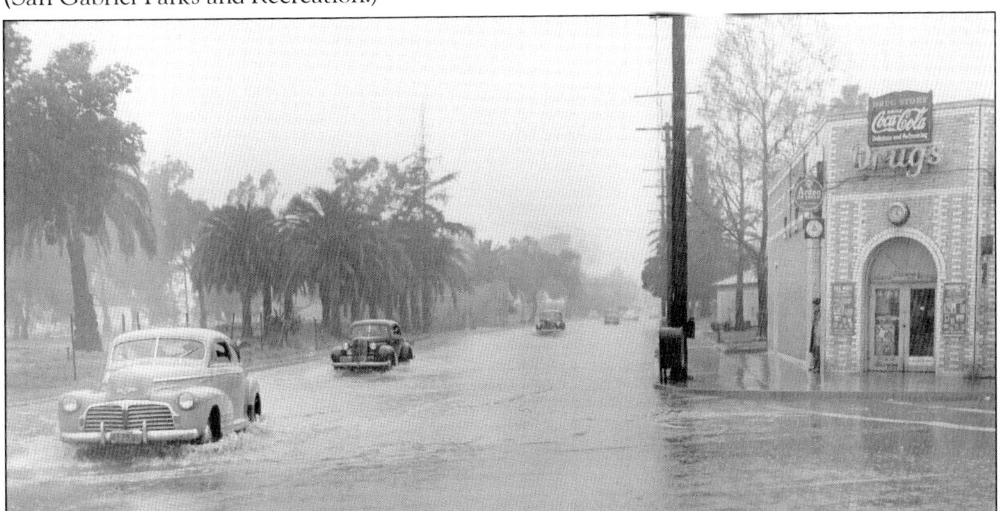

This photograph catches traffic on Mission Road at the intersection of Del Mar Avenue on a rainy day in 1947. The Del Mar Drug Store was razed in 1961 to make way for a new police facility. (San Gabriel Historical Association.)

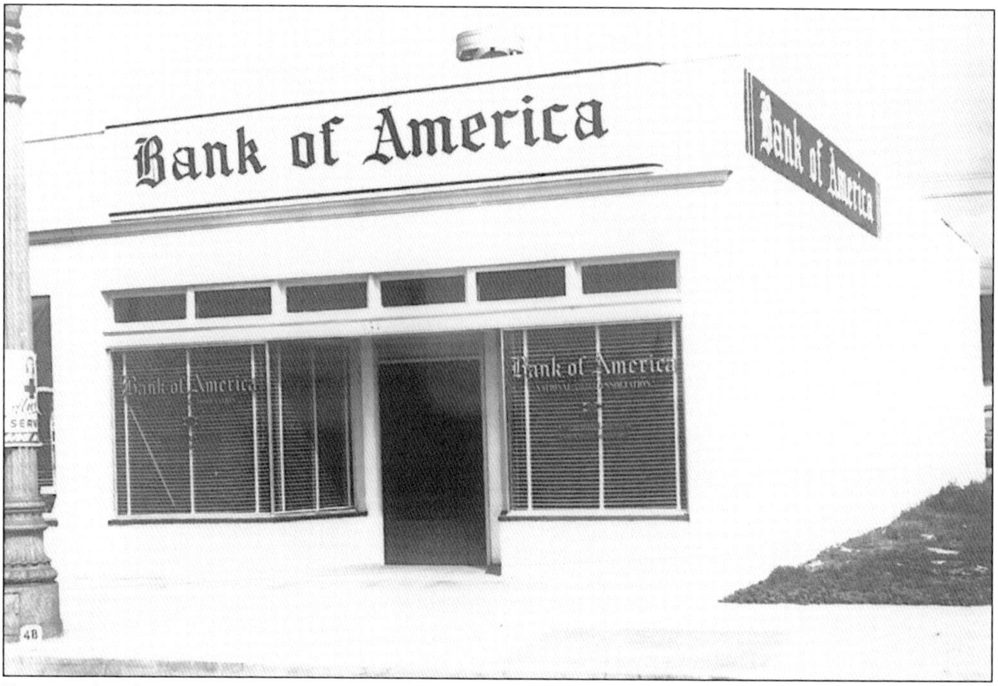

Finance has been an important part of San Gabriel's history, and Bank of America has been a part of that history since March 1946, when this facility opened at 131 East Las Tunas Drive. K.B. "Jack" Johnson was the manager of the new banking office when it opened. At that time, Bank of America had a few more than 500 branches statewide. The branch grew rapidly, and in 1949, it moved across the street to its current location at 102 East Las Tunas Drive. Although the large green building that once occupied this location has long since been replaced, the branch still remains an important institution for the community. (San Gabriel Historical Association.)

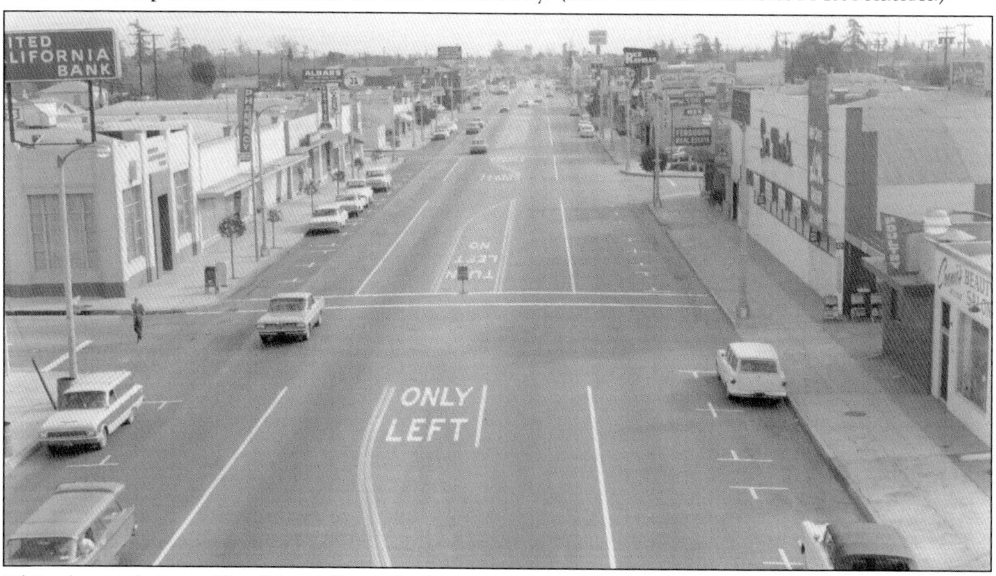

This elevated view of Las Tunas Drive looking east from Mission Drive in 1965 shows businesses, including Prudential Savings, United California Bank, Connie's Beauty Salon, La Mar's Market, Rapelje Electric, and Baskin-Robbins. (Richard Arnold Collection.)

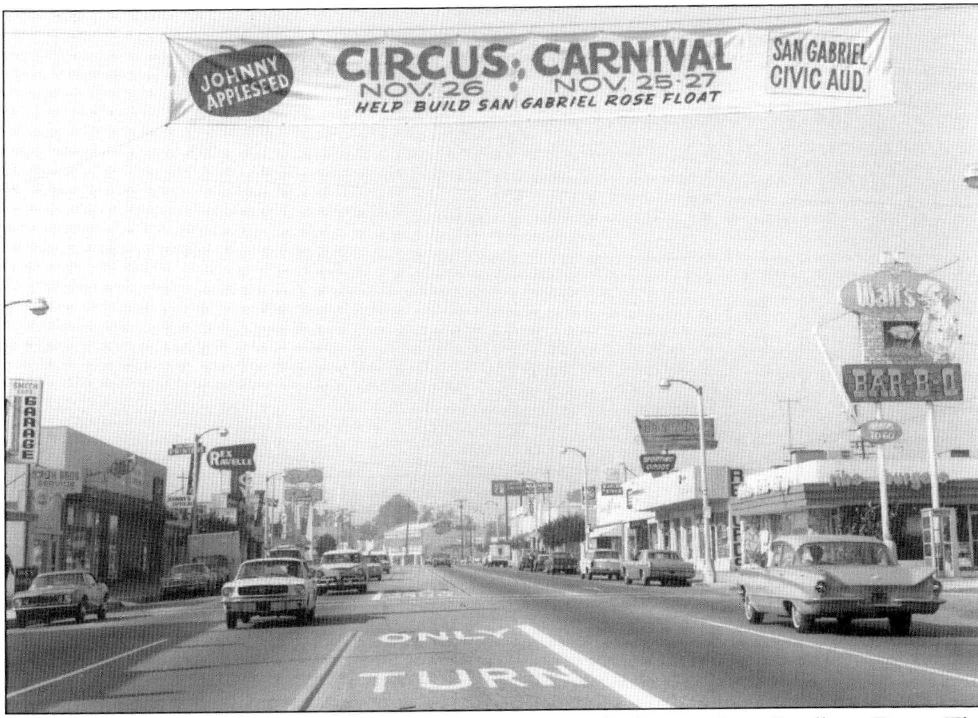

This November 1966 street-level view of Las Tunas Drive looks west from Bradbury Drive. The banner announces the circus carnival being held at the San Gabriel Civic Auditorium as an effort to raise $9,000 required to finance the San Gabriel float to be entered in the Tournament of Roses Parade on New Year's Day in 1967. A "Johnny Appleseed" theme was selected for the float. (Richard Arnold Collection.)

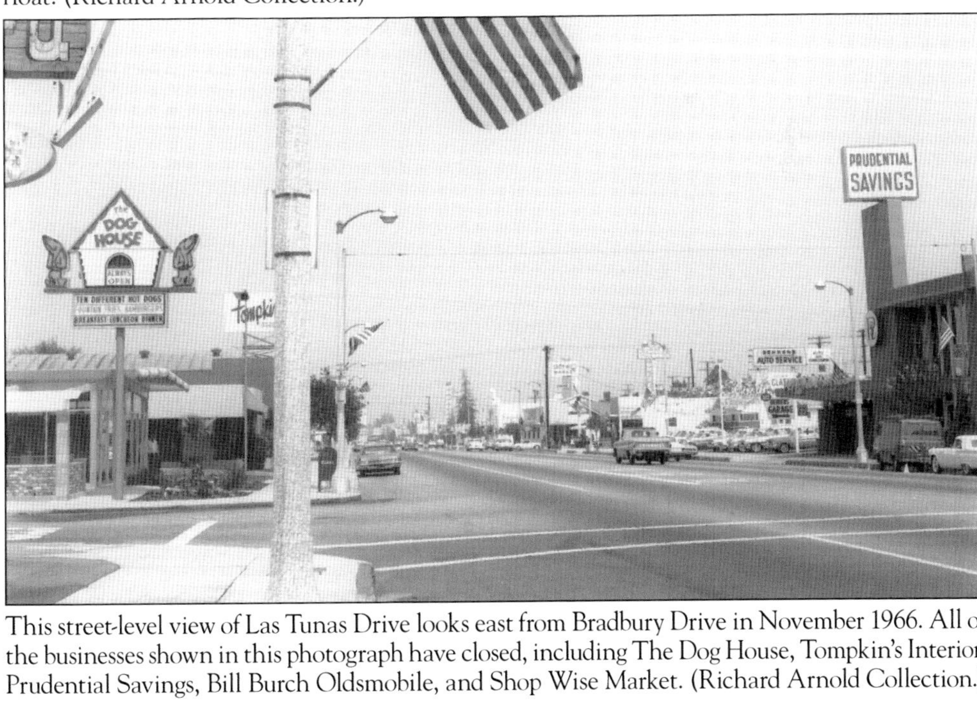

This street-level view of Las Tunas Drive looks east from Bradbury Drive in November 1966. All of the businesses shown in this photograph have closed, including The Dog House, Tompkin's Interior, Prudential Savings, Bill Burch Oldsmobile, and Shop Wise Market. (Richard Arnold Collection.)

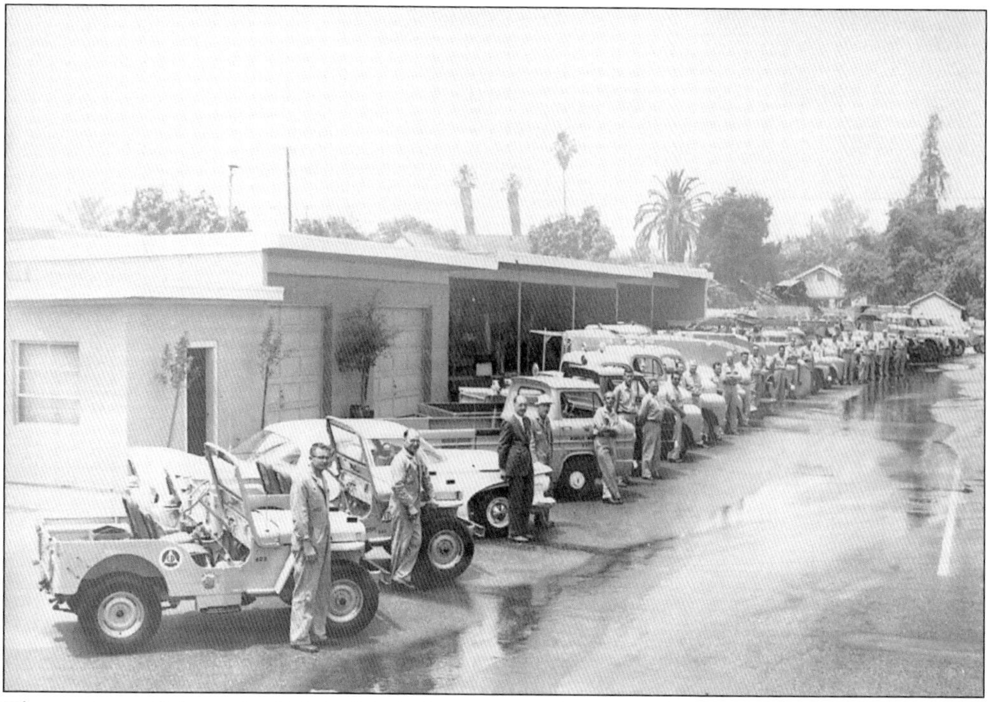

The entire staff from the Public Works Department lined up for this 1960 photograph. (San Gabriel Historical Association.)

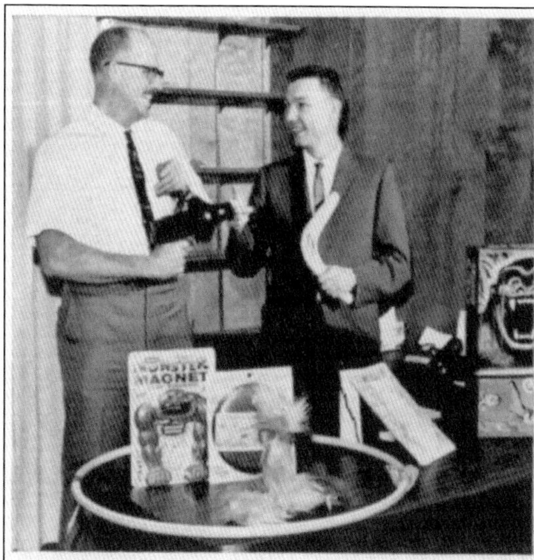

All smiles over the success of the multimillion-dollar business they've built out of fun and games, Richard P. Knerr (left) and A. K. Melin clown among some hit products in their San Gabriel, Calif., office.

This image was part of an article entitled "Can You Invent a Million-Dollar Fad?" that appeared in the January 1966 edition of *Popular Science*. The article focused on the Wham-O Manufacturing Company and invited readers to send in ideas. Childhood buddies Richard P. Knerr and Arthur K. Melin started the mail-order slingshot business in 1948. The business did not really take off until the partners spotted a man on the beach throwing a plastic flying saucer. The two bought the idea for $1 million, changed the name from the Pluto Platter to Frisbee, and watched their business grow. The two moved production to San Gabriel, where they made millions manufacturing Frisbees and thousands of other toys. In 1982, the founders sold the thriving business to Kransco Group Companies for $12 million. (*Popular Science*, Bonnier Corporation Company.)

Six

Transportation

Prior to the arrival of the railroad, early travelers found the stagecoach the most effective mode of transportation. On a journey to California from the east, travelers traveled only by day and stopped off at local hotels or stage stops at night. The stations were normally maintained at intervals of from 8 to 25 miles. The Butterfield stage line was one of the longest continuous lines ever organized, having started its operation September 15, 1858. The first stage from the east reached Los Angeles on October 7, 1858, and San Francisco on October 10, 1858.

The Butterfield line was equipped at first with the famous Concord spring wagons, capable of carrying four passengers and their baggage and 500–600 pounds of mail matter

Although San Gabriel did not have an official stage stop, Butterfield maintained a station in El Monte. The route from El Monte to Los Angeles was along what is now known today as Mission Road. It was quite common for the stage to drop passengers off at the San Gabriel Hotel, which was just north of the San Gabriel Mission. Having the two towns to stop in also broke the monotony of a trip between Los Angeles and San Bernardino.

The Southern Pacific Railroad began operating trains between Los Angeles and Colton on July 16, 1875. The San Gabriel station, located at 212 West Dalton Street (present-day Clary Avenue), was constructed in March 1874. In July 1886, a new flag stop depot was built on the northeast side of the San Gabriel Boulevard crossing, which became necessary when the East San Gabriel Hotel opened on June 1, 1888.

Mass transit in the form of the Pacific Electric Railway would be introduced to San Gabriel a number of years later. The first streetcar went through to the San Gabriel Mission from downtown Los Angeles on Wednesday, June 25, 1902. Donald Duke in his book *Pacific Electric Railway*, published by Golden West Books, notes that "the Pacific Electric was one of the greatest factors contributing to the growth of Southern California and one man built it—Henry Edwards Huntington."

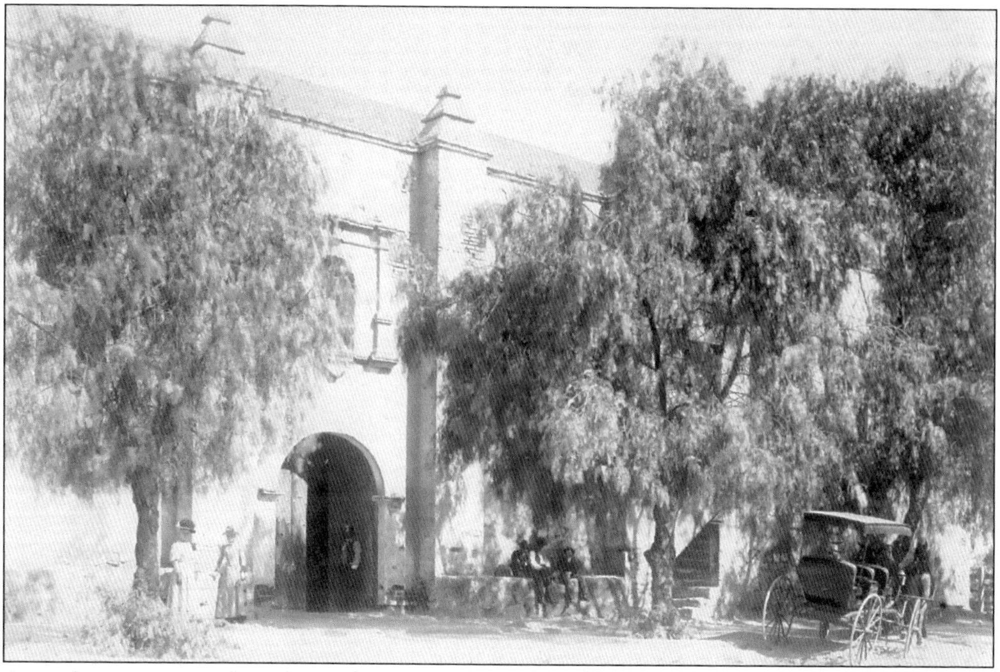

A two-horse team stands at the ready as passengers take a short rest break and pose for photographs. The six-passenger carriage was a standard mode of transportation for visitors in the 1880s. One such group was the French delegation to the Yorktown centennial that arrived in Los Angeles on Sunday, December 4, 1881. They were met by prominent citizens, including French locals, then escorted by carriage to the San Gabriel Mission, where they spent time visiting the grounds and touring the historic building. (Bancroft Library, University of California, Berkeley.)

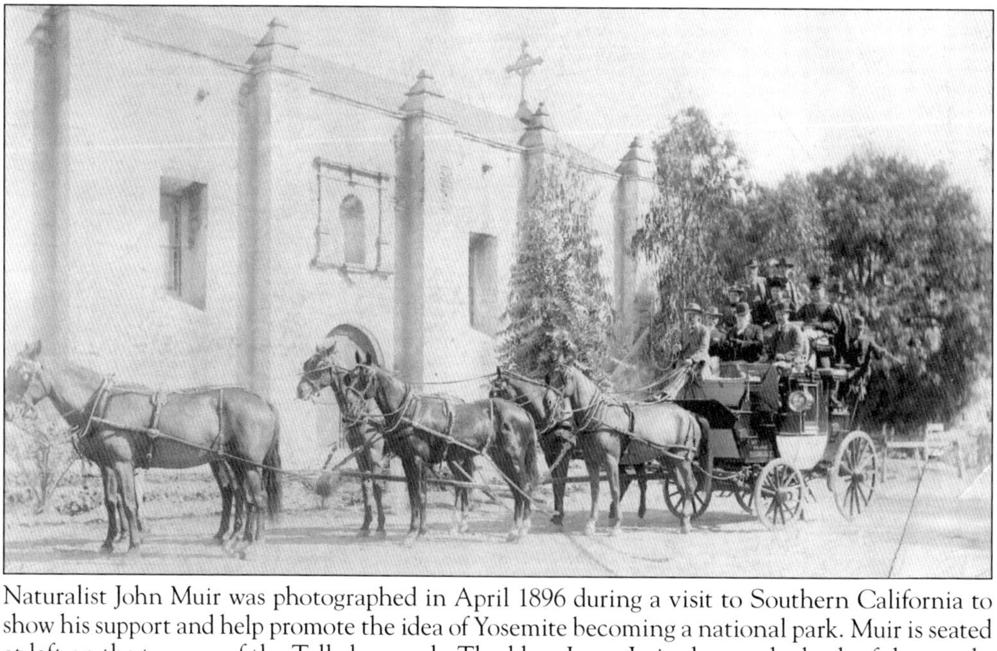

Naturalist John Muir was photographed in April 1896 during a visit to Southern California to show his support and help promote the idea of Yosemite becoming a national park. Muir is seated at left on the top row of the Tally-ho coach. Thaddeus Lowe Jr. is also on the back of the coach. (Michael A. Patris Collection.)

Henry Edwards Huntington (1850–1927) was the nephew of railroad magnate Collis P. Huntington, one of the leading members of the "Big Four" that built the Central Pacific Railroad and subsequently formed the Southern Pacific Railroad. Henry inherited a substantial amount of the family fortune upon the death of his uncle Collis in 1900, which would provide funds to eventually build street railways and interurban lines in both San Francisco and Southern California. With the purchase of the Los Angeles Railway and the Los Angeles & Pasadena Electric Railway, Huntington would form the Pacific Electric Railway, which would become the "world's greatest interurban." He made his lasting mark on history as an avid collector of fine art and rare books and as a founder of the Huntington Library, Art Collections, and Botanical Gardens in San Marino. The Pacific Electric was one of the greatest factors that contributed to the growth of Southern California. (Huntington Library.)

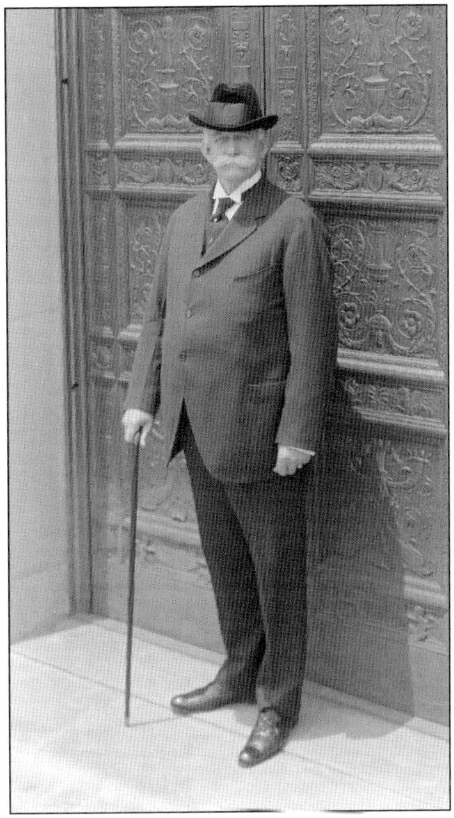

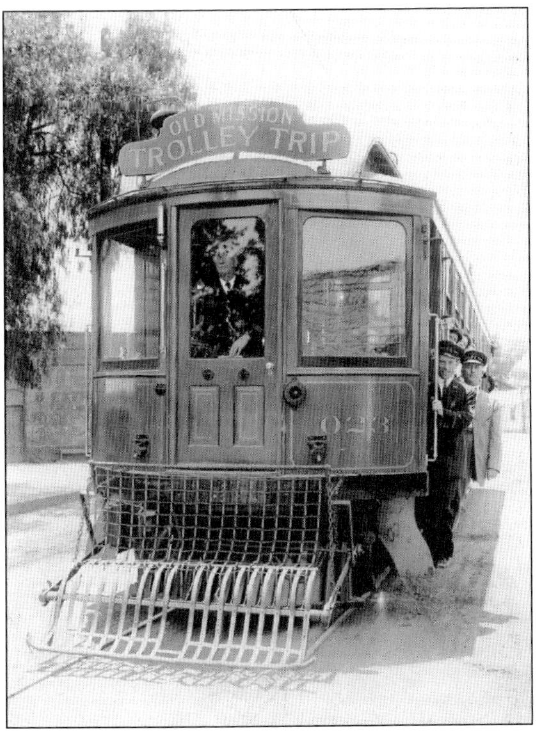

Pacific Electric Railway excursion car No. 023 pauses in front of the San Gabriel Mission to take on passengers and pose for photographs as it heads east in this 1920 photograph. Cars for the "Old Mission Trolley Trip" excursions were leased from the Pacific Electric Railway to bring guests to the mission. All of the Pacific Electric Railway cars that were not in regular service and used for excursions carried a "0" number. They were also painted blue instead of the standard red. (Huntington Library.)

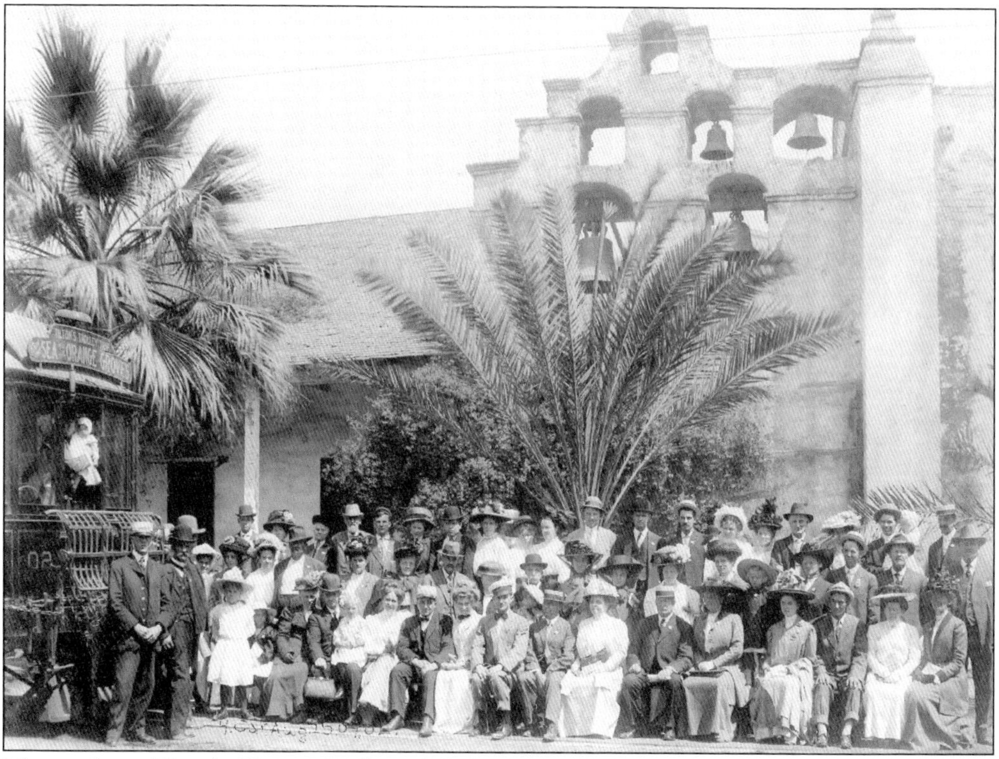

The eastbound Pacific Electric Railway deluxe car is at left as crew members and guests pose in front of the San Gabriel Mission. The destination sign board says, "Tilton's Trolley Trip—From the Sea to the Orange Groves." George F. Tilton ran the excursions on the Pacific Electric Railway, advertising "100 miles for 100 cents." The escorted and narrated excursions left the Pacific Electric depot at Sixth and Main Streets in Los Angeles at 9:30 a.m. daily and took guests to Pasadena and the Orange Groves, San Pedro-Los Angeles Harbor, the Cawston Ostrich Farm in South Pasadena, the San Gabriel Mission, and a two-hour stop at Long Beach. (Richard Arnold Collection.)

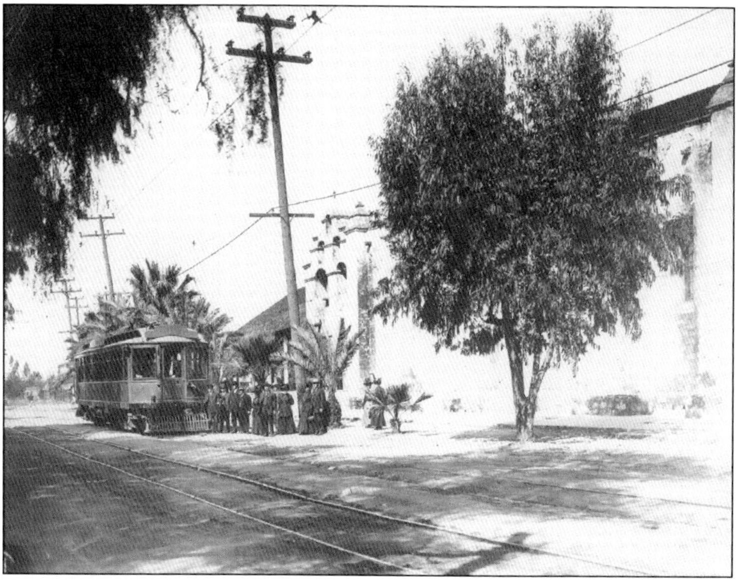

Passengers prepare to embark on the eastbound Pacific Electric Railway excursion car No. 023 after their tour of the historic San Gabriel Mission. The day's excursion, with reserved seating on the parlor car, cost a mere $1. (Harold Stewart Collection.)

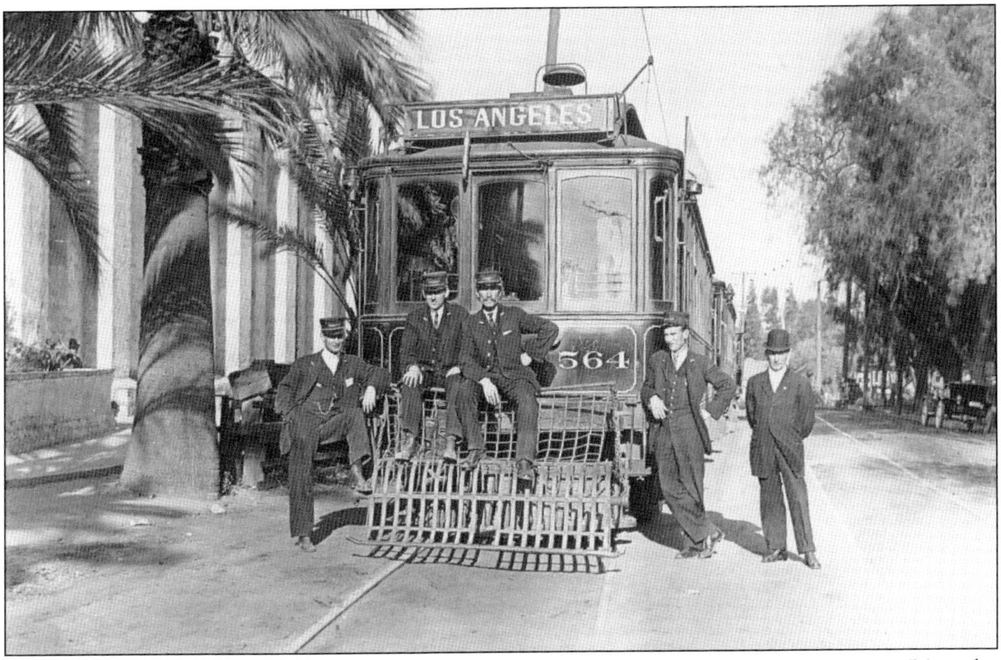

Crew members of the westbound Pacific Electric Railway special excursion car No. 564 take a break to pose for this 1914 photograph while their passengers tour the historic San Gabriel Mission. (Craig Rasmussen Collection.)

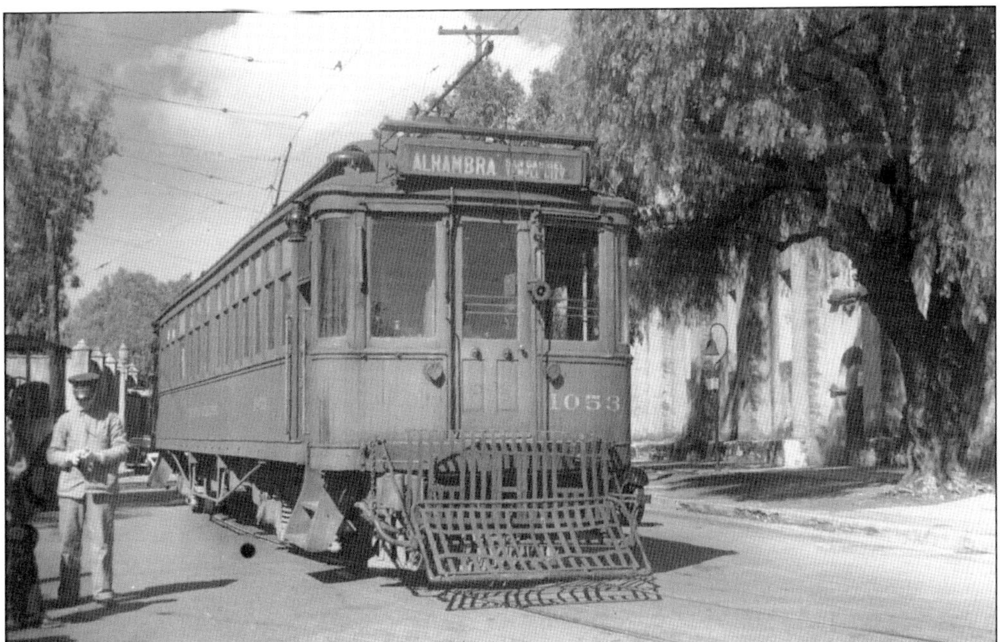

Pacific Electric Railway car No. 1053 sits idle in front of the San Gabriel Mission, which was on the Mission Loop. The interurban originated in Los Angeles, made stops in Alhambra and San Gabriel, and was bound for Temple City after dropping off passengers in front of the San Gabriel Mission, as noted on the destination sign board. (Harold Stewart Collection.)

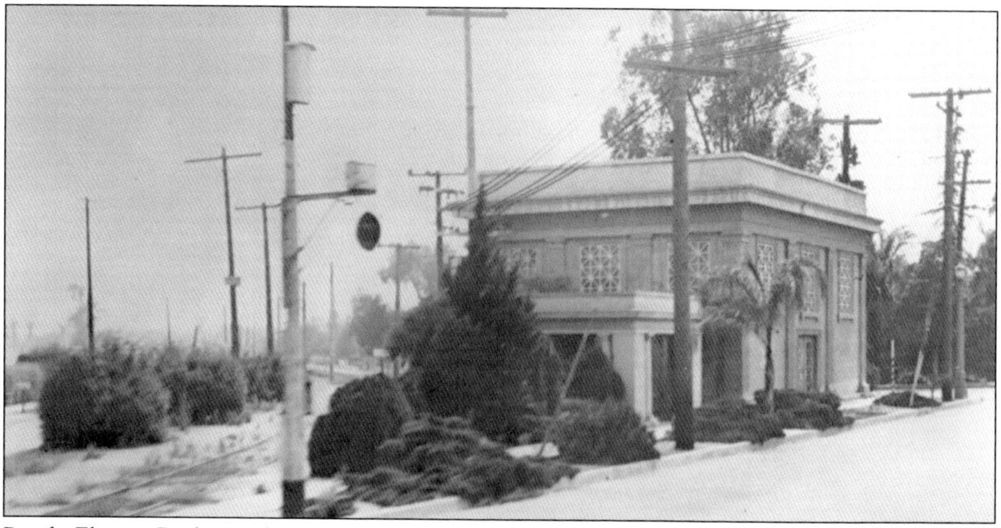

Pacific Electric Railway substation No. 52, located at Las Tunas Drive and Shorb Road (present-day Junipero Serra), was known as the Shorb Junction. Built in 1927, the substation, with adjoining passenger waiting room, replaced an older facility that was located in Alhambra. (Harold Stewart Collection.)

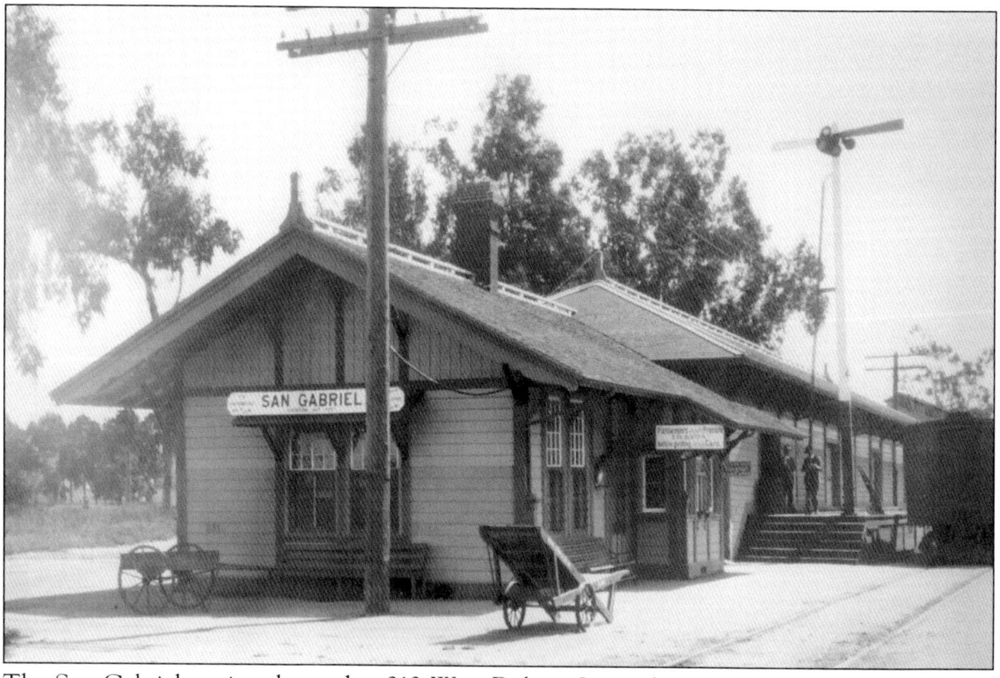

The San Gabriel station, located at 212 West Dalton Street (present-day Clary Avenue), was constructed in March 1874. The single-story building included a waiting area and freight warehouse and was considered a "major stop" for the Southern Pacific. Regular passenger service was discontinued in the 1930s, but freight shipping continued. When a new, modern station was built in Alhambra on December 26, 1940, passenger service ceased at San Gabriel. By the late 1950s, freight service to San Gabriel had dwindled, and the Public Utilities Commission authorized the Southern Pacific to close the San Gabriel station on July 22, 1958. The station was demolished in 1961. (Richard Arnold Collection.)

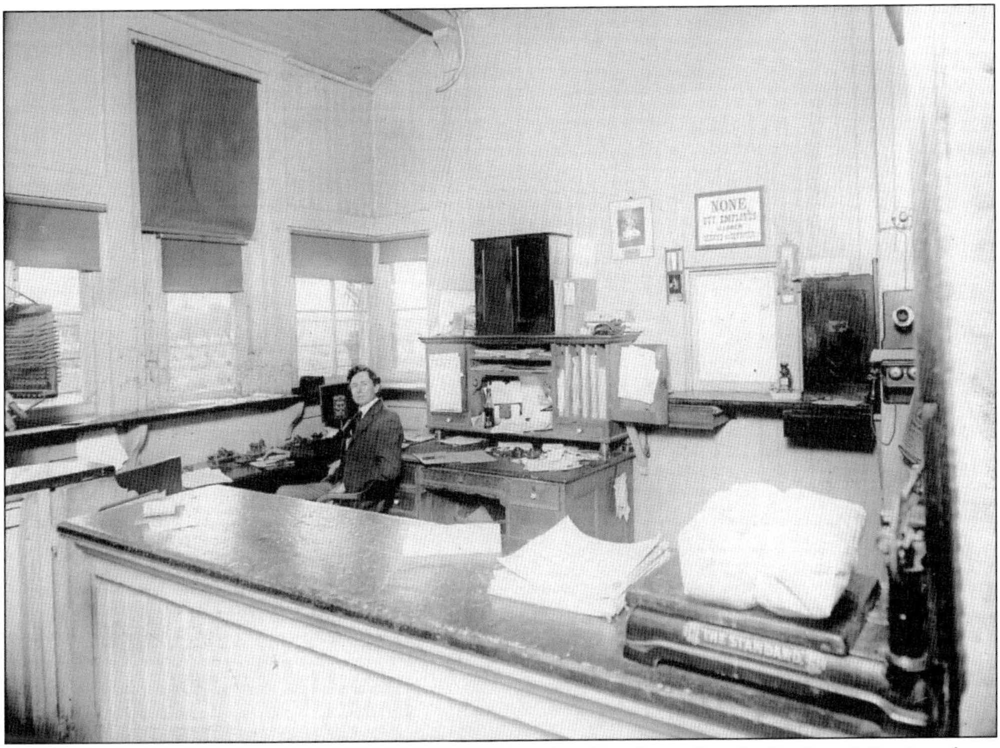

Edwin Hayes was employed as the stationmaster at the Southern Pacific Railroad Station from 1901 to 1945. When San Gabriel became a city in 1913, Hayes became one of its first city council members (then called "trustees"). In 1904, Hayes married Mary Letitia Wilson, whose father, Milton Scott Wilson, was the justice of the peace for San Gabriel Township. The family resided at 245 South Pine Street in a Victorian-style house. (Richard Arnold Collection.)

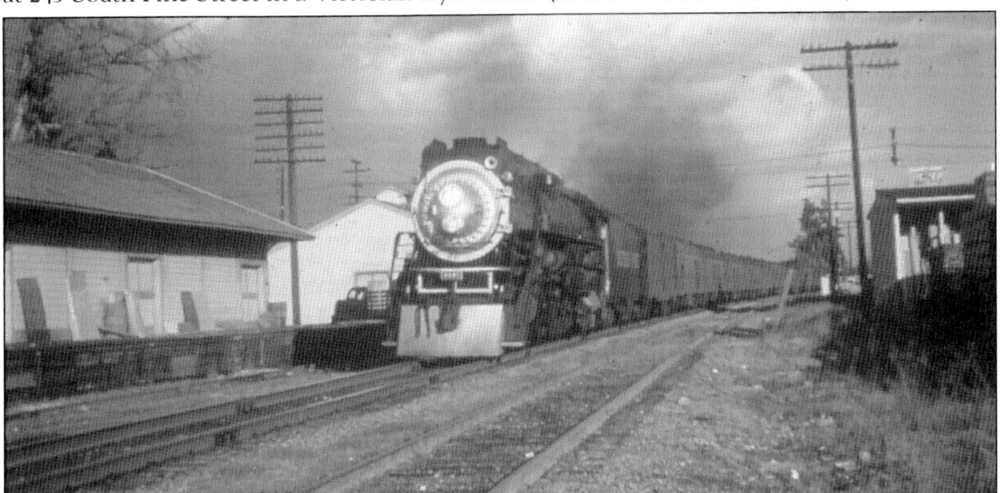

Locomotive No. 4445 (GS-4, "Golden State" Class engine) runs into town with train No. 5, the westbound Argonaut, past the San Gabriel depot at about 3:10 p.m. on November 15, 1952. Southern Pacific's number two Sunset Route train from New Orleans was nine miles from "home," Los Angeles. The old engine man's time book for November 1945 contains the notation: "4445 is the best of the 'Daylight' GS engines we've had." (Donald Duke Collection.)

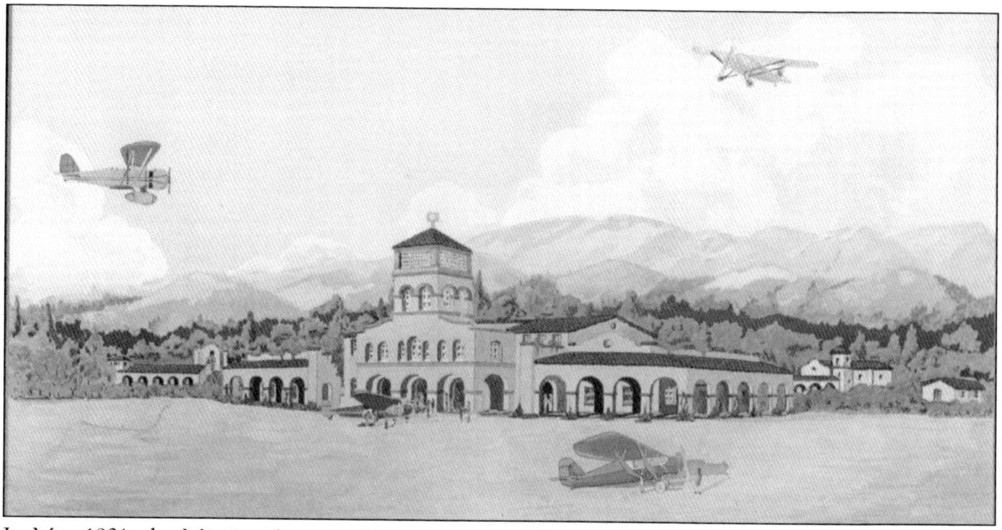

In May 1931, the Mission Airport Corporation was formed with plans to build a modern facility on 162 acres of property just south of the San Gabriel Mission. It was designed by Walker and Eisen, the Los Angeles architectural firm that also designed city hall and the adjoining Temple Building. The executive buildings and sales rooms were to be of Spanish design, connected by a chain of Gothic arches that hid the bolted steel construction hangers. This is the architectural conceptual drawing of the Mission Airport passenger terminal. (Lawrence Arnold Collection.)

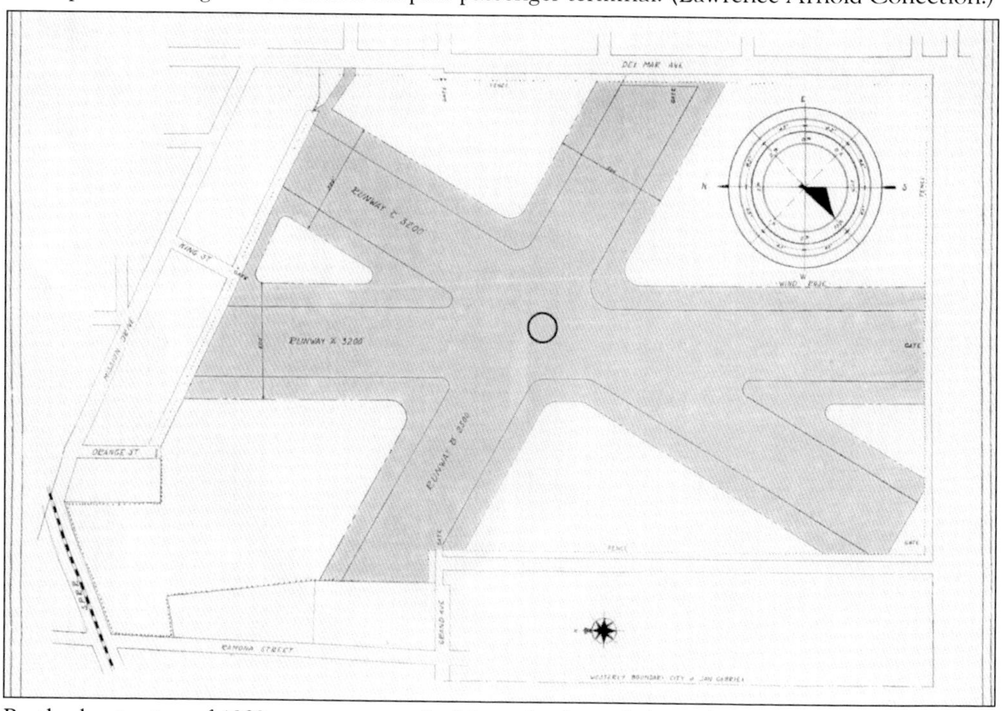

By the beginning of 1932, no structures had been built, and the only means of identifying the facility as an airport was the runway. Citizens regularly attended council meetings, complaining about the disturbance the airport caused, including stunt flying and air taxi service. During the June 21, 1932, session of the city council, a petition was approved requiring closure of the airport. (Lawrence Arnold Collection.)

Seven

THE MISSION PLAY

Shortly after writing his history of California called *California: Its History and Romance*, *Los Angeles Times* reporter John Steven McGroarty began writing an epic production that would soon be known as the *Mission Play*. Frank Miller, of the Mission Inn in Riverside, found McGroarty to be the most qualified person to write this and suggested to McGroarty that he take on the project and write the history of California as a drama.

McGroarty quickly set to writing in a room at the Mission Inn. Word has it that the play, a blockbuster in the making, took just eight weeks to write. Although he was well versed in history, McGroarty sought out the advice of well-known historians, including Rev. Zephyrin Englehardt and Charles Fletcher Lummis. Englehardt was the author of *The Missions and Missionaries of California*, and Lummis was a prolific author and fervent crusader for Indian rights.

McGroarty was less than pleased with Englehardt's criticisms of certain portions of manuscript, including his dislike for some of McGroarty's dramatics for public sale, and was taken aback by Lummis's blunt response. As noted in William Deverells's *White Washed Adobe*, Lummis chastised McGroarty in a letter about the playwright's work: "In my 53 years, I have never even found so Irresponsible a Cuss as you. Now you've got to learn–not for my sake but for yours—not to go crazy when an idea hits you. That's the time to get sane. You've got to learn to keep your Word, to be Responsible , to have some Balance. Else you'll wind up a Total Failure. Your Mission Play, and everything else will crumble unless you learn the Common Law. Wake Up."

The *Mission Play*, which told the story of bringing Christian civilization to the Western shores of America, ran for over 20 years and was one of the highest-grossing plays of all time.

By the time the *Mission Play* moved into a beautiful new playhouse, the play no longer belonged to McGroarty, and the beautiful, modern facility was owned by the Mission Playhouse Corporation. Although McGroarty was still involved with the play, it was more of an emeritus role lacking any real authority.

Two years after the final curtain of the *Mission Play*, McGroarty entered politics, serving California in the US House of Representatives from 1935 to 1939.

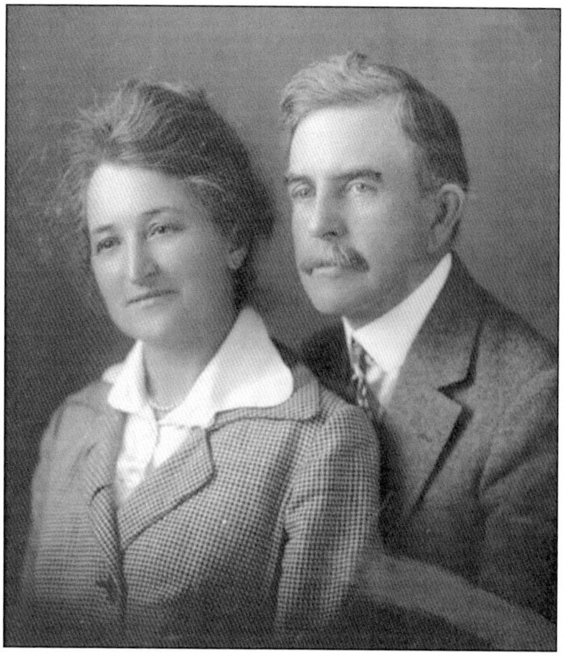

John McGroarty, author of the *Mission Play* is shown with his wife, Ida L. McGroarty, who was his childhood sweetheart. Ida was responsible for set and costume design, outfitting hundreds of actors and actresses. (McGroarty Arts Center.)

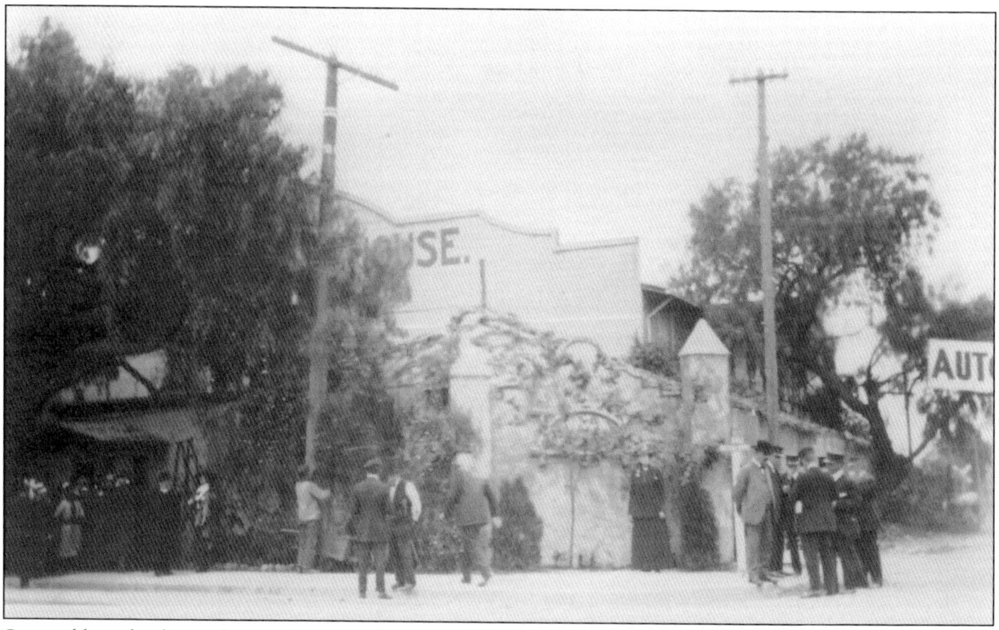

Several hundred people were in attendance on February 1, 1912, when Fathers Cassian and George, Franciscan friars from St. Joseph's Mission, turned the soil for John McGroarty's Mission Playhouse with implements supposedly used in building the San Gabriel Mission. The structure was erected on property belonging to the Catholic Church. As a Spanish orchestra played a rendition of "La Paloma," the Franciscans marched from the mission to the spot selected for the new playhouse, which was across from the mission, and were greeted by the padres from San Gabriel. Members from the Franciscan order were present for the first time since 1835, when the Franciscan order was driven from the building and had their property confiscated. (Workman and Temple Family Homestead Museum.)

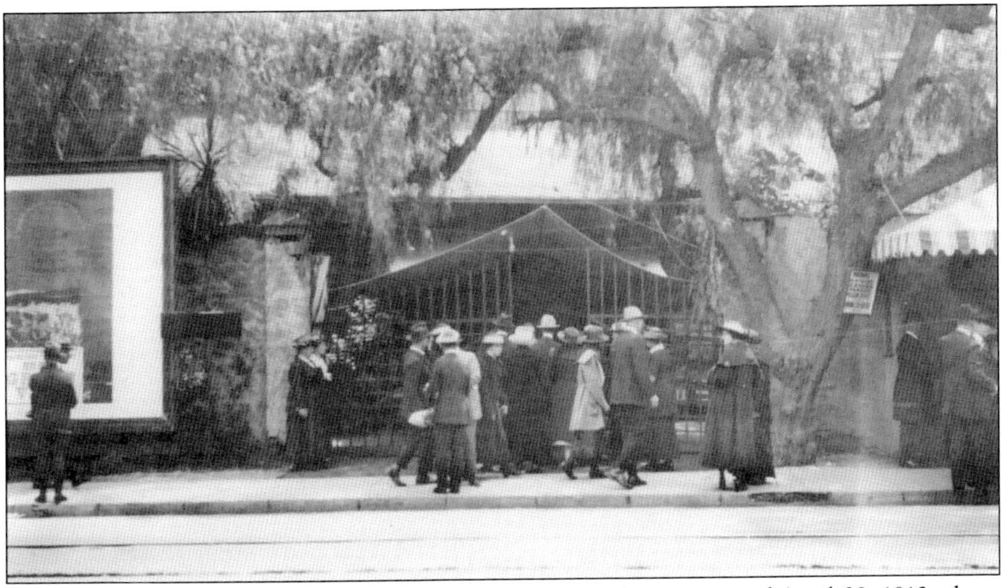

The first performance of the *Mission Play* was given on the evening of April 29, 1912, three months after the ground-breaking ceremony. The building, with a facade of mission architecture, was of simple design and within a stone's throw of the Southern Pacific Railroad. The vibration of the massive steam engines rolling along the rails shook the thin walls so violently and loudly that the actors held their lines until the noise faded. (Yale University, Beinecke Rare Book and Manuscript Library.)

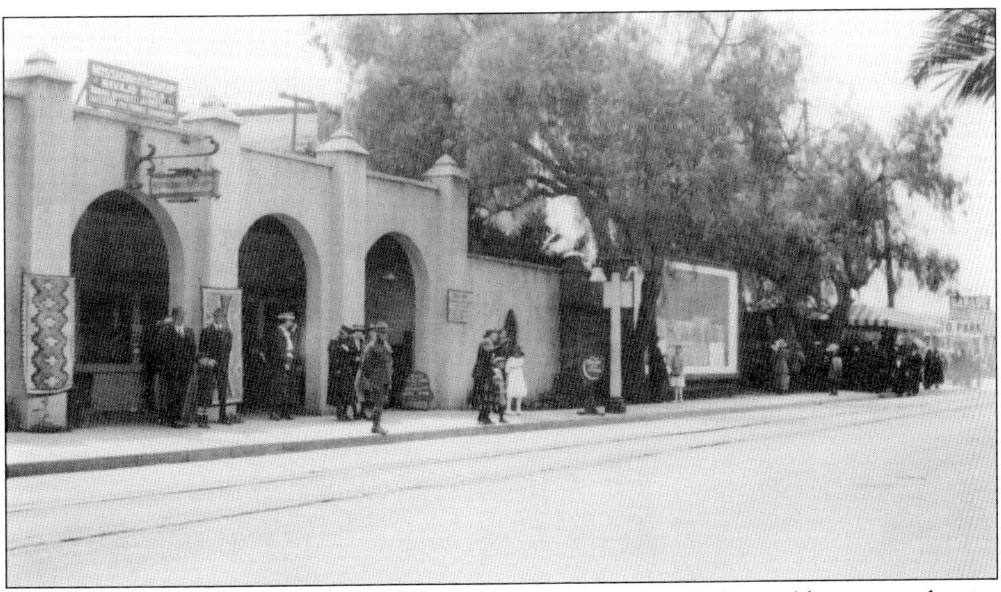

The Mission Curio and Gift Shop was located east of the first playhouse (the present-day site of Plaza Park). The shop sold souvenirs of the historic San Gabriel Mission to patrons of the *Mission Play* and tourists who came to the city to tour the mission. It was also conveniently located at the end of the Pacific Electric Railway line. (Yale University, Beinecke Rare Book and Manuscript Library.)

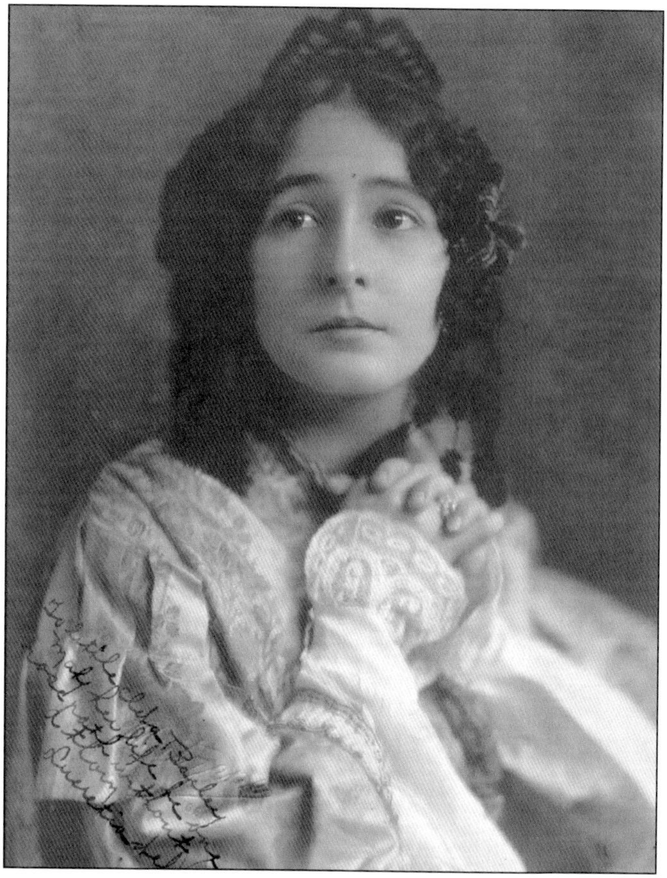

Lucretia del Valle, who played Señora Dona Josefa Yorba, the leading lady of the *Mission Play*, from late 1912 to 1917, had a charming personality, and her rich voice was suitably adapted to this character. A descendant of Fernando Villa, who came to California with Junipero Serra, del Valle reportedly wore family heirlooms as part of her costume. (David "Bodie" Bailey family archives.)

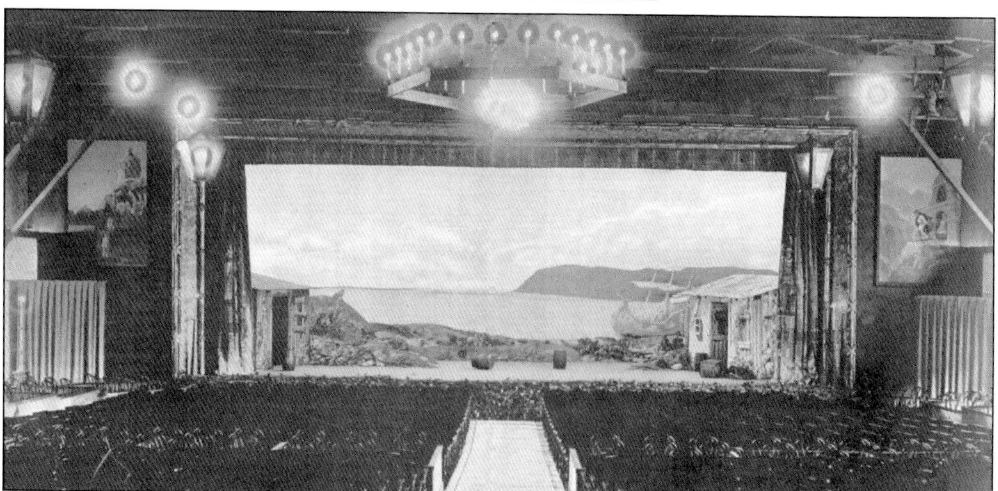

The beautifully decorated interior of the first Mission Playhouse was suggestive of the mission era. An old mission-style bell hung from the rafters to the right of the stage was rung to announce the beginning of each act. The curtain, a copy of an old Spanish tapestry, was of soft blue material with a Spanish coat of arms in dull gold. The exterior was complemented with tropical vines and shrubs that were a pleasant backdrop to the 21 miniature missions placed along the walkway surrounding the Mission Playhouse. (Richard Arnold Collection.)

Members of the Mission Play Quartette pose for this 1920 publicity shot for an upcoming performance. Shown from left to right are George Willey (tenor), Margaret Carraher (soprano), Annunciata (contralto), and Harold Ostrom (baritone). (San Gabriel Historical Association.)

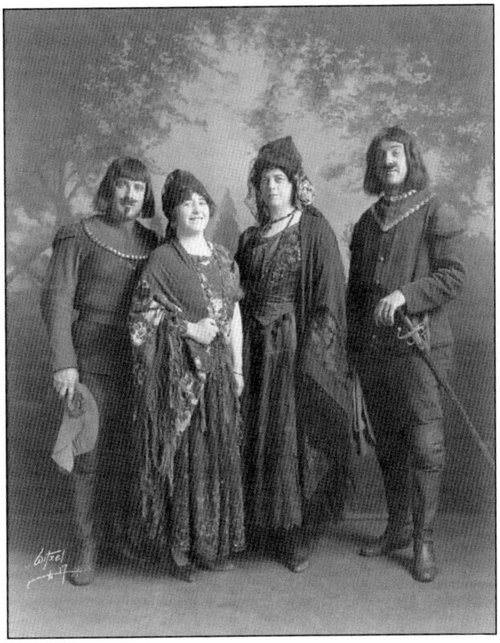

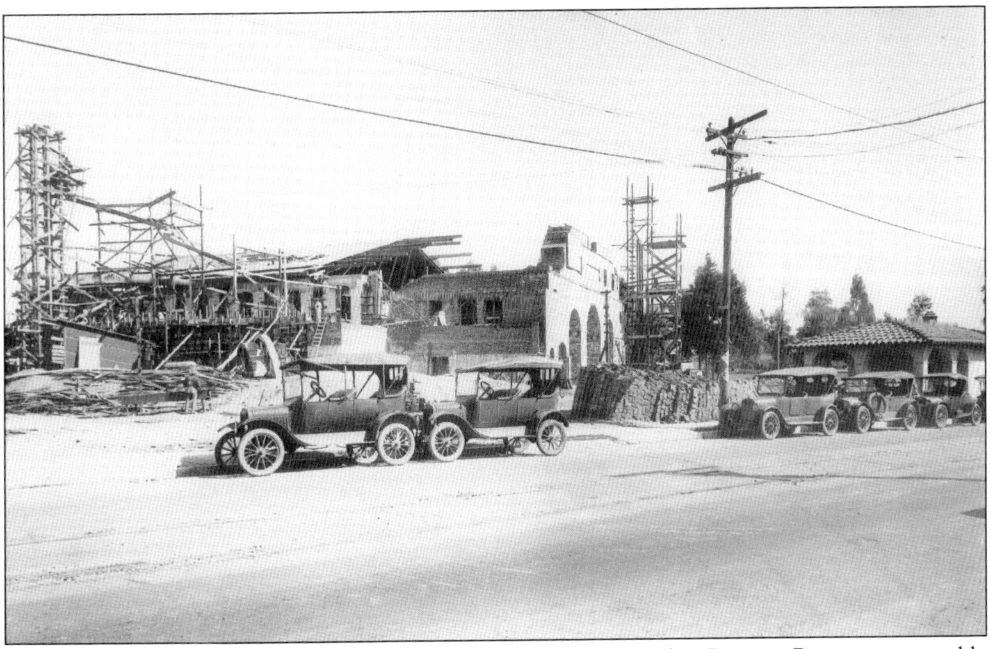

The new Mission Playhouse was designed in 1921 by architect Arthur Burnett Benton to resemble John McGroarty's favorite mission, San Antonio de Padua in Monterey County, with hopes that the new playhouse would be completed before the 1921 season of the *Mission Play* came to a close at the old facility. However, the cornerstone was not laid until 1923. A classic example of Mission Revival architecture, the structure was originally designed to allow playgoers to drive into the boxes on the sides of the theater with their own automobiles and view the productions from their own cars. Total seating capacity was set at 2,500. A permanent sliding stage was to be constructed with growing trees and shrubs. When the stage was not in use, it would be run out into the open gardens. (San Gabriel Historical Association.)

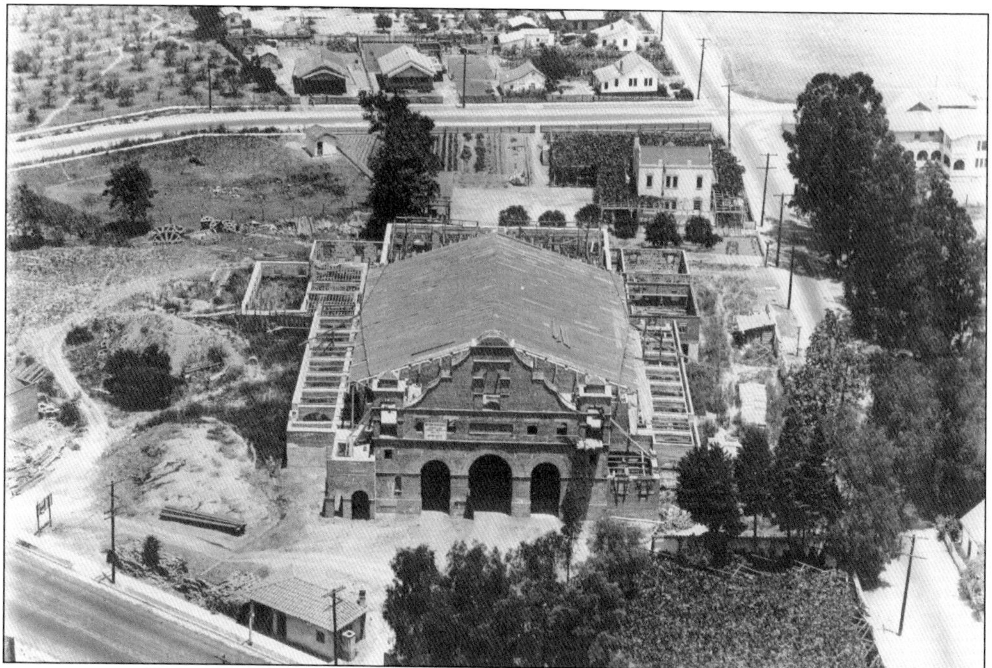

Progress was slow in the construction of the new Mission Playhouse, and by 1926, cost overruns were enormous. Architect Arthur Burnett Benton had become too ill to complete the project (he died in 1927), and it was taken over by William J. Dodd and his Los Angeles–based firm, Dodd & Richards. Many changes were made to the original design, which also caused delays. Tragedy also struck the construction site on December 15, 1922, when a laborer was killed by a 20-foot wall that became soaked by rain and collapsed without warning. (Security Pacific National Bank Collection, Los Angeles Public Library.)

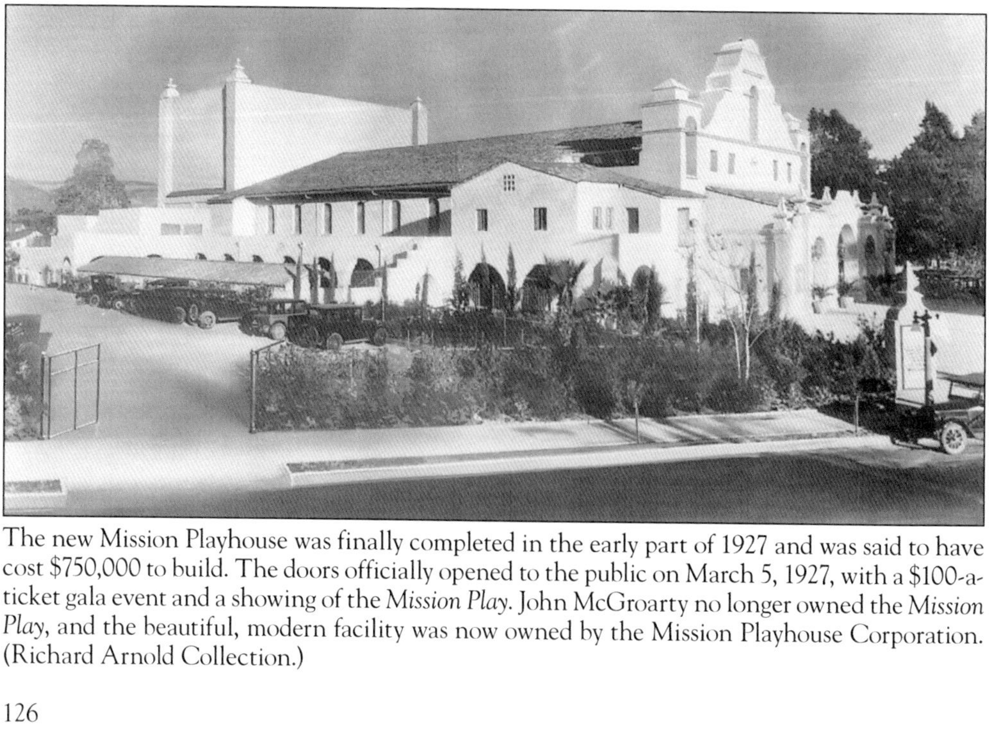

The new Mission Playhouse was finally completed in the early part of 1927 and was said to have cost $750,000 to build. The doors officially opened to the public on March 5, 1927, with a $100-a-ticket gala event and a showing of the *Mission Play*. John McGroarty no longer owned the *Mission Play*, and the beautiful, modern facility was now owned by the Mission Playhouse Corporation. (Richard Arnold Collection.)

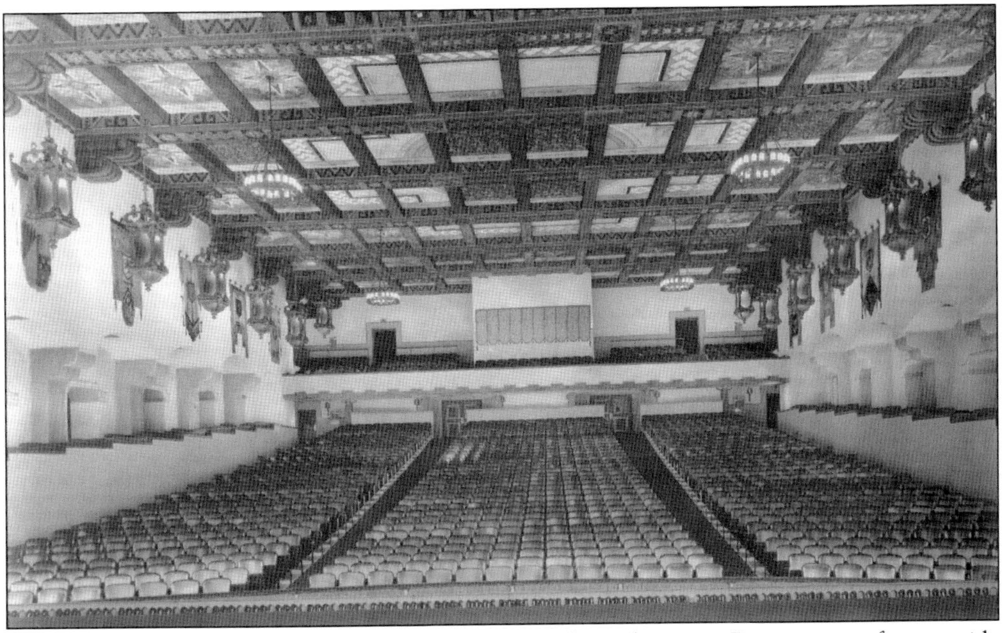

This is the interior of the Mission Playhouse as seen from the stage. Patrons enter from a wide foyer with graceful iron-grilled balconies, then head into the spacious modern auditorium. Hanging on the walls are banners of the different provinces of Spain, gifts to John McGroarty from Spanish king Alfonso XIII. The lighting in the auditorium is diffused through lanterns of wrought iron—replicas of those that hung on the decks of Spanish galleons. (San Gabriel Mission Playhouse.)

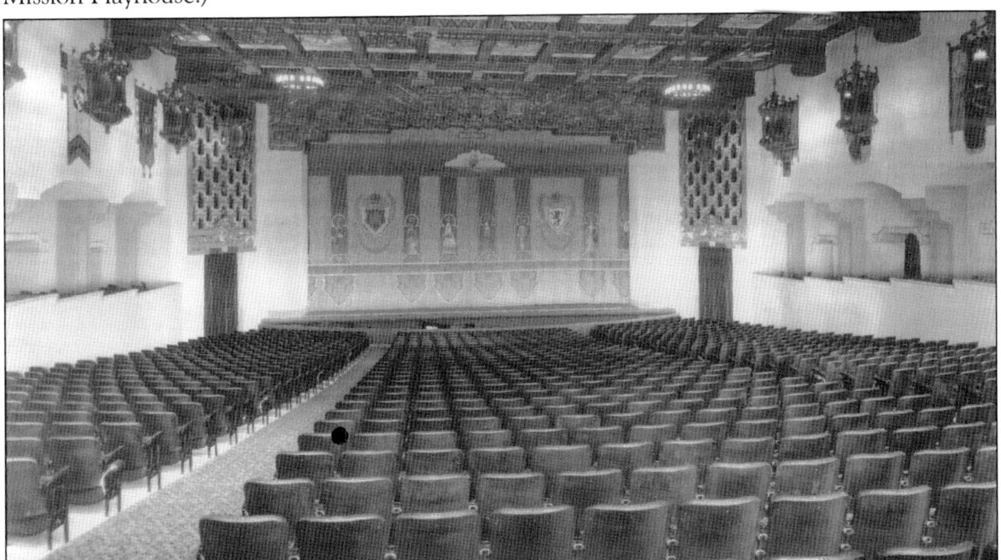

The first organ installed in the auditorium in 1927 was a two-manual 21-rank Aeolin residential pipe organ. In 1968, a four-manual, 21-rank Wurlitzer manufactured in 1924 for the 3,246-seat Albee Theater in Brooklyn, New York, was donated to the City of San Gabriel for the civic auditorium by RKO Theaters. After 15,000 hours of painstaking work by the Los Angeles Chapter of the American Theatre Organ Society, the refurbished organ was finally installed in the auditorium. (San Gabriel Mission Playhouse.)

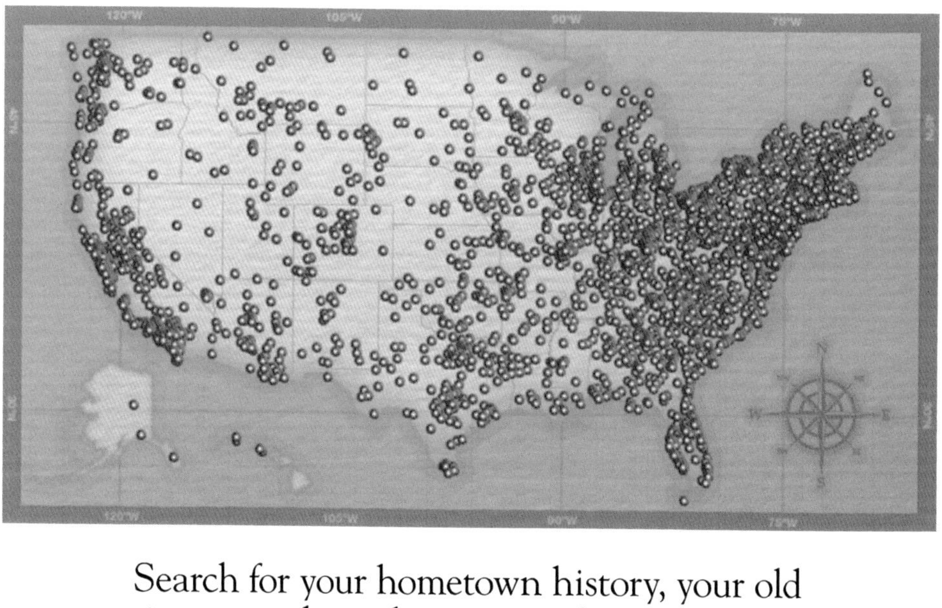